Family Problem Solving

Family Problem Solving

William J. Reid

Columbia University Press / New York / 1985

Library of Congress Cataloging in Publication Data

Reid, William James, 1928–
  Family problem solving.

  Bibliography: p.
  Includes index.
  1. Family social work. I. Title.
HV697.R35 1985 362.8'2   85-3833
ISBN 0-231-06056-4
ISBN 0-231-06057-2 (pbk.)

Columbia University Press
New York Guildford, Surrey
Copyright © 1985 Columbia University Press
All rights reserved

Printed in the United States of America

Clothbound editions of Columbia University Press books are Smyth-sewn and printed on permanent and durable acid-free paper.

Designed by Ken Venezio

To Audrey, Sophie, and Valerie

Contents

Acknowledgments

This book evolved from a project of several years duration in which the task-centered model of social work practice was applied to work with families. In this project professional and student practitioners made use of the model and discussed their work in seminars and workshops. As a result of this collaborative effort principles and procedures were tested and developed, illustrative material was generated, and, of greatest importance, all aspects of the practice model were critically examined and discussed by practitioners who made use of it.

I wish to express my deep appreciation for the efforts of the many participants of this endeavor. I feel especially indebted to several whose creative applications of the model appear in the book in the form of case illustrations: Barbara Henderer, Joe Wilson, Joan Ganeles, Louise Gibbons-McGann, Michelle Martin, Jerry Maiello, Bonnie Baron, Elaine Shick, Ira Messing, Kenneth Jacobs, Kathleen DuFresne. The last two practitioners, Kenneth Jacobs and Kathleen DuFresne, deserve double mention for their additional contributions to the project and the book in their roles as research assistants. Especially helpful were Ken's creative ideas on the use of role play and Kathleen's thinking and writing on applications of the model to single mother families. Other research assistants contributed substantially to case analysis, literature reviews, and preparation of indexes: Helene Brecker, Iris Broyde, Nina Cook, Camille Hehn, and Cara Pour. Numerous agencies provided cases for students participating in the project as well as expert supervision of the students' work. These agencies and supervisors include Colonie Youth Center (Robert Frawley), Catholic Family Service of Schenectady (Paul Bernard), and Catholic Family Service of Troy

(Ross Westhuis). An additional source of ideas and case material was a companion project supervised by Inger P. Davis, San Diego State University, who used as her principal site the Family and Children Services of San Diego.

Neither the project nor the book would have been possible without institutional resources. These were provided by the School of Social Welfare, Nelson A. Rockefeller College of Public Policy and Affairs, State University of New York at Albany. The author is indebted to the School and its chief administrative officers, Stuart A. Kirk, Dean, and John Oliver, Associate Dean. A special thanks are due to my colleague at the School, Max Siporin, for his thoughtful review and critique of a draft of the manuscript. For their thought and skill at transforming my disorderly scribbling into flawlessly typewritten pages, Gail Texter and Rose Frazier are extended my gratitude and admiration.

W.J.R.

Family Problem Solving

1. *Social Work, Family Therapy, Task-Centered Practice*

This book is about an approach to working with people who live together in intimate relationships: husbands and wives; parents and children of all ages; cohabiting couples of all gender combinations, and so on. To be simple I shall refer to these intimate pairs and groups as families. Although it is my hope that anyone in the business of helping families would find the book of interest, it is designed expressly for social work students, practitioners, and educators. It offers a *social work* model of family practice rather than a model of family therapy that social workers might use. This introductory chapter will focus on that distinction, which has ramifications not only for the approach to be presented but also for family practice in social work as a whole.

FAMILY HELPING IN SOCIAL WORK

Helping families has been a central social work function since the beginning of the profession. As Siporin (1980a) documents, ideas about family work were contained in the early social work practice theory that began to evolve after the turn of this century in the work of Josephine Shaw Lowell, Mary Richmond, Zilpha Smith, and others. Social workers were advised to work with the family as a unit, to see family members together, and to pay attention to how they interacted with one another.

The profession's close involvement with psychiatry, which began in the twenties, gave social workers even greater responsibility for families. Identified patients, whether children in guidance clinics or adults in mental hospitals, became the province of the psychiatrist while social workers dealt with "the family," or more accurately, with the remainder of the family. At the same time the dominance of psychiatric theories in social work thought hampered the development of distinctively social work approaches to the family that had begun to germinate in the holistic thinking of the pioneers of the profession. Instead social workers adopted psychopathological views of family problems which, as a result, were often treated by means of individual therapy with family members. Social workers could and did make use of psychiatric (especially psychodynamic) theory to work with family units (Regensburg 1954), but the fit between theory and the demands of family practice left much to be desired.

The family therapy movement, which became a noticeable force in the fifties, introduced a new perspective to social work practice with families. Its main theoretical and practice foundations have evolved through a remarkable interdisciplinary effort. Although social workers have been prominent in this movement, most of its major intellectual leaders have been from other professions, notably psychiatry. Whatever their professional origins, those involved in the movement have tended to identify themselves as family therapists rather than, say, as social workers or psychiatrists specializing in family practice. The growth of family therapy as an interdisciplinary specialty has been marked by such developments as training centers and programs, professional organizations, the setting of accreditation standards for family therapists, and specialized journals.

The family therapy movement evolved not as a cohesive entity but as a collection of different approaches that shared certain ideas. One attempt to capture a common core of theory embraced by these approaches has been made by Nichols (1984) in his statement of the "fundamental principles" of family therapy: "People are products of their natural contexts, the most significant of which is the family: psychological disorders are therefore not individual problems, but family problems. Although these disorders seem to be handicaps, they are actually part of

the family's attempt to maintain a viable and cohesive structure. Families may be understood as systems, operating not as a
collection of individuals but as emergent whole entities. Understanding how family systems work is greatly enhanced by concepts of circular causality, levels of communication, boundaries
and triangles" (p. 118).

As Nichols' summary suggests, the view of individual or relational problems as an expression of the dynamics of the family
system is a central tenet. To assess the problems of individual
family members one must understand how these problems are
maintained by the family as a whole. In fact, such problems
usually are best seen as symptoms of a systemic dysfunction in
the family. (Larry acts up to prevent his parents from fighting
with each other.) Intervention then must be directed to dynamics of family interaction, usually with family members seen together. Various procedures may be used to bring about change in
the problem and its systemic roots. In the session, the therapist
may interrupt accustomed patterns of interaction or challenge
views that support them, structure new modes of interaction,
help family members express and work through underlying feelings about one another, and assign tasks to be done outside the
session to bring about more functional ways of relating.

This oversimplified sketch glosses over important differences
among schools and forms of practice. It presents a conception of
family therapy that is more reflective of "systems-based" approaches than of those that have evolved from other perspectives, such as psychoanalysis. It does not describe well the
essentials of a newer arrival—behavioral family therapy. Although almost all family therapies make use of systems concepts, they may use them in quite different ways. It is not
possible to come up with precise definitions of either systems-
based family therapy or family therapy as a whole. Nevertheless, it is fair to say that the sketch presented expresses dominant themes of a movement that is growing increasingly diverse
and difficult to describe.

Whatever forms of treatment might be considered within its
boundaries, the family therapy movement has contributed enor-
mously to family practice in social work. It has advanced a sys-

tems perspective that has revolutionized treatment, not only of disturbances in family relationships but also of a host of problems—from anorexia to zoophobia—whose causes or cures may be found within the family. Accompanying the new theoretical perspectives has been an exciting array of technical innovations for effecting change in family problems and functioning. Moreover, as an interdisciplinary development, the family therapy movement has cut through outmoded distinctions between helping professions—for example, that psychiatrists should concentrate on the "sick person" and social workers should deal with "the family." Finally, the movement has stimulated new ways of studying the family and a good deal of actual research on family interaction and treatment outcome.

PUTTING FAMILY THERAPY INTO A
SOCIAL WORK CONTEXT

The family therapy movement also has created some complications for social work theory and practice. Just as the psychoanalytic movement caused social workers to become preoccupied with intrapsychic processes, the family therapy movement may be resulting in an overabsorption with family dynamics. One possible consequence is to overexaggerate the importance of the family in the formation and maintenance of problems and to neglect other units of attention, notably the individual and the environment.

Although family therapists may recognize the importance of the functioning of the individual, the rejection of one-to-one treatment relationships in the development of family therapy has led to a lack of connectedness between individual and family approaches. As Pinsof (1983) has noted, "Historically individual and family psychotherapies have been conceptualized as alternative theories and mutually exclusive treatment modalities" (p. 19). Efforts to develop models integrating individual and family treatment (Pinsof 1983; Sherman 1981) are at a beginning stage of development.

Frequently problems may be the product of interaction between individual family members and the larger environment, that is, with systems outside the family. The family system may play a subsidiary role or, regardless of its role, may not be accessible. School problems, for example, often may be just that and may be best dealt with through intervention focused on the child and school system. Often problems are the result of complex interplays between both individual and family dynamics and environmental factors. Unemployment of the breadwinner may aggravate marital tension, leading to alcohol abuse and reduced chances of finding a job. A combination of individual, family, and environmental intervention may be called for.

In consulting with students and practitioners who are "into family therapy," I quite often find their attention riveted on family system dynamics as explanations of problems, to the neglect of compelling individual and environmental factors. Or family relationship problems, which may be real enough, may be given more stress than the family wants, while concerns of individual family members or the family's need for concrete services may be pushed aside.

Furthermore, often it is not clear to what extent and how the family system contributes to individual problems. Theories that view problems of individual family members as outgrowths (symptoms) of systemic operations within the family have yet to be adequately grounded through empirical research. Few would deny a connectedness between individual behavior and family dynamics, yet there is little systematic knowledge about the specifics of these processes and how they may operate in particular cases. In its application of systems concepts, the family therapy movement has brought an eye-opening dimension to practice, but these applications have been fraught with an abundance of speculative theorizing and fuzzy concepts. Research energies have been centered in the assessment of outcomes of family treatment, rather than in study of its processes. As a result, empirical investigations have done little to clarify crucial connections between treatment theory and individual or family change.

In general, the family therapy movement has made the task of developing comprehensive theories of clinical social work more challenging. Such theories are needed to link work with individuals, families, groups, and environmental approaches. This theoretical development needs to incorporate rather than replace family therapy. It is important as a means of insuring the viability of social work as a profession, of providing guidance to practitioners, of training students, and of organizing knowledge in the field. More specifically, I am arguing for theories that will place family therapy within a social work perspective, just as there may be a need for theories that incorporate family therapy within the perspectives of other disciplines—psychiatry, nursing, and so on.

The assumption here is that family practice in social work has been shaped by a configuration of factors, principally the particular functions social workers perform, the range of settings they work in, the kinds of problems and clients they serve, and their professional training. Functions that are more characteristically carried out by social workers than by other related professionals include helping families with practical problems (financial and housing needs, for example) and social problems associated with illness and disability; locating resources and linking families to them; facilitating transitions of people from institutional to family and community life; mediating conflicts between organizations and families; and serving as public agents to safeguard the well-being of children (for example, investigating suspected child abuse and neglect and providing institutional, foster care, and adoptive placements). These functions are discharged in (and molded by) a wide range of settings, including mental health, medical, family agency, child welfare, geriatric, court, and school.

Compared to those served by allied professionals, the families that social workers work with are more likely to be poor, involved with community organizations, and not seeking help offered. These characteristics are likely to lead to change efforts occurring simultaneously with both the family and its environment. They are also likely to result in cases in which contact is brief or episodic, or in which one or two family sessions may occur as a part of treatment centered on work with individuals. Given their broad range of functions, social workers in many settings are likely to work with families around problems that are not necessarily reflective of family pathology such as illness, disability, or care of a family member. These families may be functioning quite well and may need only a limited amount of help focused on the immediate problem. Models of family therapy that seek "big change"—for example, in the family's structure, or in family members' underlying feelings about one another—are not really appropriate.

The diversity that is so characteristic of social work also can be seen in other respects. In some settings social workers may work intensively with a small number of families; in others, case loads might number in the hundreds. Qualifications may vary, from no professional training, to bachelor's and master's degrees.

This mix of characteristics, together with social work's traditions in work with families, leads to a different view of family treatment than that of the conventional image of a therapist and family in a consulting room absorbed in the intricacies of familial relationships. Social workers may work with or "treat" a family in preparation for the discharge of a family member from an institution, may help a mother take action to secure the return of her child from foster care, may have crisis-oriented interviews with distraught parents who have brought their injured child to an emergency room, may help mediate a conflict between a family and a manager of a housing project.

From a social work perspective, it seems fruitless to try to make precise distinctions between family treatment and other kinds of work with families. For example, work with a family may involve an effort to restructure relationships between parents and a delinquent son, as well as to help the parents cooperate with the son's school and probation officer to resolve some of the youth's difficulties outside the home. There is little point in viewing the restructuring effort as family therapy, and involvement with the family and community agencies as something else, particularly since the latter activity may also utilize the same knowledge of family dynamics as the former.

It makes more sense to develop a framework that spans both conventional family therapy activities and methods of intervention with families that may not usually be labeled as "therapy."

This framework would include ways of carrying out distinctive social work functions, particularly those involving the relationship between the family and the community, and work with family members as individuals. Further, it would need to be adapted to the diversity of social work practice—the variations in setting, problems, client characteristics, practitioner training, and so on. For this purpose what is needed is a model with adjustable settings—for example, one that can be set to meet the requirements of a well-functioning family but can be adjusted for work with disturbed families, or one that has different settings for practitioners with differing amounts of training.

In her attempt to develop a coherent framework for social work practice, Meyer (1983a) has advocated use of an eco-systems perspective that directs the social worker to attend to "the fit between the person and the situation with an emphasis on the interface" (p. 56). The practitioner selects a practice model depending on her assessment of "what is happening at the interface" (p. 56). This kind of ecological viewpoint captures whatever might be distinctive about social work; it is one shared by a growing number of theorists of the profession (Siporin 1980b; Germain and Gitterman 1980; Maluccio 1981; Hepworth and Larsen 1982; Hartman and Laird 1983). This viewpoint incorporates a systems view of the family, but regards the family as just one of several intersecting systems and family therapy as one modality for effecting change.

In order to develop and implement this thrust in social work, there is need for greater integration at the level of practice theory and method. One means of achieving this synthesis is to incorporate theories and methods from family therapy into practice models in social work that are designed for a range of client systems, including individuals and families. Examples include psychosocial casework (Hollis and Woods 1981), the life model (Germain and Gitterman 1980), behavioral social work (Schinke 1981; Gambrill 1981), and task-centered practice (Reid and Epstein 1972; Reid 1978; Epstein 1980; Reid 1981; Fortune, 1985). In fact this process has already begun. In most general models, explicit attention now is being given to family treatment (Hollis and Woods 1981; Gambrill 1981; Reid 1981; Hepworth and Larsen 1982; Garvin and Seabury 1984). Hartman and Laird (1983) have recently presented a family practice model within an ecological social work perspective. These efforts are a welcome start but much more needs to be accomplished, particularly the construction of a greater variety of full-scale social work models for helping families.

All of this is not to argue for an end to the interdisciplinary thrust of the family therapy movement. On the contrary, a continued flourishing of this development will have many benefits for social work practice. The argument is for a development of a different kind, one that will extract concepts and methods from the family therapy movement and order them within general social work practice models. Both developments should be able to proceed in a mutually beneficial fashion. General models are dependent for substance on the contributions of specialists. Specialists can gain insights from applications of their methods within broader perspectives.

The present book is one attempt to meet the need for incorporating family treatment methods into a more comprehensive approach to social work practice. It enlarges one such approach—task-centered social work—by expanding, quite considerably I hope, its family practice component. Into this expansion has been put a number of ingredients: theoretical and technological developments emanating from the field of family therapy; research on family life; recent contributions from relevant task-centered literature and results of ongoing research and development designed to test and modify innovations in task-centered family practice. The product is an integrative model for work with families that is tied to a larger practice system. The model can be used as a part of that system, as a self-contained method of intervention, or in conjunction with other approaches.

The volume in itself does not meet the need for a comprehensive social work approach that incorporates a fully developed family practice model. Rather, the book concentrates on presenting such a model as an addition to a practice system that includes, in other publications, models for work with individuals, families, and groups, and for agency management (Reid and

Epstein 1972, 1977; Garvin, Reid and Epstein 1976; Reid 1978; Epstein 1980; Parihar 1983; Fortune 1985). An effort is made, however, to present herein the essentials of the larger intervention system and to show how the family practice component relates to it. Also, work on family treatment applications has led to new perspectives, concepts, and methods that have implications for task-centered social work as a whole.

A brief statement of task-centered social work follows. This summary will make the goal just presented more understandable and will provide necessary background for a discussion of a second objective for the book.

TASK-CENTERED SOCIAL WORK

As a service approach, task-centered social work is a way of helping people with problems of living. Whether used with individuals, families, or groups, certain basic concepts and procedures remain constant. Helping efforts are concentrated on problems as perceived by clients. Although practitioners provide input that may affect the clients' perceptions, the client system must acknowledge the problem and expressly agree to work on it. Goals and strategy of service also are made explicit and agreed to. The practitioner avoids hidden agendas, such as private goals she may hope to achieve in the "best interests" of the client system.* Clients are thus regarded as consumers of service who have the right to decide what changes they want and to be informed of what the social worker has in mind for them.

Assessment and resulting intervention are guided by a theory of self-perceived problems and how people solve them. Problems result from wants that people are unable to satisfy, and in one form or another are an inevitable part of the human condition. Most problems get resolved or at least reduced to a tolerable level by people's problem-solving actions in combination with environmental responses. The human being is viewed optimistically as a resourceful problem-solver, rather than pessi-

---

*Throughout this book I use the pronoun "she" for professionals and generally "he" for clients and other persons.

mistically as a victim of pathology or circumstances. Sometimes, however, solutions are blocked by obstacles within the client system or environment or by lack of available resources. It is these problems that are brought to the attention of social workers.

Problems as well as the obstacles and resources that make up the contexts of the problems are viewed from a multisystems perspective. Individuals, families, groups, and organizations are seen as systems whose internal dynamics and interactions can be understood in systemic terms. Within this framework the practitioner can draw on any type of theory that may fit the case at hand. It is assumed that no one theory is adequate for all contingencies. At the same time any theory that purports to explain behavior is viewed cautiously, as a source of hypotheses to be tested with evidence from the case. The practioner's role is to help the client system define and understand its problems and to facilitate problem-solving actions. As a part of this process, the current psychological and situational contexts of the problems are explored. The model is present-oriented, though historical events still influential in the clients' lives may be examined.

Change in problems is brought out primarily through actions or tasks undertaken by clients in the session or in their life situation, as well as through tasks undertaken by the practitioners. Work proceeds collaboratively, with emphasis on stimulation and support of the clients' own problem solving capacities. Obstacles that block the clients' task work are identified and efforts are made to work them through. Resources that would facilitate this work are brought to bear. Various techniques for helping clients plan and implement tasks, such as clarification of incentives and rehearsal, are utilized. Relating to clients with empathy and caring are integral parts of the practitioner's contribution, but they are not sufficient conditions for change.

The task-centered approach is a structured form of practice. Its procedures are clearly spelled out and follow suggested sequences. The expected duration of service is planned in the initial phase. In most cases service is short-term—eight to twelve sessions over a three-to-four-month period. The model is empirical in several senses—in its preference for research-based knowledge, in its demand for evidence from the case to support theoretical hypotheses applied to the case, in its reliance on data to evaluate case progress, and in its use of research to develop its methods.

The task-centered system has been cited as a major approach in clinical social work (Turner 1979; Hepworth and Larsen 1982; Germain 1983; Meyer 1983b; Garvin and Seabury 1984). Adaptations have been developed for most settings in which social workers practice, including child welfare (Salmon 1977; Rooney 1981; Rzepnicki 1985); public social services (Rooney and Wanless 1985) school social work (Epstein 1977; Reid et al. 1980); corrections (Hofstad 1977; Bass 1977; Goldberg and Stanley 1978; Larsen and Mitchell 1980); industrial (Taylor 1977; Weissman 1977); geriatric (Cormican 1977; Diekring, Brown, and Fortune 1980; Rathbone-McCuan 1985); medical (Wexler 1977); family service (Hari 1977; Reid 1977; Wise 1977); and mental health (Ewalt 1977; Brown 1977; Newcome 1985).

From its beginning the task-centered approach has been used as a method of helping families. Although the first major work on the model presented it as a general system of practice (Reid and Epstein 1972), the majority of illustrative and research cases therein concerned family problems. Since then there have been various specific applications in the family area (Wexler 1977; Ewalt 1977; Wise 1977; Bass 1977; Reid 1977; Tolson 1977; Reid 1978; Gibbons et al. 1978; Butler, Bow, and Gibbons 1978; Rooney 1981; Reid 1981; Rzepnicki 1981; Wodarski, Saffir, and Frazer 1982; Fortune 1985). Nonetheless, the task-centered system had only modest beginnings in theory and methods *expressly* designed for work with families. Research on the model, as well as clinical experience with it, suggested areas for development, including better theory and methods for assessing family systems, a broader range of techniques for working with the family as a unit, improved strategies for effecting change in factors underlying target problems, and more effective means of helping families develop skills for coping with problems in the future. Finally, as discussed, there appeared to be need to incorporate within a social work practice approach developments in the family treatment field. The task-centered model seemed an appropriate vehicle for this purpose.

Whether a practitioner is helping adult children develop a plan with a community agency for the care of their aged mother or is helping a family with problems of interpersonal conflict, she can draw on the same body of concepts, principles, and methods. In both cases problems would be defined, and family members would be engaged in working together on tasks to effect solutions.

In addition to its ability to span a wide range of family problems encountered in social work, the model has other features designed to fit the characteristics of social work practice. Tasks for practitioners as well as clients provide a way of conceptualizing work with the environment. Basic concepts and procedures of the model apply to work with either individuals or families, facilitating movement from an individual to a family focus. The collaborative, problem-solving, short-term orientation of the model is suited to well-functioning families who need, want, or can accept only a modest amount of help. The simplicity of the basic structure of the model and the action-oriented cast of the intervention strategy lend themselves to practitioners who may have yet to acquire theoretical or technical sophistication in family practice and to clients who may lack verbal skills. The approach can be used at a more advanced level and, in fact, must be to achieve certain objectives; however, its basic methods are relatively easy to grasp and to use.

It is understood, and should be underscored, that the value of this practice model, or any practice model, lies not so much in its faithful application as a whole but rather in the pieces that can be taken from it by discerning users. Most practitioners who work with families are eclectic in orientation and are constantly on the lookout for new ideas and techniques or new ways of integrating what is already available. The present work, I hope, will provide a fruitful area for this search.

In one sense the present model provides a way of organizing a variety of theoretical and technical developments concerning work with families. While it shows how these developments can be combined within a problem solving framework, it also offers users discrete components that can be fitted into almost any form of family treatment. These include procedures for problem formulation; a framework for assessing family interaction; a survey of in-session tasks for the family involving problem-solving, negotiation, skill training, role play, sculpting, and other activities; a typology of out-of-session tasks and considerations in their use; methods for helping family members achieve understanding of their problems and situations. In addition aspects of the empirical and theoretical foundations of the model may be of interest to readers regardless of their practice orientations, for example, reviews of research relating to family interaction concepts and intervention methods, and discussions of the role of structure and collaboration in family treatment.

A RESEARCHABLE MODEL

A principal thrust of work on task-centered social work has been to construct an approach that would lend itself to development through continuing research. It is assumed that research has a vital contribution to make to any form of treatment, not only through testing the effectiveness of methods but also by stimulating technical and theoretical innovation. Although research can contribute to any type of family treatment, progress will be facilitated if the practice model is "research friendly"—that is, if it is systematically organized into specific steps and procedures that can be identified, replicated, tested, and evaluated, and if guidelines and techniques for study are incorporated as part of the model. Progress through research will be slower when the strategy and method are put together in a complex, unpredictable form by the therapist. Even though this style of treatment may be quite effective in the hands of a skilled and knowledgeable clinician, it is difficult to isolate and study particular elements.

A second purpose of the book is to present a model that can be systematically applied, evaluated, and developed through single-case and group studies. Even though the approach to be presented can be used "as is," the assumption is that there is considerable room for improvement in any form of family treatment. The need lies not only in constructing more effective and efficient approaches but also in better articulation of the methods of family therapy so that these methods can be more readily learned and disseminated.

Ongoing research is vital to obtaining these ends. It is expected that much of this work will take the form of single-case studies and small-group experiments, many of them done by students. An appreciable number of master's and doctoral projects involving applications of the task-centered model have in fact been conducted (Rooney 1978; Tolson 1977; Brown 1980; Diaz 1980; Rzepnicki 1981; Jackson 1983; Thibault 1984; Cattaneo et al 1984). Even when studies are done as unpublished course projects, they can have important learning values for students and also may be informative for instructors interested in model development.

The work presented in this volume is in fact the outgrowth of a developmental research undertaking centered at the School of Social Welfare, the Rockefeller College of Public Affairs and Policy, the State University of New York at Albany. The program has involved a series of trials of the family-centered, task-centered model by practitioners, students, and the author in a variety of settings, and provides the source of most of the case illustrations used in this book. In the majority of these case applications, data in the form of tapes of clinical sessions, structured practitioner recordings, and self-report instruments completed by family members have been collected and analyzed. This empirical work has been combined with extensive reviews of theoretical, clinical, and research literature that might inform the development of the model.

The book, I hope, will be of particular value to instructors and students involved in single-case research. Several useful volumes presenting methods of single-case study have appeared in recent years (Jayaratne and Levy 1979; Tripodi and Epstein 1980; Bloom and Fischer 1982). The present volume adds to this literature by offering a model of family treatment that lends itself to single-case designs, along with methods of study that may be used in conjunction with it.

Although I have emphasized research and development relating to task-centered family treatment, it is important to remember that the model itself incorporates components widely used in work with families. As a consequence, the model offers a framework for research on particular components generally used in treatment, especially tasks. In fact, the model can be viewed as an approach to the study of the therapeutic use of tasks.

PLAN OF THE BOOK

The book is organized to facilitate its use for practice, research, and training purposes. For each of these purposes, users are provided with a summary of its objectives, strategies, and procedures, as well as illustrative applications. These are outlined in the following chapter. Selective additions and amplifications are provided in remaining chapters: the distinguishing emphases of the approach (chapter 3), dimensions of family interaction (chapter 4), intervention strategies and methods (chapters 5, 6, and 7), an application to a type of family (chapter 8), and research and recording procedures (chapter 9). The plan results in some repetition between the second and remaining chapters, a disadvantage that is outweighed, it is hoped, by the usefulness of the overview.

2. *Objectives, Strategy, and Procedures*

This chapter presents an overview of the purposes and design of the family practice model. The first section sets forth the purpose and focus of the main elements of its strategy. The main procedures of the model are then presented in a step-by-step fashion, with emphasis on its initial plase. The outline of procedures for the middle phase is particularly concise since three subsequent chapters are devoted to its components. The chapter concludes with three illustrative cases.

The chapter is not intended to be an abridgment of the book but rather a succinct expression of what is needed to apply the model. The chapters that follow provide elaboration but also introduce additional theory, rationale, and methods. The hope is that potential users will read the book as a whole and then use the present chapter as a convenient point of reference when applying the model.

OBJECTIVES AND STRATEGY

The first order of business of task-centered family treatment is to help alleviate *target problems*—that is, problems that are expressly identified and agreed upon by family members and the practitioner as the focus of work. Change in target problems represents a desirable goal in its own right and fulfills the service contract. At the same time, target problems are part of a larger *context* that must always be taken into account. The context of a problem can be seen generally as a configuration of

Portions of this chapter have previously appeared in Reid (1985).

factors in the family and its environment that may interact with the problem. The context includes obstacles to solving the problem and resources that can be applied to work on it. These obstacles and resources in turn can reflect almost any aspect of family life, including functioning of individual family members, patterns of family relationships, and environments of which the family and its members are a part.

An effort is made to help families alleviate target problems in ways that will exert a positive influence on the context of the problem. Whereas significant contextual change is not a fixed objective in all cases, it is generally sought as a means of facilitating solutions, of preventing recurrences and side effects, and of strengthening the family's problem-solving abilities. Contextual change is essentially defined and limited by the nature of the target problem, and is not simply any change that would help the family. Practitioners move from the target outward by degrees, giving priority to contextual change most directly relevant to the problem at hand.

It should be obvious that the boundaries between a target problem and its context are seldom clear-cut or fixed. Basically the distinction is between a particular issue defined and specified in a given way (the target problem) and a host of factors that bear upon the issue (the context). Contextual change does not necessarily mean structural realignments or other major modifications in family life. It may be as minor as a subtle shift in attitude of one family member toward another.

The primary means of bringing about change in target problems and their contexts are through tasks carried out in the session (*session tasks*), by family members at home (*home tasks*), or by family members or the practitioner in the environment (*environmental tasks*). Task work is facilitated by familial or environmental *resources* that the practitioner attempts to identify and mobilize. It may be blocked by *obstacles* that the practitioner tries to help the family explore, understand, and resolve. Examining and understanding resources and obstacles so that they can be put to work, or worked through, is carried out collaboratively by the practitioner and family members (*contextual analysis*).

The treatment strategy is guided by principles that maximize the family's own problem-solving activities and potentials. It is assumed that generally families can be best helped if they are provided with an orderly, facilitative structure in which to work out immediate problems and to develop problem-solving skills, with the practitioner in the roles of guide and consultant (chapter 3). Although the family's limitations are realistically appraised, emphasis is placed on identification of strengths, competencies, and resources within the family. Accordingly, the family members are helped to devise their own solutions with the practitioner's assistance. Should these efforts be blocked by obstacles, increased attention is paid to contextual factors that may be responsible for the obstacles. The practitioner assumes more of a leadership role and pushes for greater contextual change as is necessary to help the family work through obstacles preventing problem solution. These principles serve to organize contributions from a broad range of approaches to family treatment (chapter 3).

Applicable Problems and Situations

Within the task-centered system, work with family members together is generally preferred over one-to-one treatment when the targets of intervention are clearly family problems. In this category fall difficulties in family relations, such as marital discord and conflict between parents and children, as well as troubles affecting the family as a whole (for example, an impending eviction). Seeing family members together for such problems facilitates assessment, problem formulation, task planning, and review, and provides opportunity for in vivo work with families on problem solving, communication, and other types of tasks that can be done in the session.

The choice of intervention modality is not as clear-cut when target problems are centered in individual difficulties, such as depression, alcoholism, delinquency, or school underachievement. Traditionally, individual treatment has been applied to such problems, but family therapy is being used increasingly. In task-centered practice, conjoint treatment would be indicated when either one of two conditions obtain: when the problem appears to be related to family processes, as in the case of a wife who is depressed over her marriage, or when the family may provide an effective resource for resolving the problem regardless of its causes—for example, a child having trouble with his studies may be helped by the parents' assuming a more active role in tutoring, structuring time for homework, and providing rewards for improved academic performance. In general, if a client is a member of a family, and most are, almost any problem area needs to be examined with an eye to involvement of the family in treatment.

In the present model, choice of treatment method is determined fundamentally by the problem as it is defined by the client in consultation with the practitioner. When problems are unequivocally family problems, or when it appears that family involvement would facilitate their solution, the practitioner normally suggests group sessions attended by family members related to the problem (a marital pair, parents and a child, etc.). No premium is placed on total family attendance, although one is cautious about interviewing combinations of family members that would reinforce dysfunctional boundaries, such as seeing an enmeshed mother-child pair and not the isolated father (Nelsen 1983).

Working with family members together enables a more systems-focused approach in which family dynamics can be more readily observed, altered, and put to work than in one-to-one treatment. The results of intervention research comparing individual and conjoint treatment appear to support this contention (Gurman and Kniskern 1981).

Family sessions are not always the way to go, however. Clients may not want them; they may not work well for one reason or another (a high level of conflict is a common cause); family members may have private concerns, such as whether or not to remain in the family, that they do not wish to share; or members may need to put distance between themselves and their families (Northen 1982).

There are no hard criteria for such decisions. A principle for the task-centered model as a whole is to view family sessions as preferable when indicators discussed earlier obtain—that is, when problems are defined in terms of family relationships or as a general family concern, when they appear reactive to family processes, or when their solution can be facilitated by the resources of the family. Under these circumstances the practitioner starts with, or attempts to initiate, family sessions and normally holds to this course unless contingencies, such as those discussed subsequently, arise. Then a combination of individual and family sessions may be in order, or it may be preferable to switch completely to individual treatment. In keeping with the multisystem and integrative orientation of the model, a flexible approach, one responsive to the problems at hand, is called for.

Assessment

The gathering and evaluation of assessment data are primarily determined by the target problems. From these focal concerns, the practitioner branches out into other areas of the family's functioning and situation. The intent is not, as in some models of practice, to gather and sift a large body of information about these areas to serve as a basis for determining what the client's difficulties are. Rather, the practitioner's purpose is to secure information that will provide guidance in work with problems whose essential outlines have already been determined, not on the basis of what is "wrong" from a theoretical perspective but on the basis of what is troubling the family.

The practitioner's assessment activities are responsive to difficulties encountered in resolving problems. If problems move readily toward resolution, a minimal amount of assessment data may be obtained. When obstacles are encountered or when the complexities of the problem make it difficult to arrive at suitable tasks, more understanding is required. Assessment data are obtained and processed within whatever mix of theoretical frameworks seems to provide the most useful understanding of the problems, with priority given to formulations that have research support or that can be specified in empirical language (chapter 3). Inquiry is guided by a multisystems perspective that views individual family members, the family itself, and the family's environment as a network or ecology of systems (chapter 3). While diagnostic attention may be given to any system, from individuals to organizations, that may be contributing to the problem, the family system is usually the most important source of assessment data. Interest is centered on communication and interactive events, especially in relation to dimensions of control, involvement, alliance, and flexibility (chapter 4).

Contextual Change

Although the model is directed at alleviating target problems, considerable attention is paid to contextual change, particularly when target problems are narrowly defined or lack stability. A discussion of the ways in which positive contextual change can occur will add to the theory of the model as well as serve as a vehicle for illustrating the model's strategies and methods.

First, contextual change can occur as a direct consequence of alleviation of a target problem. In some cases, changes in target problems can produce ripple effects, setting in motion "beneficial" cycles of interaction. In other cases, work on the target problem itself can bring about change in attitudes, expectations, or interaction patterns that "go beyond" the problem, even if obstacles are not encountered. For example, the process of negotiating a specific disagreement may give participants new appreciation for each other's feelings about a number of considerations related to the disagreement, or may result in some modification of how each relates to the other. In general, work on session tasks, as well as successful attainment of tasks outside the session, can help family members improve communication, problem solving, and coping abilities.

Second, efforts to change the target problem may be accompanied by concomitant attempts to modify factors closely related to the target problem. This strategy can be illustrated by different approaches that might be taken to help John and Betty work out a target problem involving care of their infant son,

Tony. Betty, who has just resumed working part-time, is upset over John's apparent unwillingness to assume greater responsibility for care of Tony so she can increase the hours she spends working. Her husband, a draftsman, could do some of his work at home. In fact, he had agreed to get permission to do so before Tony was born but has been putting this off. John admits that he did promise to arrange to work at home but says that his work situation has become tense, and he is reluctant to make any demands at this point. Remarks made by Betty and John in the ensuing discussion give the practitioner reason to believe that John was opposed to having a child at this time and viewed Tony somewhat as Betty's project; Betty in turn seemed to resent John's hands-off attitude and his lack of appreciation for her assuming most of the child care responsibilities for Tony.

A practitioner might deal with the target problem in one of two ways. She could concentrate on resolving the immediate problem through session tasks in which the couple worked out a compromise about care of Tony. Issues concerning John's reluctance to have a child and Betty's feelings of not being appreciated would not be taken up. On the other hand, in addition to dealing with the target problem, the practitioner, perhaps through additional session tasks, might help the couple clarify these issues and attempt to achieve some resolution of them. In the first approach, the focus is limited to change in the target problem. In the second, an effort is made to alter the context of the problem.

It is seldom completely clear whether contextual factors should be dealt with or to what extent. In the example just given, it could be argued that resolution of the target problem might be sufficient. A change in the problem would presumably bring about some positive change in its context. The partners could be given responsibility for dealing in their own way with remaining issues. In fact, it might be better to allow the issues to remain dormant for the time being to give both Betty and John time to adjust to their new roles as parents. But justification for going further also can be found. Any solution to the immediate problem might be short-lived, or comparable problems might flare up unless these issues are satisfactorily dealt with. Moreover, the contextual change being attempted would have a generally beneficial effect on their relationship.

Third, contextual change may occur in the process of working through obstacles that prevent resolution of target problems. For example, in one case, the target problem consisted of a conflict between a father and his daughter over her coming home excessively late, and on occasion staying out all night. Efforts to reach a compromise between father and daughter on this issue were undermined by a mother-daughter coalition against the father. The obstacle was defined as this triangular pattern. Working through this obstacle involved session tasks between father and daughter, accompanied by a calculated effort to prevent mother from siding with daughter (or daughter turning to mother), and session tasks between the parents who were asked to develop a plan for dealing with the problem. Home tasks called for the daughter to come home at a mutually acceptable time and for the father to give her driving lessons if she did. The mother's task was to demonstrate support for the contract between father and daughter. These tasks not only alleviated the target problem but brought about at least temporary modification of a "problem-breeding" coalition.

The final way in which contextual change can occur is through use of resources within the family as a means of resolving the target problem. Although most successful tasks in family treatment involve use of resources within the family (strengths, skills, coping abilities, and so on), reference here is to more explicit use of the family as a resource. Perhaps the clearest examples occur when the target problem involves difficulties that a member is experiencing outside the family. (For purposes of the present discussion I assume the member is a child.) In some situations these difficulties can be best tackled through work on dysfunctional patterns within the family that may be causing the problem or that may constitute an obstacle to its resolution. In other situations, however, the connection between the child's difficulties and family functioning is not clear, but the practitioner can identify resources within the family that might be brought to bear on the problem. In applying these resources to the problem, benefits beyond problem alleviation can occur. For example, in another case, the target problem concerned behavior difficulties that David, age fifteen, was experiencing at school. He would "mouth off" to teachers who tried to reprimand him for minor infractions. The mouthing-off had resulted in repeated suspensions. David had recently begun to live with his father, having left his mother with whom he was having serious conflicts (The parents had divorced some years ago). His relationship with his father, which had not yet jelled, was beginning to develop tension around the school problem.

The practitioner used the father as a resource in work on the school problem through a series of session tasks. The tasks stressed role plays which were used in part to avoid tempting the father to lecture to his son about the school difficulties. Instead, the father took the role of his son, with the son in roles of a critical teacher or provocative peer. In these tasks, the father was able to model for his son means of handling the kinds of situations that were getting him into trouble and to do so in specific and convincing ways. What might be useful for the son was emphasized by the practitioner in the post-task discussion. (Other types of session tasks as well as home tasks were used to reinforce the theme of how the father might help the son.) The immediate objective was to alleviate the school problem; at the same time, father and son were being given the opportunity to develop their relationship around a meaningful issue, while avoiding disruptive conflict.

In the task-centered approach, behavior problems of individual family members are seen differently than in models that view such problems both as "symptoms" of systemic dysfunctioning in the family and as serving a function for the system—probably the dominant position in the family therapy movement. (See Nichols' summary quoted in chapter 1.) The major difficulty with the symptom/family system formulation is that it assumes that family systems are sufficiently powerful and sufficiently decipherable to provide the best explanations of the problems of an individual family member.

In actuality a large inferential leap, if not an act of faith, often is necessary to connect the behavior of the individual to some complex and poorly understood family process, especially when other systems may be influential. Sometimes a family systems explanation may be the best available, but it may not be. In the present theory, problems are seen as having multiple sources in one or more systems—the individual, the family, and its environment. The connection between the problem and its sources usually is not clear and often is unknowable, and, fortunately, need not necessarily be known in order to resolve it. It is quite possible to make use of systems concepts and a systems viewpoint without regarding the problem as a symptom of a dysfunctional family system. One can "think systems" without "thinking symptoms."

When one sees a behavior difficulty as a symptom, the next question becomes what it is a symptom of, and one's attention is drawn to the "what," which is typically difficult to discern. There is also the risk, especially with beginners, that "symptom thinking" can deflate the importance of the problem and sidetrack efforts to deal with it directly. Finally, this mind-set can result in an overemphasis on what is defective in family functioning. A family can be functioning quite well despite a problem, but it may need to take novel action to solve it.

It may be preferable to move from the problem to immediate contextual factors that may be maintaining it or blocking solutions, or that could be used as problem-solving resources. For example, a father may be drinking excessively because of pressures at work or to relieve a sense of inner emptiness. His family may play a part in the drinking problem but its role may not be clear, and even if discerned, may not prove central. Hence, his drinking is not symptomatic of family dysfunctioning. The solution to the problem may lie in some combination of change in his work situation, recognition on his part that it may be better to bear his emptiness than to try to fill it with alcohol, *and* novel actions on the part of his family—for example, to make his life easier when he does not drink, harder when he does.

As a rule, for marital, parent-child, and other problems that are defined as difficulties in family relationships, family systems concepts usually provide the best framework for assessment, even though this framework may need to be supplemented. Such problems can be regarded as direct expressions of system dysfunctioning or as "representative" problems as described below, rather than as symptoms of anything larger or more malignant than themselves. In some cases, other parts of the family system may need to undergo change before the problem can be resolved, but significant systemic change may not be necessary. Concentration on such problems may lead to contextual or systemic change via the means described above.

Forming a Relationship

From the moment they encounter one another, practitioner and family members begin to form a relationship that will endure during their period of work together. Since this relationship influences the willingness of family members to reveal and work on problems, it will be considered prior to discussion of procedures for problem formulation.

The practitioner attempts to develop a relationship in which family members feel understood and accepted, and in which she herself is trusted and respected by the family. She tries to do this by responding empathetically to the family members' problems in a way that shows her understanding of these problems as the family members experience them, and by showing respect for the family members' values and opinions.

In the initial encounter the practitioner may make certain gestures as a means of facilitating the development of a relationship, such as engaging in self-disclosure or highlighting similarities between herself and family members. These efforts are designed to demonstrate or to emphasize likenesses between the practitioner and the client and to encourage the revelations of personal material. Unfortunately, such efforts at "joining" the family (Minuchin and Fishman 1981) appear to be somewhat calculated when referred to as "techniques." It may be useful therefore to view them in a somewhat different context.

Suppose I am in a situation—for example, on a vacation trip—in which I have encountered a family that I would like to get to know. To get on more familiar terms with the family I would naturally try to find some common ground in which similarities between the family and me would be highlighted. I would probably adapt my style of speech and vocabulary to some extent to match that of the family. I would probably disclose some things about myself and expect that the family would reciprocate with some self-revelations of its own. If the father is stretched out in a comfortable position, I might do the same. I would engage in these behaviors more or less naturally without giving much thought to them. I would not see them as "joining" techniques, à la Minuchin, even though I would have engaged in imitation, self-disclosure, mimesis, and so on. An outsider would probably see my behavior as quite appropriate and not calculated or manipulative. These efforts to get more familiar with the family also would be carried out in the context of conversations about various topics.

This perspective can be applied to a practitioner's first encounter with a family. Paradoxically, at this stage it may be better to proceed with engagement as one might do in trying to get on more familiar ground with any family, without too much attention to technique. There are, of course, some differences between a therapeutic and a social encounter. The practitioner and client are not about to engage in a symmetrical relationship. And of course, the content is not small talk but the clients' problems. Still, the comparison to a social situation may help the practitioner avoid extensive self-consciousness during this phase.

Although relating to the family as a client bears basic similarities to relating to an individual client, some important differences should be noted. In relating to a family one is relating to a natural group, if not a microculture, and hence must be aware of such considerations as power and status, conflicts, norms, and expectations, as well as differing needs of individual members. Thus, when parents and children are seen together, the practitioner shows respect for the authority of the parents while demonstrating an understanding of the predicaments experienced by all family members, including a problem child.

PHASES AND PROCEDURES

What follows is an outline of steps of the model at its current state of development. The outline assumes that sessions are conducted with at least two family members seen together who are able to articulate problems—for example, a married couple or a parent, and at least one older child. Structured recording guides for each phase may be found in the Appendix.

Initial Phase

The initial phase ideally is accomplished in a single two-hour session, though it may involve two or more sessions. Whatever its span, the following steps are involved.

1. Problem Survey. The practitioner elicits statements from each family member on what each sees as the problems to be worked on. She permits the family to present its problems in its own style. She allows give and take among family members but makes sure that each has a chance to voice his or her opinions about the problems for which help is sought. The practitioner's role at this point is primarily that of facilitator of the family members' presentations. Questions are few and are aimed primarily at clarification of meaning and detail.

2. Initial Problem Exploration and Formulation. After each family member has been heard from, the practitioner explores more actively the areas of difficulties that have been presented. Her exploration is guided by hypotheses about what family members view as problems and not by notions of what the underlying issues "really" are. In other words, she attempts to help family members explain what is on their minds rather than investigate her own ideas about what might be wrong. In this process, she may help clients verbalize thoughts and observations that they have been reluctant to reveal in the initial problem survey, or she may raise questions about areas of difficulty that have not been presented as problems.

As the exploration proceeds, the practitioner begins to organize points of concern into tentative conceptions of problems. The emphasis at this point is on *what* the trouble is as the family members see it and not on how things got that way, although the practitioner may need to be tolerant of the clients' needs to trace the origins of the problem. At this point, it is not necessary to require a large amount of detailed knowledge on the frequency of the problem or the intricacies of its operation. But enough detail is needed to describe it adequately for subsequent prioritization and to see if it may be combined with other issues. Sweeping or vague statements of issues need to be specified. Family members may agree that "we fight all the time." The practitioner wants to know about what and how. Who does what to whom, how, and under what circumstances is a question that is repeatedly asked in different ways at this stage of the process.

Sometimes a problem is expressed originally in terms of some very specific, often transient issue. When asked what she sees as problems in the family, Jody says only "My mom won't let me go to Sandy's party on Thursday." Or sometimes it is stated as a series of specific behaviors: "Mike doesn't keep his room straight, won't take out the garbage like he's supposed to, talks back when he is asked to do something." Although expressions at this level should be taken seriously and in fact provide essential details of potential target problems, they may be too limiting to provide adequate focuses for work, or may result in an unwieldy number of issues.

An attempt is made to explore more general problems that are reflected by these very concrete difficulties. The practitioner tries to help the family formulate problems that are specific enough to clarify what will be worked on and when, but not so limited that their solutions would not make an appreciable difference in the life of the family. Thus, in the first case above, the practitioner, after some exploration, might offer the thought that Jody and her mom seem to be at odds about Jody's choice of friends. In the second, the practitioner, again after some more exploration, might suggest that there seems to be a tug-of-war between Mike and his parents about what chores Mike is to do and when he is to do them.

In some cases family members may want help with only a very specific issue that is of importance to them and may so limit their request at the outset. For example, a couple may want help with reaching a decision about adopting a child, or parents may be divided on how to react to their daughter's plans to live with her boyfriend. A request for limited help of this kind can properly serve as the sole basis for work even though the practitioner may see all sorts of additional "problems" in the picture. Family members should always be asked if they want help with other things, but the practitioner should be prepared to take "no" for an answer without giving clients the impression that something is wrong because they do not wish to work on other issues.

Related to the level of abstraction in problem formulation is the question of what is the "real" problem. A simple answer to that question is that all problems are "real" to someone. It is usually impossible, and fruitless, to search for the one problem that has some quintessential reality that others lack. Other formulations are more useful. As noted, one can view specific problems as being expressions of larger problems, that is, as falling at different levels of abstraction. It is also possible to see how some problems are aggravated by others. A coalition between father and daughter may be regarded as a contribution to difficulties in the interaction between mother and daughter. It would be hard to demonstrate that the coalition was the real problem, the fundamental cause. It is reasonable to assume that all problems have multiple causes. If any problems have a special degree of reality, they are those that clients say are causing them discomfort.

Rather than viewing some problems as more "real" than others or seeing problems as symptoms of underlying disorders, we have found it useful to think in terms of the *representativeness* of problems. Some problems appear to be relatively isolated or encapsulated, or at least their links to other problems are not clear. A couple whose relationship has been going smoothly suddenly may find themselves in a terrible stew over whether or not the aged father of the wife should live with them. The conflict may stir up deep emotions. The wife is enraged that her husband does not accept her feelings of affection and indebtedness toward her father. The husband reacts strongly against sharing his wife and household and expects his wife to see his position. A power struggle may ensue. But these conflicts are the product of this particular issue. If the old man should decide on his own to live with another daughter, the conflicts would be expected to dissipate and the marital relationship to return to normal.

Other problems, doubtless the majority encountered in work with troubled families, are clearly representative of other issues. A conflict between mother and daughter over her daughter's choice of friends may be representative of conflicts in the dyad over dominance and autonomy. This is not to say that the problem is merely a symptom, to be "replaced" by another of equal intensity once it is solved. The battle over the daughter's choice of friends may have unique qualities—for example, the mother's reliving her own adolescent peer conflicts through her daughter. But the other issues are there and might be expected to give rise to other problems.

It is assumed, however, that a solution of a representative problem can affect others linked to it as obstacles are encountered and worked through. In fact, other problems may need to be modified before the representative problem can be resolved. Focused work on a limited problem then can have important consequences for the system. The representative problem can be seen as an arena in which family dynamics find concrete expression. To the extent they can be changed at all, these dynamics often can be altered more effectively by addressing specific manifestations than by attempting to wrestle directly (and often unsuccessfully) with the "big issues."

Because they do reflect these larger issues, representative problems can be expected to be stubborn. When progress does not occur, practitioners may feel tempted to shift the focus to underlying patterns or to "more significant" problems, particularly if the problem at hand seems minor. Such a move often is a mistake. The practitioner usually finds herself confronting the same obstacles on other fronts or, worse still, lacking any clear focus for work. Meanwhile, whatever progress has been achieved on the representative problem may be lost. It usually is better strategy to stay with the target problem and its obstacles, or at least to "keep it alive" while attention is broadened to other areas.

Although problems in the model express the concerns of family members, the practitioner has the responsibility of constructing formulations from the typically fragmented, shifting, and contradictory complaints and observations that emerge from family members' presentations of problems as they see them. She must also begin to understand the nature and context of these concerns. To carry out these functions, the practitioner needs to listen with a sensitive and knowledgeable ear to the flow of client "problem talk" that dominates the beginning of treatment. Families rarely present *the* problem or problems in a clear, concise, and considerate fashion. The practitioner must deal with a description that unfolds from numerous discrete statements made by different family members. Several perspectives can fruitfully be brought to bear as a means of comprehending and organizing these communications.

Speaker. Problem descriptions are made by individuals. Rarely do family members speak in concert, even though case examples sometimes give this impression. Noting who puts most of the problems on the table gives us an idea of who is the most anxious to see changes brought about, or who within the family will give clues about family relationships discussed consequently.

Content. Perhaps the next most obvious aspect of a problem description is that it is about something. From the vantage point of the speaker, the description indicates that something is undesirable. The "something" has a location in the system, usually pertaining to the behavior of another family member (Sandra is always mouthing off) but maybe relating to some aspect of family interaction (We don't get along), to an external system (Carl's teacher is giving him a hard time), and now and then to the speaker's own actions (I lose my temper too much). Characteristics of whatever is undesirable are described. As statements accumulate, it becomes possible to determine who or what are the focal subjects of the speaker's concerns and what in general he or she finds objectionable.

Responsibilities and Consequences. Sometimes by implication and sometimes directly, problem statements reveal the speaker's attribution about who or what is responsible for the difficulty and who is being hurt by it. Often where the problem is located and how it is characterized reveals the speaker's thoughts about responsibility, as in, "Harry doesn't care how he acts." But sometimes the problem is located in one place and responsibility in another (David is failing in school, but it's really his father's fault). Responsibility, as used here, incorporates the family members' perceptions of causation, which, even if inaccurate, can give clues about how family members view problems and one another (She gets that temper from her mother).

Acknowledgment. "For whom is what a problem?" is the question here. A family member who acknowledges a problem says in effect, "This is troubling or aggravating me," but may or may not see himself as the cause of the difficulty or take responsibility for it. Indeed most problems acknowledged by family members appear to take the form of complaints about one another. When the person complained about does not acknowledge the problem, it can be said that he has a problem attributed to him. The designation of "attributed problem" is useful as a means of distinguishing between self-perceived difficulties and those attributed by others. If we say that Mr. L has a "drinking problem," it is important to know if Mr. L sees it that way or if the problem is the construction of others.

Relationship Patterns. As already seen, how family members define problems reveals their relationships with one another. Connections may be fairly obvious. Thus, complaints by a father about lack of obedience and threatening behavior on the part of his son who, in turn, complains of being grounded excessively is indicative of a pattern of mutual coercion (chapter 4). Often, however, links between defined problems and relationship patterns are more subtle or suggest complexities in relationship patterns that will need to be explored further.

For example, at one point in the interview, a mother complained about her son's butting into conversations between her and her boyfriend; at another point the mother remarked that the son was interested only in himself and was not willing to listen to any problem she might have. Those disparate complaints suggested complex and inconsistent patterns of emotional involvement with her son. She appeared to need him as a confidant but also wanted him out of her space when her boyfriend was present.

The in vivo interactions occurring when problems are presented always are instructive. Who dominates the initial problem presentation, who defers to (or contradicts) whom, who participates and who remains apart, and who sides with whom are several possible facets of basic interactive processes, regardless of the content of the discussions. Issues concerning control, involvement, alliances, or flexibility (chapter 4) may be revealed by how the family discusses a problem. The practitioner's awareness of these issues becomes part of her understanding of context at this point as she relates to the family's expressed concerns. She may, however, inquire into a relationship difficulty that emerges in the presentation of problems. If family members acknowledge it as an area of concern, the practitioner may suggest that it be considered by the family as a possible target problem. If a relationship pattern is preventing the family from agreeing on a problem, then the practitioner usually focuses attention on the pattern as the problem to be dealt with.

3. Formulating Problems. The practitioner attempts to identify shared acknowledgments of problems and, where possible, to recast problems expressed in individual terms as problems of interactions between family members or as problems of the family as a whole. These reworkings of the problem are checked out with the family.

Fred, do you share your parents' concern that your school work is a problem?

Joyce, you think that Harry never wants to part with a dime—and Harry says you are an impulsive spender—so this seems to add up to a disagreement about how your money should be handled.

Each of you seems to think that someone else in the family causes these arguments. That's natural, but at least you agree that continued arguing is a problem.

The major reason for securing shared acknowledgments and putting problems in terms of interactions within family units is to begin to create a climate of joint responsibility for the family's difficulties. Sometimes it may not be possible to move very far in that direction in the initial interview. Family members may not get beyond the point of blaming each other while defending themselves. The practitioner can still introduce an interactive theme by putting the difficulty in terms of one family member's concern for (or objections to) another's behavior. "You don't like Dan's drinking habits," "The two of you are worried about Tim's difficulties at school." In any event, the practitioner tries to help each family member articulate some change he or she would like to see in the family so that each has some investment in at least one problem. To be avoided are problem formulations in which one family member is given or accepts total responsibility for the family's troubles.

Helping clients put problems in interactional form is one way of "reframing" the difficulty (Segal 1981; de Shazer 1982; Fisch, Weakland, and Segal 1982). More generally, reframing gives family members a different definition of the situation, one that may help them see the problem in a new light. Often the reframing consists of redefining the problem in less negative, more constructive terms. Thus, the parents' complaint that their teenage son doesn't do what he is told may be reframed as a disagreement about the amount of freedom he is entitled to—a reframe that may make the problem formulation more palatable to the son and that may start the parents thinking about his need for independence. (See also "positive explanation," Chapter 5.)

Finally, as noted, the practitioner may suggest problem formulations based on difficulties that family members refer to or act out in the interview but do not verbalize as problems. These formulations, which may be used to broaden the family's conception of its difficulties, are offered as possibilities for the family to consider and react to. If there is recognition that the difficulty the practitioner has formulated is in fact a concern, the problem may be added to a list for ranking by the family, as discussed in step 5 below.

4. Special Situations. The procedures described for eliciting problems from family members and their subsequent exploration are based on assumptions that the relevant family unit is present in the initial interview and that members have problems they are ready to divulge. When this assumption does not apply, additional or alternative procedures may need to be used. In some cases, it is the practitioner and not the family who initiates contact. The most common examples in social work are child protective cases involving suspected abuse or neglect. The family usually is not seeking help and may not be willing to reveal any problems it may have to the practitioner. Or a child may be in placement, and the only problem the family sees concerns return of the child. The practitioner on the other hand may have in mind certain requirements that may need to be met before the child can be returned. Many of these cases involve "mandated" problems, which essentially are problems that are defined not by the family but by the community and its representatives, including the practitioner. Essentially, the social worker needs to reveal to the family at the onset the general shape of these mandated problems (Rooney 1981). As Rzepnicki (1985) has suggested and demonstrated, a reasonable next step is to work with the family and relevant community agencies in an effort to negotiate problem definitions that are acceptable to those involved.

In another kind of situation one family member, usually a child or adolescent, may be a reluctant participant. A family may have sought help for a youngster's problems in the school or in the community. In the initial problem presentation, the parent or parents may describe the problem primarily in terms of the troublesome behavior of the child. The child may refuse to participate or may do so only in a minimal fashion; or, instead of revealing a problem that he wants to work on, he may defend himself against the parents' accusations. If efforts to draw the youngster out do not succeed, the practitioner moves ahead with the parents' definition of the problem and attempts to help the child accept it. At the same time, she expresses understanding of the child's predicament from his point of view and expresses the hope that he will be able to reveal difficulties that he wants changed (see chapter 9).

In still another kind of situation, the case may open with an interview with one or more family members, usually a spouse or parent(s) whose presenting problems concern behavior of mem-

bers of the family not present. The practitioner follows procedures presented in this chapter and elsewhere (Reid 1978) for
eliciting and formulating the client's problems. The formulations are kept tentative, however, and the contracting phase is
deferred until other relevant members of the family can be seen.
If the client present is not willing to involve other members or
does not want the practitioner to make this attempt herself, then
the case proceeds with the single client. The issue of involving
other family members may remain an open one to be taken up
later.

In all of these situations and in others, there may be need to
obtain information from community agencies such as courts,
schools, or hospitals before coming to closure on the problem
formulation. The final formulation of the problem and contracting may be deferred until such information is obtained.

Finally, more than one interview may be needed to complete
the initial phase. Illustrative cases are those in which family
members have difficulty articulating problems or are generally
suspicious of the practitioner, or where problem expression is
blocked by conflict within the session. While it is generally desirable to come to closure on at least one target problem in the
opening session, it is recognized that this ideal cannot always be
attained.

5. Determining Target Problems and Goals. The initial problem
exploration should usually produce several issues that have
been clarified in the preceding step. The practitioner states
these roughly in the order of their presumed importance to the
family. Considerations presented in the preceding sections provide guidelines for the formulations. The problems then are
ranked by family members in the order they would like to see
them solved.

The practitioner records and reviews the rank orderings and
suggests a way of proceeding based on data the family members
have supplied. Generally the practitioner suggests which problem she thinks should be dealt with first and indicates how other
problems can be worked in. Normally the problem suggested for
immediate work is the one selected as the most important by

most family members present. If the family is split on its choice, then the practitioner usually selects the problem that seems most amenable to change on grounds that it is important to achieve some progress quickly. The second problem can be phased in almost immediately (the following week), and the two then can be worked on together.

Even if the family agrees on the "number one" problem, there may be grounds for suggesting that it not be taken up at once—it may need further clarification, it may be laden with more conflict than can be handled, and so on. It may make more sense to begin with a more readily manageable problem of lower priority in order to start positive changes in motion and to set the stage for work on the more important issue. Reasons for these variations are shared with the family, and its approval is obtained.

Generally no more than three problems are chosen as targets at this point. However, the problem list can be modified as work proceeds. Problems can be revised, added, or dropped, and priorities can be rearranged.

To provide clarity of agreement and focus, the problem is expressed in the form of an operational or working definition. Given the multidimensional nature of problems in task-centered family practice, the following format has been found useful in problem description. A problem is briefly described and located in a phrase or sentence (the problem statement), which is followed by names or initials of family members acknowledging the difficulty. This format is illustrated by a case in which two problems were formulated.

Problem 1: *Carl's difficulty with school work (Mr. A, Mrs. A, Carl).*
Problem 2: *(Mr. and Mrs. A's quarreling over how to handle Carl (Mr. and Mrs. A).* (The working definition is completed with a fuller (one paragraph) description of each problem. This description provides details on the frequency, severity, and other pertinent characteristics of the problem. The second of the problems above might be described as follows):

Mr. and Mrs. A have been quarreling often, about two or three times a week, about Carl's school work. Mrs. A has tried to persuade Mr. A that Carl needs outside tutoring or that he should spend more time helping him with his studies, while Mr. A thinks the problem can be handled by convincing Carl of the importance of doing his homework and withdrawing privileges if he does not. Their arguments have been confined to the issue with Carl and have not "gotten out of hand" up to this point.

An alternative format is to list specific conditions that help spell out the problem. This format is especially useful if the problem consists of a configuration of discrete but related issues. The statement spanning these issues may be fairly global but the enumeration of conditions provides needed specificity. In problems involving pervasive conflict, the conditions enumerated may take the form of examples of current difficulties.

For example, a problem might be stated as *Gail and Barry have trouble communicating*. Under this very global problem statement might be listed such specifics as

a. They can't agree on whom to have as friends.
b. They have trouble making their sexual needs clear to one another.
c. They get into sullen silences following minor quarrels. For example, they didn't speak to each other the rest of the day after an argument about who was to make the coffee at breakfast.

Although a problem statement as general as the one given is far from optimal, it may be the best that can be formulated initially with a family that is vague or scattered in its complaints. This may be preferable to simply listing difficulties as discrete problems, especially if family members see them as interconnected.

Even if not written out, this kind of factual description of the problem should be pulled together by the practitioner and reviewed with clients. Presenting the working definition at this point is for the purpose of showing what a problem looks like at the brass tacks, empirical level. A definition at this level provides a clearer point of reference for subsequent discussion than the more abstract formulations presented previously.

Although target problems so defined may be relatively clear, they are by no means simply arrived at or fixed. They are constructed from complex, interrelated, and shifting realities. It is always a challenge to extract entities called "problems" from these realities. As the family's involvement and the practitioner's understanding grow and as events take place, original problem formulations may change (Tolson 1984).

Once initial agreement on problems has been reached, goals for each problem are clarified. Goals reflect what family members hope to achieve in effecting solutions for the problems. Often the practitioner can suggest goal statements based on prior discussion of the problem or the way the problem is formulated. For a problem of conflict between mother and daughter over the daughter's boyfriend, the goal naturally might be some reduction in conflict. It may be neither realistic nor necessary to call for elimination of conflict on this issue. Or if the problem of natural parents is the loss of their child to the welfare system, and they have made it clear that they wish to have their child back, then the goal again is rather apparent. However, if the problem was stated as "missing their child" and it was not clear what they wanted to do about it, there then could be several goal possibilities: reducing their feelings of longing, securing visiting arrangements or trying to get their child back. When the goal is not apparent, the practitioner needs to explore possibilities with the family members, beginning with those who appear to have the greatest stake in solution of the problem.

6. *Orientation and Contract.* Once agreement on target problems and goals has been reached, the practitioner explains the approach she plans to use. The explanation makes clear that service will concentrate on the target problems and their immediate causes, that the practitioner's major role will be to guide the clients' own problem-solving efforts (organized in the form of tasks), and that service will consist of a number of interviews, usually eight to twelve.

The orientation to the model can precede the initial problem survey, and should if clients have questions at the beginning about the service the practitioner plans to offer. However, delaying the orientation to this point enables the practitioner to be more specific about what is to be done.

Client approval of the service plan is obtained. In the process clients' questions are answered, or a rationale for different parts of the service plan are given. Some explanation of the reason for the service limits usually should be offered. The best rationale that can be given simply is that short-term service, according to a considerable amount of research, is usually as effective as a longer period of service—that whatever can be gained from counseling usually is gained quickly (chapter 3). Clients can be advised that service limits can be reconsidered as the agreed-upon termination point approaches, and more service can be offered if it seems indicated in their particular case.

Basically, the family's acceptance of the service plan as offered, explained, and qualified by the practitioner constitutes the service agreement or contract. It should be explained that the agreements are open to revision. Service limits as well as problems and goals can be modified with the clients' consent. It should be understood, and also can be explained, that the initial contract is an expression of a process of proceeding by explicit agreement and is designed to give the family clear control over the objectives of treatment.

7. *Detailed Exploration of the Target Problems.* The target problems established in step 5 are explored in greater detail. The amount of time to be devoted to this step and what exactly is to be covered will depend on what has been revealed about the problem in previous steps. The following data, if not already obtained, are secured for each problem: (a) approximately when the problem began and outstanding facts about its course to present; (b) its severity and frequency during a brief period, from one to two weeks prior to the interiew; (c) what efforts have been made to solve it; (d) obstacles preventing solution of the problem and other relevant contextual factors. When problems are complex, or if it is difficult to elicit data, detailed exploration may be concentrated on the first problem. It is likely that material pertaining to other problems, will emerge, particularly contextual data.

Explorations and assessment of problems and their contexts are activities that start in the first encounter with family members and continue through the final session. From the beginning these activities are guided and informed by the family's problem-solving efforts. If the family moves forward quickly toward solution of its problems, exploratory and assessment activities may be minimal. They are intensified if this forward movement does not occur. Continuing exploration of the problems themselves is concerned with obtaining information about their occurrence as a means of additional specification, of monitoring change, and as a basis for problem focusing and contextual understanding. The question guiding this kind of exploration is, "What is happening?" It is accented toward eliciting the facts and details of how problems play themselves out.

Interwoven with the problem exploration is investigation of contextual factors. This activity is largely a search for obstacles and resources that have a bearing on the problem. An obstacle is essentially anything that stands in the way of problem resolution.

Little can be done about some obstacles thay may constitute limitations or constraints in a case. Thus, a father's physical incapacity may interfere with tasks requiring mobility, and the tasks may need to be adjusted to the limitation. If a task (or problem) is blocked completely by unmodifiable obstacles, then the formulation of the task (or problem) needs to be altered. While fixed obstacles must be understood and reckoned with, our search is concentrated on obstacles "with give."

Because obstacles keep problems alive, they are equivalent to active causes of the problem. The concept of obstacle is preferred because it focuses on what needs to be worked through and avoids the difficulty inherent in "explaining" problems through the logic of causation. Any problem can be seen as the result of multiple causes extending from factors directly responsible for its existence to remote etiologic origins. The practitioner is not interested in tracing causal chains back through time, even if this were possible, but rather is concerned with locating current factors whose modification would make a difference in the problem—hence, the preference for obstacle over causes. Past causes are of interest only insofar as they aid in understanding present obstacles.

Whereas obstacles maintain problems, resources facilitate their solution. Interest here is centered on the strengths that one may find within the family or in its external involvement. To identify resources, the practitioner needs to be sensitive to possibilities and explore promising leads. This calls for a switch from the usual problem-pathology focus that practitioners tend to gravitate toward in work with troubled families. Obviously, a considerable amount of attention needs to be given to the family's difficulties, but at the same time an unrelenting preoccupation with what is wrong will blind the practitioner to resources that may be used in solving the problem. One key is to evaluate the functioning of family members, even problem behavior, with an eye to potential strengths. More is called for here than simply reframing or interpreting behavior in a positive light. Rather, one identifies the constructive elements of action in order to use them. In a father's attempt to break up his daughter's relationship with an "undesirable" boyfriend, there might be some elements of concern for her welfare that could serve in the daughter's interests.

In her exploration, the practitioner tries to identify obstacles that can be modified and resources that can be put to work in the present. Not a great deal is accomplished by dwelling on entrenched causes or latent potentials.

The here-and-now orientation of the model does not deny the importance of eliciting selective historical data as they pertain to the development of the target problem. In the initial assessment, the practitioner usually is interested in determining when the problem (as currently defined) first appeared, the outlines of its course since that time, and how the family has coped with it. In exploration of the coping responses, the practitioner gives special attention to successful and unsuccessful ways of dealing with the problem. As has been observed by strategic therapists (Fisch, Weakland, and Segal 1982), problems can be maintained by unsuccessful solution efforts, which may, in fact, become part of the problem. Patterns of coercive symmetry (chapter 4) in which family members attempt to force their own solutions on one another provide a common illustration of this phenomenon. One also needs to ask about responses to the problem that, in the family's view, have worked. Even if they turn out to be part of unsuccessful solution efforts, they are likely to persist because they have been seen as successful. They may also provide clues as to what might be genuinely useful in helping the family develop a problem-solving strategy.

In exploring the history of a problem, the practitioner's attention is centered on data informing action that can be taken in the present. What are family members revealing about earlier events that may shed light on their current responses? Simple immersion in historical material is not sufficient. A conscious effort needs to be made to relate the past to the present. In work with married couples, current perceptions and reactions of spouses to one another may be influenced by old wounds in the marriage. A wife's negative reaction to her husband's going out for an occasional evening with men friends becomes more understandable when we learn that earlier in their marriage such a night out led to an involvement with another woman. Once brought to light, the wife's anxiety about her husband's fidelity can be dealt with as a current issue.

Important historical material of this kind is frequently brought up by clients, either because they perceive its relevance or because it is still alive in their minds. Pertinent material may be elicited by questions concerning when and how the problem developed, or by asking clients to recount whatever past events may have bearing on it. Often important historical data emerge later in treatment, in analysis of current obstacles.

Throughout this exploratory process, the search is for points of leverage to effect immediate change rather than for a "thorough understanding" of how the family works. The ideal of obtaining a clear and accurate picture of the causal patterns that produce family problems probably is mythical in any case. For example, take the common problem of the delinquent or predelinquent adolescent. There are numerous theories to explain the phenomenon but none has gained general acceptance. Delinquency, like most family problems, is an outgrowth of the complex and poorly understood interplay of cultural, societal, biopsychological, and family dynamics. We really cannot satisfactorily explain why Peter is in continual difficulty at school or why Paul sets fires. Explanations are at best tentative and partial. We hope to identify enough in the way of controlling factors to provide some guidance for our change efforts, but still we must rely to a large extent on standard interventions that appear to be somewhat successful on the average. The process can be better characterized as informed trial-and-error than applications of proven theories and methods.

Still, we assume that the better informed the trial and error is, the more helpful we can be. Data that would shed light on contextual factors are obtained in relation to what appears to be relevant to the problem at hand. The organizing concepts and formulations presented in the next two chapters provide guidance for the effort, or at least a framework and vocabulary that may be helpful in integrating theory, knowledge, research, and experience available to the practitioner.

8. *Initial Session Task.* The practitioner structures a session task on which family members work together for a few minutes on the first problem to be dealt with. The task serves both as assessment and a therapeutic function. It provides the practitioner with in vivo data on how family members interact; more specifically, it provides data on their problem-solving and communication skills. Additional facets of the problem also may be brought to light. As a therapeutic device, it provides family members with an opportunity to begin to develop a solution to one of their problems and to begin the process of developing more constructive ways of interacting. The task may involve all family members present or some other combination, such as a dyad, depending on the problem and communication patterns exhibited thus far in the session.

9. *Post-Task Discussion and Planning Initial Home Task.* After the session task has been brought to a close, the practitioner responds to the family's effort. Participants in the session task are given credit for positive aspects of their interactions. What has transpired in the task may lead to additional clarification of the problem. For example, some pattern of communication may be noted, and the practitioner may inquire if the pattern is similar to how the family members communicate at home.

The practitioner then generally helps the family develop one or more home tasks that can be carried out by family members prior to the next session. Usually the session task will have set the stage for the development of home tasks. In some cases, family members will have arrived at some type of action plan addressed to some aspect of the problem. The practitioner may need only to make sure that the plan can be set out in the form of specific actions or tasks that family members understand and agree to carry out. In other instances, some directions for task planning will have emerged and can be built upon. When the session task does not provide momentum, the practitioner may need to determine what family members think they can begin to do about the problem. Their ideas then become the stimuli for task development. If the family cannot provide ideas, the practitioner then suggests task possibilities for one or more tasks. Tasks are planned and, if necessary, rehearsed, incentives are established, and other task-implementation procedures are used (chapter 7).

In general, tasks are designed to be simple enough so that likelihood of their attainment is high, but they still should make a significant "bite" in the problem. They should be clearly stated, calling for specific, feasible actions, and they should be expressly agreed to by family members who are to carry them out. The principle of balance in who carries out tasks is important. Generally each participant in a problem should take on some task responsibility.

Home tasks may be augmented by environmental tasks undertaken either by the practitioner (practitioner tasks) or by family members. For example, the practitioner may agree to confer with school officials about reinstatement of a child who has been expelled, or an unemployed parent may agree to contact an employment agency. Depending on the problem, only environmental tasks may be used.

II. Middle Phase

The middle phase of treatment, which ideally begins with the second or third interview, consists of a series of weekly or twice-weekly sessions. Major procedures are briefly described below, and are discussed in detail in chapters 5, 6, and 7.

1. Task and Problem Reviews. The interview opens with a review of tasks attempted since the previous session and of developments in the target problems. Generally the *task review* is attempted first, although it may be temporarily displaced by developments in the problems, particularly if major changes for the better or worse have occurred. Should that be the case, the task review can be deferred until developments in the problems have been considered.

The task review covers what the clients or the practitioner have actually done in relation to the tasks agreed upon. Successful efforts or "good tries" by clients are credited. Difficulties in task implementation are explored. The resulting data may be used to guide subsequent task development.

Review of changes in the target problems *(problem review)* is actually an elaboration of the task review, which normally includes information on developments in the problems. Changes in the frequency and severity of problem occurrence are obtained, as well as additional detail on the characteristics and context of the problem.

What happens next in middle-phase interviews depends on the outcome of the problem and task reviews and related contextual factors. Several options are presented below, followed by consideration for their differential and combined use.

2. Problem Focusing. In family treatment, problems often are cast at a fairly general level or, if specific to begin with, may expand or shift. Tendencies toward diffuseness and instability in problem formulation are more of an issue in family than in individual treatment for several reasons.

Family members may be hard put to articulate amorphous interpersonal issues and to maintain agreement about their nature or relative importance. The family's concerns may jump from one issue to another depending on the course of interactive or environmental events. Finally, given the complexities of family interaction and constraints on communication in group sessions, hidden or underlying problems may surface after the initial contract has been formed. When the problem focus becomes blurred or unsteady, the practitioner faces a dilemma. On the one hand, she wants to avoid drifting aimlessly with the flow of the system. On the other, there is little point in rigid adherence to obsolete problem formulations. *Problem focusing* may be called for. In this procedure the practitioner attempts to make explicit connections between the issue on the table and agreed-on target problems. If some reasonable link can be made, work may proceed, perhaps with a modified conception of the target problem. There may be need for further focusing, however, on what is to be dealt with in the session.

If a link is not possible, the practitioner has three options: (1) to deal with the unrelated issues as a temporary diversion, which may be the only course of action if the issue is of crisis proportions (Rooney 1981); (2) to take the position with the family that the issue, while of legitimate concern, is tangential to the original target problem(s) and would be better left for the family to deal with; and (3) to formulate the issue as a new target problem, possibly replacing an original problem that is no longer of major interest. Which of these options is best pursued is largely a judgment call, but whatever is done there should be clarity with the family about what is being worked on, and agreement with the family about any significant changes in the formulation of the problem.

3. Contextual Analysis. During the course of the review of tasks and problems, obstacles to task achievement and problem change usually are encountered. As noted, the essential difference between a target problem and an obstacle is that the former is a difficulty that the family and practitioner have contracted to change, and the latter is a difficulty standing in the way of progress toward resolution of the target problem. An obstacle may reside in the functioning of individual family members, in their interactions, or in external systems. Obstacles may range from minor matters to issues of greater magnitude than the target problem itself.

Whereas obstacles block progress, resources facilitate it. Resources are usually found in strengths and competencies of individual family members, in the ties of loyalty and affection that hold families together, and in the intangible and tangible supports provided by external systems. However, a given characteristic may serve as either an obstacle or resource depending on its function in relation to the problem.

In *contextual analysis* the practitioner helps the family identify and resolve obstacles as well as to locate and utilize resources (chapter 5). The discussion is led by the practitioner, who relies on focused exploration, explanations, and other methods designed to increase the clients' understanding. The process may overlap with the problem and task reviews, when obstacles and resources may emerge and be explored. The practitioner may help individual family members modify distorted perceptions or unrealistic expectations of one another. Dysfunctional patterns of individual behavior or family interactions may be pointed out. Obstacles involving the external system, such as interactions between a child and school personnel, or the workings of a recalcitrant welfare bureaucracy, may be clarified or resources within these systems searched for. An effort is made to avoid concentrating attention on the problematic functioning of any one family member or explanations that would provoke defensive reactions. Whenever possible explanations are couched in terms that show the constructive intentions of family members ("positive interpretations"). The focus is on interaction rather than on individual behavior.

4. Session Tasks. Session tasks enable family members to work together on their problems as well as to improve problem-solving and communications skills (chapter 6). Tasks involve family members communicating directly with one another as in the initial session task, with the practitioner in roles of observer, facilitator, and coach. The tasks are designed by the practitioner to achieve limited objectives, which include negotiating a conflict, planning an activity, arriving at a decision, clarifying feelings and expectations, learning and practicing problem-solving communications, or putting a resource to work, as in the role-play example given earlier.

Before setting up the first of these session tasks, the practitioner explains their purpose—to help family members work out their own solutions and to improve their ability to communicate with one another—and may go over certain "ground rules" that will facilitate their work. For example, participants may be advised to talk directly to one another, to concentrate on the problem at hand, to avoid abusive language, and to be as concrete as possible when discussing problems or solutions.

Session tasks may be followed by short discussions involving all family members. The practitioner may comment on what was accomplished or demonstrated by the task or may point out obstacles to task performance. Efforts of the participants are praised whenever possible. Possibilities for home tasks may be identified. The post-task discussion may also provide the basis for structuring another session task.

Most session tasks are addressed to problems and obstacles. The practitioner normally proposes a particular kind of task for a given problem or obstacle. For example, if the target problem consisted of family members not spending enough time together, an appropriate session task might involve their planning joint activities. It is assumed that work on such straightforward tasks often will be blocked by various obstacles, usually in the interaction between the participants. These obstacles can be addressed by additional session tasks. For example, a couple attempts to negotiate an issue between them but fails to do so. One reason seems to be that they appear to be "talking past" one another and not listening to what they each are saying. This pattern is called to their attention but they continue to exhibit the same communication problem. The practitioner, observing that their emotional involvement in the issue may be preventing them from correcting the communication difficulty, devises a task in which they communicate about a less volatile issue, beginning each of the responses with a paraphrase of what the other has just said (Jacobson and Margolin 1979). Alternatively, obstacles arising from session tasks, particularly if they reflect larger issues, may be dealt with through the methods of contextual analysis.

5. Home and Environmental Tasks. Tasks undertaken outside the session by family members and the practitioner are addressed to bringing about change where change matters most—in the family's life at home or in the community. Ideally these tasks should be an outgrowth of problem-solving efforts in the session. They should be a means of implementing or extending this work.

When session tasks are not used or do not provide a sufficient base, planning for tasks outside the session is derived from the problem and task reviews, from problem exploration and focusing, and from contextual analysis. Regardless of the source of task possibilities, the practitioner is guided by one central question: who can do what about the problem between this session and the next? Developing tasks makes use of a set of procedures, the task planning and implementation sequence. Alternative task possibilities are generated, and explicit agreement is reached on the tasks to be done. These tasks are then planned in greater detail with attention as needed given to motivational factors and potential obstacles. Brief rehearsals and practice of tasks may be employed. Task plans are summarized at the end of the session.

Task development may consist of fairly lengthy problem-solving work involving the practitioner and family members. Although the purpose of this step is to arrive at viable tasks, a good deal of preliminary work may be required. For example, it may be necessary to help parents and their adolescent son negotiate rules about homework before particular tasks can be devised. (If a session task format is not feasible, the practitioner may need to remain directly involved in the negotiation process.)

A fundamental principle is to concentrate on alleviating target problems through relatively simple, straightforward tasks. These tasks may be designed to effect contextual change in passing, but the target problems should be the first priority. Structural dysfunctions, underlying pathologies, and so on are left alone unless they intrude as obstacles. To the extent they do, practitioners then can shift toward tasks more directed at contextual change—tasks, including paradoxical varieties, that may be aimed at structural modifications. This progression from the simple to the not-so-simple fits the needs of social workers who deal with a wide range of family types, from normal to highly disturbed, across a wide variety of problems and settings, and who may not be expert in family therapy. Many families do not want a change in structure, many problems do not require it, and many practitioners lack the skill to effect it.

Certain functions, limitations, and planning requirements can be identified for each of the major types of home tasks, *shared, reciprocal,* and *individual.* Shared tasks, which family members do together, provide a means for continuing at-home problem solving and communication tasks worked on in the session; for enabling family members to work together on practical projects, such as home improvements; and for affecting relationships between family members. In respect to the latter function, family members can be brought closer together through activities that are mutually enjoyable, or alignments can be strengthened or weakened. For example, two sets of shared tasks—one set involving both parents in some activity and the other involving siblings in a separate activity—can be used to strengthen the boundary of the parental subsystem and weaken a coalition between a parent and child.

Reciprocal tasks make use of the principle of reciprocity in arranging for exchange between family members. Exchanges may involve comparable behaviors, as is usually the case among family members who occupy equal status, such as husband and wife. In another form, compliance to rules may be exchanged for rewards, or noncompliance for penalties—the form reciprocal tasks usually take between unequals, such as parents and children.

Whatever their form, reciprocal tasks require that participants express a willingness to cooperate and regard the exchange as equitable. Although it is important to work out the details of the exchange in the session, a "collaborative set" (Jacobson and Margolin 1979) is esssential to insure that participants are prepared to accept reasonable approximations or equivalents of expected behavior, rather than letter-of-the-law performance, and are willing to adjust expectations in the light of unanticipated circumstances. All of this suggests that work in the session toward clarifying and negotiating conflicts around particular issues precedes the setting up of reciprocal tasks to deal with issues at home. If reciprocal tasks are "tacked on" at the end of session without sufficient preparatory work, they are likely to fail.

Individual tasks, which do not require collaborative activity or specific reciprocation, serve several important functions in the model. First, they provide opportunities for family members to volunteer independent problem-solving action for the common good. Much problem solving in everyday family life seems to occur this way. Family members may do what needs to be done to help solve a problem without expectations of immediate payback, though they may expect that others eventually will do their share. Second, individual tasks are useful in situations of conflict too intense to allow for collaboration or exchanges between family members. For example, a husband and wife may agree to take on tasks with provisions for self-administered rewards if completed (Weiss, Birchler, and Vincent 1974) . An adolescent who is rejecting parental authority may be willing to pursue tasks in his or her self interest that also may help alleviate a family problem. A third function for individual tasks arises when the lack of autonomy in a relationship is an obstacle to change. For example, a diabetic youngster who is being smothered by overprotective parents might undertake a series of tasks designed to enable him to be responsible for his own medication. Finally, individual tasks can be used to involve a family member left out of reciprocal or shared tasks undertaken by other family members.

Practitioners make use of formulations concerning task functions in suggesting task possibilities to clients, in responding to the client's ideas for tasks, and in the give-and-take of the planning process. These formulations, as well as other knowledge, inform the practitioner's contribution to collaborative work with the family. However, they do not provide a set of rules for "task assignments."

III. Termination

In the task-centered model, the termination process actually is begun in the initial phase when an understanding about the expected direction of service is reached with the family. This agreement can be modified at any point during the service contract, preferably before the final interview. In some cases, brief extensions beyond agreed-upon limits may be called for to complete work on target problems, especially when there has been evidence of progress. In other cases, termination may be delayed until some decisive event, such as a court hearing about the return of a child, has occurred. In still other cases, a second service contract consisting of an additional eight to twelve sessions may be arranged to work on additional problems (Reid 1978).

The principle is to use termination in a flexible way to help families achieve realistic goals and to end service with a feeling of accomplishment. Extensions should be arrived at in a deliberate manner, related to explicit objectives, and based on an expressed desire of the family to prolong the service.

The terminal interview should begin with a review of the family's progress during treatment. It helps the family examine what has been accomplished and sets the stage for subsequent consideration of what it may wish to work on after treatment has terminated. The review should begin with examinations of change in the target problems. For each problem, the practitioner should determine the extent and direction of change from the point of view of each family member present. Remaining issues relating to these problems as well as other problems of concern to family members then should be explored.

The family's plans for dealing with difficulties they are currently facing should be considered, with emphasis on how the aproaches used in the model can be applied to them. Plans for a follow-up session, or needs for additional help and how it may be obtained, can be discussed. The family's sense of having made some progress, which should be present in most cases, is highlighted and reinforced.

6. *Differential Use of Interventions.* The model presents three principal types of intervention aimed directly at problem resolution: contextual analysis, session tasks, and home and environmental tasks. Of the three, home and environmental tasks are used consistently throughout the course of treatment. Every session should end with the planning of at least one such task to promote implementation of change where it matters most, in the family's life situation. Variation in use of procedures generally involves relative emphasis given to planning these tasks, to session tasks, and to contextual analysis. Influential factors include the nature of the problem or obstacles to be addressed, the family's problem-solving abilities and style, the level of conflict in the session, and the practitioner's own orientation.

A general guide is to follow the overall strategy of the model, which calls for giving the family the opportunity to do as much of the problem-solving work as it is able to. Thus, first consideration usually is given to session tasks that are tried out in the initial session and subsequent to it. If these appear to be successful, they can become the central modality for much of the planning of tasks, even for those outside the session. Problems or obstacles involving difficulty in face-to-face communications lend themselves particularly well to this approach. In fact, session tasks can be used in sequence to provide learning in problem-solving communication (chapter 6.).

When the value of session tasks proves to be limited because of conflict among family members or for other reasons, more stress will be placed on other modalities. Complex obstacles in the family system, particularly those operating ouside the awareness of family members, may call for greater use of contextual analysis as a means of determining what tasks in and out of the session may be most effective. Some families can make better use of contextual analysis than others, and some practitioners are more comfortable and skilled than others with this approach.

An alternative to reliance on either session tasks or contextual analysis is to emphasize planning of home and environmental tasks with the family through an open discussion format. In this approach, the practitioner can still give the family a good deal of opportunity to develop its own solutions and can provide input more easily than she can in the session task structure. This strategy may be preferable when problems or obstacles can be resolved by tasks with which the practitioner may have a good deal of expertise, such as ways of managing child behavior problems or of dealing with external systems. An attempt still would be made to work toward the use of session tasks.

When a target problem fails to respond to any of these methods, the practitioner, retracing her steps, usually raises question about the formulation of the problem. Is the problem still something the family wishes to work on? Exploration of family members' opinions and feelings about this issue may lead to a new and perhaps more fruitful way of formulating the problem, or in some cases to a decision that not much can be done about it.

CASE ILLUSTRATIONS

Because the model incorporates a variety of options for different situations, a large number of cases would be needed to illustrate the full range of possibilities. The three cases that follow provide examples of characteristic and important features.

Mrs. Johnson contacted a family agency because of problems concerning her sixteen-year-old daughter, Nancy, and the resulting fighting in her family. In an initial interview, the parents, Nancy, and her fourteen-year-old brother, Mark, presented their views of the problems. Mr. J began the session with a stream of complaints about Nancy. Her "attitude" toward him and his wife was "hostile." She did not accept his beliefs or standards. Any attempt to communicate with her was futile. He then turned to the problem that precipitated their contact with the agency: Nancy's insistence that her boyfriend, Mike (age nineteen), be allowed to visit in their home over the weekend.

Mr. J had objected to Nancy's relationship with Mike ever since Nancy's pregnancy and abortion about six months earlier, but had accepted it because Nancy was determined to see him anyway. He even tolerated his coming to their home but did not want him there all weekend (Mike would stay over Friday and Saturday night, using a spare room). He saw Mike as an unwelcome intruder whose presence deprived Mr. J of his privacy.

Joining in, Mrs. J complained of Nancy's nagging her to get permission to do things her father might not allow. If Mrs. J refused, Nancy would become belligerent and insulting. On top of this, Mrs. J usually would be the one to patch things up between Nancy and her father. Nancy said little, but expressed bitterness that her parents were trying to disrupt her relationship with Mike. When asked about his views of the problem by the practitioner, Mark commented in a somewhat detached way that the fighting between his mother and Nancy was the main difficulty.

From the family's presentation of the problems and their interactions in the session, the practitioner was impressed with the father's lack of real control and Nancy's efforts to get what she wanted through her mother, who was put in the middle. Further exploration made clearer the mother's "peace keeping" role and her discontent with it. The practitioner presented this picture as an additional problem to be considered.

In ranking the problems that had been brought up, the family agreed that the issue of greatest priority concerned the conflict over Mike's visiting. They accepted the practitioner's formulation of "mother's being in the middle" as a second problem.

The family was seen for seven additional sessions. The main interventions were structured around problem-solving tasks in the session and at home. These tasks were designed to achieve a compromise around Mike's visiting and, in the process, to work on the dysfunctional interaction patterns that had been identified. Initially, these tasks were designed to bring about more direct communication between Nancy and her father as well as more cooperation between the parents. It become apparent, however, that the interaction pattern was more complex than originally thought. Mrs. J was not the only peacemaker. Mr. J frequently assumed this role with Nancy and her mother. The parents were then coming to each other's rescue without taking responsibility either individually or jointly for dealing with Nancy's behavior. In subsequent family problem-solving tasks, each parent agreed to take responsibility for settling his or her differences with Nancy without trying to rescue the other. At the same time, an effort was made to encourage the parents jointly to develop rules that each could apply consistently in dealing with Nancy.

Midway in treatment, a compromise was reached on Nancy's relationship with Mike. Mike could spend one night a week at the J's home but would not be there on the weekend. Interestingly enough, the solution was suggested by Mark, who had remained somewhat on the sidelines in the family discussions. The plan was implemented and, perhaps to everyone's surprise, held up.

The case ended on a positive note. The immediate problem had been worked through and the family members, in their evaluation of treatment, indicated that their situation as a whole was better. In her consumer questionnaire, Mrs. J commented that the experience had been a "good lesson in problem working."

The case illustrates several features of the model. Focus was on the specific problem the family most wanted to solve. The major intervention strategy was based on tasks in which family members struggled toward a solution in their own way. At the same time, dysfunctional patterns of intervention that might underlie this and other problems were explicitly identified with the family and worked on as a part of the problem-solving tasks. Not all cases present such opportunities to achieve contextual change. In this case, they were present and were well-utilized by the family and practitioner.

The second case illustrates additional concepts of the intervention strategy presented in the chapter. Specifically, it demonstrates the process of identifying obstacles and resources and developing tasks to resolve the former and utilize the latter.

Mrs. N requested help from a counseling center for her son Donald, age 15, who was presenting behavior problems at school. The N household consisted of Mrs. N (divorced), Don, and an older sister. Don had frequent difficulties in the classroom and in his interactions with school personnel, including temper outbursts, swearing at teachers, and "cutting up" in gym. These episodes often led to temporary suspensions from class or from school.

A second problem involved Don's presumably sexually active relationship with a girl about his age. In an individual session,

Mrs. N expressed her fears that the two were not using contraceptives. She had been unable to discuss the issue with him. Reciprocal tasks involving Donald and his mother were designed to tackle the school problem. Although the details of the task were complicated, in brief, Donald was to improve his behavior at school to the point where he would not be suspended. If he succeeded, his mother would provide a monetary reward; if he failed, he was to be "grounded." The tasks appeared to bring about a modest change for the better in Donald's behavior, but not enough to avoid suspensions. Over the course of several joint sessions with Donald and his mother, the practitioner explored possible obstacles and resources relating to the problems. In table 2.1 are listed obstacles (and resources) identified and the interventions attempted as a means of resolving (or utilizing) them.

Table 2.1. Obstacles, Resources, and Interventions: N Case

Obstacles	*Interventions*
1. Donald's lack of skill in asserting self with school personnel.	Use of role play in the session to help Donald learn how to express feelings of being treated unfairly without losing control.
2. Donald's self-reported "feeling of power" when he shows aggression toward school personnel, which was related to his belief that they treated him unfairly.	Use of contextual analysis to help Donald see that aggression resulted in loss of power and that properly assertive response might give him greater feeling of power.
3. School not informing Mrs. N about Donald's suspension. She was thus dependent on information from Donald, which was not always accurate, in providing rewards and sanctions.	Practitioner task to remind school personnel of agreement to keep Mrs. N informed, with successful results.
4. Donald's getting gratification in having time with mother when he is grounded for a suspension. Donald had acknowledged his	Reciprocal task altered to make time with mother a reward for improved behavior and to avoid mother's giving additional time

wanting to have more time with his mother but not the connection between grounding and the added time. When grounded he and mother did spend more time together.

5. Donald's suspected wish to disrupt Mrs. N's relationship with her boyfriend, Harry. By being a school problem, Donald perhaps believed that he might discourage Harry, who had commented unfavorably on his school behavior. Donald was openly antagonistic to Harry but had not verbalized any link between his school behavior and his desire to have Harry out of the picture. Mother had told Donald, however, that Harry might break off the relationship because of Donald's behavior with him and at school. Evidence concerning obstacle sketchy and incomplete.

when grounded. Shared tasks involving activity between Donald and mother to satisfy his need for maternal attention.

Exploration of Donald's possible rivalry with Harry for mother's attention, and his recognition of mother's need for adult relationships; Mrs. N advised not to hang her difficulties in her relationship with Harry around Donald's neck. Interventions made in tentative, low-key manner given quality of evidence.

Resources

1. Mrs. N's ability to handle provocation without losing her composure.

2. Open, informal communication between Don and sister..

Interventions

Session task in which Don took role of provocative teacher, with Mrs. N assuming Don's role; Mrs. N modeled ways of handling provocation.

As a task, Mrs. N requested that sister talk to Don about contraception, resources, and getting information; sister did, leading to resolution of problem.

As the example shows, contextual data are obtained in relation to possible obstacles and resources. The first two obstacles are "located" in Donald's functioning, the third in the external environment, and the last two primarily in his interaction with his mother. One theme connecting several obstacles appeared to be the incentives supporting Donald's school problem: a desire for power, need for maternal attention, and rivalry toward mother's relationship with Harry. Another theme seemed to be the symmetrical involvement between Don and his mother. Although the relationship was characterized by mutual concern, which was a source of strength, their tendency to relate as equals and their emotional interdependency seemed to stand in the way of Mrs. N's enforcing rules consistently and to feed Don's antipathy toward Harry.

In keeping with the model, obstacles are identified in relation to family members' continuing struggles with their problems, including their work on tasks and their responses to intervention. Once identified, an effort is made to address the obstacles through contextual analysis and session, home, or environmental tasks, as illustrated by the interventions. Obstacles are understood in relation to whatever theoretical framework seems to best fit the circumstances at hand. In the example given, there are applications of learning, cognitive, and labeling theories as well as use of insights from psychodynamic and structural perspectives. The formulations of obstacles are viewed as partial and tentative. No attempt is made to arrive at any overarching explanation of the many complexities of the problem or of the case, although an attempt is made, as shown in the preceding discussion, to identify patterns that might tie together different obstacles and serve as the basis of identifying others.

A good deal of attention is given to evidence that might bear upon formulation of an obstacle. Speculative theorizing— as one might be tempted to do, in regard to the Don-mother-Harry triangle—is avoided or at least recognized for what it is. Interventions based on speculative formulations are put in the form of probes or experiments, designed in part to gain additional data.

Premature closure on a particular formulation is avoided in favor of consideration of plausible alternatives. For example, although it was clear that Don was antagonistic to Harry and wanted his mother to break off the relationship, there was no strong evidence of a connection between this issue and Don's school problem. The link is based on inference. An alternative explanation, that the problem at school and with Harry are independent of each other, cannot be ruled out.

Although the client's resources are brought to bear in any task, deliberate attention to the capabilities and strengths of the family can suggest promising task possibilities. As the example suggests, resource-based tasks can not only offer fresh alternatives but also avoid obstacles that may prove to be difficult to tackle. Thus, Mrs. N may not have been able to communicate with Donald about contraceptives, but his sister could.

Finally, the case illustrates use of interventions on different systems levels. Although the primary unit of treatment is the mother-son dyad, interventions are also addressed to Donald and his mother as individuals and to the school system.

The setting for the final case is a ward of a psychiatric center. Terry, age twenty, had been an inpatient for several months. She had been admitted following an acute psychotic episode in which she threatened to harm herself and her infant daughter, Kim. She had been hospitalized on two previous occasions following violent outbursts and apparently psychotic behavior. A high school dropout, Terry had never been competitively employed. She lived with Jake, a man in his late twenties, who had a drinking problem and had not been regularly employed for several years. Kim currently was being cared for by Terry's sister. Terry and Jake had one previous child who had been placed in adoption. The couple's relationship had been tempestuous with numerous episodes of violence. Terry currently was on probation for stabbing Jake during one of their quarrels.

Jake, who was anxious to start living again with Terry, complained that the hospital was messing up their lives by keeping her there, and he had been pressuring Terry to try for an immediate discharge. Because Terry's involvement with Jake was central in her life, her social worker suggested that he participate in developing a discharge plan. Terry and Jake were agreeable to this. The practitioner opted to use the task-centered model and to see the two of them together.

During the initial phase (two joint sessions), Jake asked hostile questions about why the hospital had kept her so long, while

Terry said that they only needed an apartment. She later added her need for a job and her wish to obtain her G.E.D. (General Education Diploma). Jake saw their problem primarily in terms of Terry's "crazy" behavior. He was afraid she would "go off" and hurt him or the baby. When things got tense he would storm out. Terry replied that his drinking up the food and rent money drove her wild.

Although Jake wanted Terry and Kim to move in with him and his family until they could find a place of their own, Terry was hesitant. Perhaps she was not ready to leave the hospital just yet. As this discussion developed, the practitioner pointed out that both the court and the hospital were insisting on her spending a period of time in a transitional unit and described a "supervised apartment" program as one possibility. Terry was unsure; Jake was opposed to any further delay in her discharge, though he wanted her to remain in treatment as an outpatient so she could continue to receive medications.

Target problems and goals were developed, and a service contract calling for six to eight sessions was set up. In terms of goals, the contract called for both Terry and Jake to get jobs, for Terry to enroll in a G.E.D. program, and for both to be able to discuss differences without Terry losing control or Jake's leaving. The last goal was derived from the practitioner's interactional formulation of the individual complaints of each and was accepted by both. A goal for Terry to move from the hospital ward to a supervised apartment was added as a "mandated" problem/goal—one required by the court and the hospital as a condition for her discharge.

In the joint session, tasks were devised and worked on. Terry started employment in a sheltered workshop; Jake carried through on job search tasks and found a part-time job. In order to provide Terry with an incentive to move ahead with the sheltered workshop program and to permit her and Jake to have time alone together, she was given passes for dates with Jake as rewards for satisfactory performance. Terry and Jake helped devise this task plan, and it worked well from their point of view. Modeling, role play, and rehearsals were used in session tasks to work on the couple's communication problems. The social worker, a male, made use of a female co-therapist to model how problems might be discussed without loss of control. The couple practiced skills that were modeled. In addition, the practitioner, through tasks of his own, obtained information about Terry's social security status, and worked out details regarding her participation in the sheltered workshop and supervised apartment program, including negotiating with the court worker about the length of time she would need to remain in the sheltered apartment.

Although these tasks seemed to go well, Jake continued to press for Terry's discharge "without going through all that apartment shit." Terry became increasingly resistant to Jake's insistence that she demand to be released right away.

In an individual session, Terry revealed that she didn't think she was ready to start living with Jake but was unable to confront him. She was afraid of his reaction and of getting into a fight. Her fears of Jake, her inability to stand up to him without becoming violent, and her difficulty in sticking to positions she believed in were taken up as obstacles. How she might tell Jake in a session task was planned and rehearsed in a role play. Jake was also seen individually (with Terry's approval) and advised generally of Terry's reluctance to leave the hospital at this point. In a joint interview immediately following, the two discussed the issue in a session task making use of the role play. Terry told Jake, "I am not ready to live with you yet. I am scared I'll get sick again." Jake became angry and shouted obscenities, but he eventually calmed down and agreed to go with Terry to look at a supervised apartment.

In remaining interviews, Terry and Jake were able to discuss their situation and differences in session tasks without loss of control. By termination, which occurred on schedule, Terry had decided to stop seeing Jake, who did not attend the last session. She thought she had accomplished a lot in the sheltered workshop program; she had actually been "promoted" to more challenging work and was ready to move into the supervised apartment and start the G.E.D. program. Although she felt positive toward treatment, she thought she needed to proceed on her own with these plans. For Jake, the outcome was less positive.

He continued to hold his job but blamed the hospital and the social worker for the breakup of his relationship with Terry.

The case illustrates a number of facets of the model. First, it shows how the approach relates individual treatment to treatment of a family (or in this case, a unit that had been functioning as a family). Terry and Jake each had individual problems and tasks (around finding jobs) as well as problems and tasks in common (the communication problem). The unit of attention shifted between an individual and a couple focus, depending on the problem and the progress of the case.

There are, of course, some issues here, not the least of which are the difficulties inherent in maintaining an adequate family focus when one member is already in treatment and may remain the client of primary concern to the service agency. Second, one sees how the model can be used in an environmentally complex situation so typical in social work, in which the demands and offerings of several organizations and programs must be interconnected. Third, it illustrates a variety of session, home, and environmental tasks and how they can be combined in a single case. Finally, the case provides an example of task-centered family practice within the context of a typical social work function, discharge planning. Work with Terry and Jake as a couple was suggested by the general problem situation in the case. This strategy was a means to an end—to develop and implement as good a plan as could be achieved under the circumstances. It could be argued that part of Terry's essential task work in achieving a viable exit from the hospital was to resolve, in one way or another, issues in her relationship with Jake. Her move away from Jake may well have been a step toward freeing both from a mutually destructive relationship.

3. *Foundations*

In this chapter certain basic aspects of the task-centered family practice model are considered. The dimensions are fundamental to the purposes, organizations, and methods of the approach. Discussion of these foundations of the model should help clarify and justify its distinctive features. It also will provide an opportunity to raise and deal with a number of issues in the field of family treatment.

AN INTEGRATIVE THRUST

Task-centered social work was conceived of as an integrative or open system of practice. It set forth certain value premises, a modest body of theory, an intervention strategy, and an array of helping methods, but it did so in a way that facilitated the incorporation of compatible developments in clinical theory and practice in general. The intent was to create not an eclectic stew of ideas and techniques but rather a coherent system in which useful components of other approaches could be recast into the task-centered framework.

The broad conception of family practice suggested in the initial chapter provides a basis for one kind of integration—linking traditional social work activities with families to the family therapy movement. Another kind of integration involves the joining of intervention strategies from different schools of family therapy within the task-centered system.

The methods of contemporary family therapy tend to be organized in the form of different schools, among them structural, strategic, Bowenian, and behavioral. Although differences among schools are often more terminological than substantive, most schools do have their distinctive points of view, concepts, and techniques (Kolevzon and Green 1983). The development of such diversity has, of course, immensely enriched the teaching and practice of family therapy. Besides, diversity is inevitable in an endeavor in which there are not reliable means for determining the best methods in general or for a given situation.

Some family therapists eschew this diversity and concentrate on mastering one approach. Probably the majority fashion some form of eclectic practice to suit their own predilections and case loads (Walsh 1983). There are difficulties either way. A single-model therapist is handicapped by whatever limitations in theoretical perspective or range of application exist in her chosen method. Imbued in the vocabulary of one approach, she may have difficulty in translating concepts from another, even though the concepts may convey knowledge that would be useful within her own conceptual framework. Moreover, a particular approach may be better suited to certain family situations than others. Given the tendency of model proponents to avoid putting limits on the potential range of effectiveness of their approaches, and the lack of relevant research, the optimal fit between treatment model and family situation may not be readily apparent, or even ascertainable.

While practitioners can master the model or models best suited to their case loads, case loads do vary, or problems within a case may vary, and clients who may appear made for a particular model may want no part of it. Also, social workers are a mobile breed, and they may find an overly limited repertoire of treatment methods to be a disadvantage in the job market.

Practitioners who are comfortable centering their practice within one school usually are interested in adding to their repertoire by incorporating techniques from other approaches. Differences among schools in theoretical and practice vocabularies can make this process difficult. For example, if unfamiliar with the terminology of learning theory and behavioral theory, a practitioner might not even bother to read an article entitled "A Stimulus Control Model of Change in Behavior Couples Therapy: Implications for Contingency Contracting" (Jacobson 1978).

As it turns out, the main point of the article can be expressed in language that any human service professional could understand; many would find the point worth considering. What she may want is not another model to practice by, but one that would present conceptual and technical contributions from different schools in terms she can readily understand.

The full-fledged eclectic practitioner, if such an individual really exists, faces another, perhaps more formidable set of problems. In effect, she needs to build her own practice system, in which diverse offerings from different schools can be placed, and to develop her own rules about what methods from what approach to use under what circumstances. Moreover, she must decide what to select from a wide and burgeoning array of models. In a sense, integrative approaches attempt to do all that, and thus can perhaps be a source of some guidance, at least to practitioners who are attempting to achieve an eclectic orientation to practice.

Problems of diversity present themselves in a different form when one is introducing social work students to family therapy. An educator may be justifiably reluctant to limit her students to one approach, particularly since the students as interns or later as beginning practitioners may be in settings where other models may be in use or more appropriate. A survey of different approaches has obvious drawbacks: students often find brief exposure to a sequence of schools to be intellectually stimulating but poor preparation for beginning practice.

One solution to these predicaments is the development of integrative approaches that incorporate compatible concepts and methods from different schools and, more important, that are open to the continual incorporation of such elements. Although such approaches are themselves models of practice, they are models of a different order—by design hybrid and open to expansion. Work of this kind has already begun to appear (Pinsof 1983; Feldman and Pinsoff 1982; Nelsen 1983; Segraves 1982; Birchler and Spinks 1981). Integrative models can provide a wider range of theoretical and technical alternatives than any single system and hence can encompass a wider range of clients, problems, and situations. Although these models may not be able to provide the detail found in single systems, they can show how this detail can be fitted in and organized.

To realize these advantages, an integrative approach must extract elements (concepts, propositions, principles, methods, and so on) from different practice models, translate them into a common vocabulary, and build them into a framework that provides a way of ordering their application. This ordering should include guidelines for the combined and differential use of the incorporated elements. Finally, criteria for the selection of elements need to be made clear. How these requirements are met in the present approach will be considered.

The process of extracting elements from different schools and transposing them into a common framework and vocabulary has been basic to the development of the task-centered approach. The process is well-illustrated by the concept of "task" itself, which in the model refers generally to planned problem-solving action. Various methods from different family treatment approaches involve actions that can be conceptualized as tasks of one sort or another: homework, behavior exchanges, contingency contracts, directives, paradoxical injunctions, enactments, and so on. The use of a common concept provides a degree of unity to this diversity and facilitates comparisons of apparently diverse techniques against certain standards. For example, it might be assumed that the client should have an incentive or rationale for carrying out a task. For a behavior exchange contract of the type used in behavioral treatment, the client's incentive in doing the task is presumably having another family member behave in a desired manner in exchange for some behavior on the client's part. However, one would need to determine if the exchange in fact provided an adequate incentive. For a paradoxical directive of the type employed in strategic therapy, the incentive or rationale may not be readily apparent, since the connection between the client's task (such as provoking an argument) and relief from his problem may not be clear. Presumably a rationale can be found in the client's willingness to accept the practitioner's authority; if so, the client-practitioner relationship and how the task is set up become critical considerations (Haley 1977).

It is assumed that different approaches have their special contributions to make and that these contributions can be sorted out and ordered according to two principles. One principle is that the practitioner should facilitate the family's autonomous problem solving to the extent possible, interceding only to the degree necessary to remove obstacles to forward movement, to identify resources, or to facilitate change in the immediate context of the problem. In operation the principle calls for use of problem-solving tasks in the session and client-generated tasks to be carried out at home. Obstacles addressed are normally those impeding productive, face-to-face interactions among family members in the session. Contributions from earlier task-centered approaches (Reid 1981), Bell's (1981) family group therapy, the problem-centered model (Epstein and Bishop 1981) and behavioral treatment (Jacobson and Margolin 1979; Stuart 1980, Gambrill 1981) are emphasized at this level. If obstacles prove to be embedded in underlying patterns of family relationships, then session and home tasks aimed at changing these problems are attempted. Contributions from structural therapy (Minuchin 1974; Minuchin and Fishman 1981; Aponte and Van Deusen 1981) and strategic approaches (Haley 1977, 1980; Madanes 1980; Stanton 1981b; Fisch, Weakland, and Segal 1982; Bross 1982) are drawn upon here. Following this principle, the practitioner moves incrementally to the use of more intrusive methods aimed at contextual change in response to obstacles preventing solution of target problems, regardless of the nature of the problem. In other words, she does what is necessary to fulfill her contract to the family to help resolve the target problems agreed upon.

The other principle attempts to relate the situation the practitioner confronts to the "best" intervention options available. A well-developed and apparently successful approach may have been designed for a particular kind of situation, consisting of certain types of problems and contexts. Strategies and procedures have been worked out and there is research evidence demonstrating their effectiveness. Other approaches may lack well-developed or tested methods of treatment for the situation, even though these approaches could be used with it. In other words, for some situations there may be one or more provisional treatments of choice. Suppose the practitioner agrees to help a couple with a problem of not being able to settle differences without quarreling. Several tested models of communication and negotiation training are available (chapter 6). This work would be drawn from in setting up session tasks aimed at increasing the couple's capacity to negotiate differences. These tasks would be supplemented by others if obstacles were encountered, but the basic strategy might continue to be limited to a communication training focus on grounds that other options, including more intrusive methods, would not do better. If the target problem, however, initially was defined as a structural difficulty in a family (mother and son are too involved with each other; father is isolated), then tasks based on the structural approach might be used at the outset. Such an approach might also be used initially in a case where the target problem was substance abuse on the part of a young person living at home, and where the problem seemed reactive to the family situation (Stanton, Todd et al. 1981). It is possible that quite different task sequences could be used simultaneously for different problems in the same case—for example, one sequence based on a communication training model, and another based on a structural approach.

The second principle provides exceptions to the first. The practitioner generally uses progressively more intrusive methods as obstacles are encountered. But she may start with or move directly to a method if it appears to be the best available for a problem. The task-centered model provides some guidelines about when certain treatments of choice may be appropriate, how generally they can be applied, and where further theoretical and technical detail can be found. There still remains, however, considerable room for practitioner judgment and choice.

In our developmental work, elements from available approaches were considered if they were compatible with task-centered value premises and structure and would appear to augment the model. They were more likely to be selected if there was research evidence supporting their effectiveness and if they could be cast in explicit, testable form. In some instances, promising elements were reshaped to fit requirements of the model; in others the requirements themselves were relaxed.

The schools most heavily drawn upon fall within a grouping that Levant (1984) has referred to as "structure/process models"—communications, structural, strategic, and behavioral approaches. With their emphasis upon here-and-now interactional and behavioral phenomena, they fit well to the basic orientation of the present model.

It should be emphasized that no attempt is being made to fully synthesize these or other approaches into some master model, or even to create another form of family therapy. Rather, selected elements from different approaches have been incorporated into a more comprehensive system of practice, task-centered social work. In this system the course of intervention is guided by whatever seems to be the most efficient and effective way to resolve agreed-upon problems to the clients' satisfaction. If the problems are of concern to the family, an effort usually is made to involve the family, but the kind of involvement depends on what may be the best way to proceed with the problem. In many situations, family involvement may be irrelevant, impractical, or even contraindicated. Often the practitioner would like to involve the family in treatment of an individual client but either the client or family is unwilling. In still other cases there is movement in and out of a family focus as the case progresses. For example, a practitioner may involve family members around a particular problem but not others. Comprehensive models, such as psychosocial, behavioral, ecological, or task-centered models, can facilitate the practitioner's efforts by providing unified frameworks and technologies. For example, in the task-centered approach, movement from work with an individual client to work with the family does not require a reorientation in thinking or knowledge of radically different techniques, but rather calls for building on to what is already familiar.

The point has particular relevance for students in field practica who must often deal with a diversified case load and complex "part-family" cases with very little knowledge of theory and technique. It is hoped that the task-centered practice system is one that will provide students with the conceptual tools to move between individual and family work, and that the present addition to that system will facilitate moving in a "family direction."

Structure

All family treatment approaches have some degree of *planned structure*. Sessions with the family normally occur on a schedule, such as once a week, and the length of the session usually conforms to a fixed period of time, such as 50 minutes or an hour. Beyond this, therapy models vary considerably. At one extreme there may be no plan of events for the individual session or no predetermination of the number of sessions or length of contact, as in "symbolic-experiential" family therapy (Whittaker and Keith 1981). Somewhat more structured are models like the brief therapy approaches developed at the Mental Research Institute (Segal 1981) which have fixed durational limits (ten sessions) and in which the therapist normally closes each session with some form of directive to the family. Fully structured models may specify not only the number of sessions but a planned sequence of events for each session. Some communication training programs provide examples (Jacobson and Margolin 1979).

As can be seen, the notion of planned structure refers to prior organization of the treatment process. It is used here to describe an aspect of a treatment model rather than the style of individual practitioners, whose practice may be quite structured even if the model they draw from is not.

The task-centered model is a relatively structured form of practice. The opening phase is divided into steps culminating in the treatment contract. For sessions in the middle phase there is a choice of formats, each beginning with a task review and closing with a summary of the next round of tasks. The final session follows a particular plan. Guidelines for retracing steps, a hierarchical principle for choice of interventions, and the planned short-term nature of service provide additional elements of structure.

Although the model orders treatment into a series of stages and steps, it does not specify content, as might a program providing a certain kind of training or following a particular theory. Whereas the model may suggest general strategies for dealing with certain kinds of problems it does not offer, for example, the kind of problem-specific sequence of therapeutic maneuvers that Haley (1980) does in his approach to working with families of disturbed young people.

The "openness" of the model has both advantages and disadvantages. It permits practitioners to make use of a wide range of theories and techniques but does not necessarily suggest which to use. At the same time, the model provides some guidance on these matters and provides in itself a core of theory and procedure that should enable the practitioner to provide significant help in most cases.

A major function of the structure of the task-centered model is to provide practitioners with a set of guidelines for working with families. The structure may offer particular advantages to practitioners, including students, who are inexperienced or untrained in family treatment and are without much access to expert supervision. It offers answers to questions of "How do I begin?" "What do I do now?" "What do I do after that?" "How can I correct my mistakes?" Procedures for problem formulation, contracting, devising and reviewing tasks, monitoring progress on problems, and retracing steps enable the practitioner to go from A to B to C, and if necessary back to A. The structure is supported by a philosophy that gives the practitioner license to accept the family's thinking about their problems and to build on their own problem-solving efforts. This coalesence of structure and philosophy is expressed in session tasks that permit the family to work toward its own solutions. The practitioner can assume the role of facilitator of the family's problem solving, rather than having to become a mastermind of therapeutic strategy. Moreover, the session tasks give the practitioner the time and opportunity to observe, reflect, and plan her subsequent interventions.

This is not to say that more knowledgeable and experienced practitioners will find the structure unhelpful. For some it helps systematize a style of work they would do in any case and provides a framework for integrating other methods of interest to them. Others may make use of the structure selectively, with variation from case to case.

For the family, the structure of the model can provide clarity of purpose and a systematic way to work on its problems. Treatment that is broken down into described steps and activities is easier to comprehend and helps clients assume collaborative roles. The degree of organization provided by the model is welcomed by clients who like to do things in a methodical way and may offer needed controls for "underorganized" families.

Still, clients may want the opportunity from time to time to proceed in a less structured fashion. Thus a family may wish to talk over a recent crisis or problem with the practitioner at some length and in an unstructured way. In response to such needs, or for their own clinical reasons, practitioners can permit less structured exchanges to take up part of the session, or can alternate between more structured and less structured sessions (Knopf and Reid, in press). A practitioner can, of course, depart from the session structure and still remain within a task-centered framework. Normally departures involve more extended explorations of a problem with a family. Using procedures discussed subsequently, the practitioner can help the family move from problem exploration to the development of tasks.

The structure may be useful if only pieces of it are used. In one of my cases, involving a separated couple, the husband appeared at the third session, glum and withdrawn. Staring at the floor he would mutter that he had "nothing to say" regardless of my questions, reflections, or whatever. So much for the session tasks I had carefully planned. He was able to talk with his wife about some instances earlier in their marriage that bothered him. This was not exactly what the model called for, but I felt any communication was better than none. Finally, I tried to engage the two of them in a "brainstorming" task in which they would come up with ideas about what, if anything, they might do together during the coming week. The wife was full of suggestions, but the husband lapsed back into his moody silence. Somewhat out of desperation, I shifted the task to one in which the wife and I would do the brainstorming and the husband would pick out whatever suggestions had the slightest appeal to him. So we did this, as husband remained silent. His next sign of life was a grunt after one suggestion had been made—that they go to a movie but not discuss anything serious. He would go along with that, he said, and a home task was planned. Although the structure of the model was used only at the close of the session and in an odd way at that, it still helped salvage what might otherwise have been the terminal interview.

Finally, the structure of the model has important advantages for research and development efforts. I assume that systematic testing of a model and the use of resulting data to enhance its performance provides a potent means of building effective practice approaches. If so, then it can be argued that such research and development undertakings can be carried out much more readily with an approach that is well structured than with one that is not. With a high degree of structure to work with, a researcher-clinician is able to study the operation and effects of specific components of the model in relation to specific targets. For example, in the present model one can identify different types of session tasks, characteristics of their execution, the practitioner's intervention immediately following, and their immediately apparent effects. When communication between family members reaches the "name calling" stage, what subsequent practitioner interventions appear to be the most effective? In relatively unstructured forms of practice, in which family communication and related interventions are subject to much greater variation and entanglement, it becomes much more difficult to sort out answers to such questions.

Empirical Orientation

A strong empirical stance has been one of the essential characteristics of the task-centered approach. In general this has meant reliance on scientific knowledge, methods, and perspectives to the extent possible in both the construction of the model and its use in everyday practice. Specifically, a number of components of our empirical orientation can be distinguished: (1) emphasis on research-based knowledge of human functioning and of tested methods of intervention, (2) a commitment to a continuing program of research and development as a means of testing and improving the model, (3) a data-oriented approach to assessment and treatment planning, (4) the definition of concepts and methods in empirical or measurable terms, and (5) an openness to alternative explanations for behavior and a preference for parsimonious explanations supported by data.

In developing the model, preference has been given to knowledge based on empirical research over knowledge derived from clinical experience, although the latter is by no means eschewed. An effort is made to spell out theoretical concepts in measurable terms and to avoid theorizing what cannot be tied to empirical evidence. There has been a commitment to a continuing program of research designed to test and improve the model. The empirical orientation of the approach also is expressed in work with clients. Research-based knowledge is used to understand the family and its difficulties. Problems to be treated as well as concepts used to understand client functioning are operationalized in terms of specific behaviors or circumstances. Data on the pretreatment frequency and severity of the problems are obtained, and the course of change in these problems is subsequently monitored. Standardized research instruments may be used to obtain additional data on the problems or characteristics of the clients. Although theories of human functioning may be brought to bear in an effort to understand target problems and client functioning, these theories are tested in the case at hand. Alternative theoretical explanations are explored in the light of case data, and preference is given to the most parsimonious explanation that is best supported by the evidence. As a case proceeds, data on the immediate outcome of interventions are obtained and used to guide subsequent intervention. Data on case outcome as a whole are used to evaluate the methods employed in a case.

An empirical orientation of the kind described is more difficult to actualize in family treatment than in some other forms of practice. Although a good deal of research on family life is available and can be drawn upon, knowledge of dynamics and change in family problems is in a rudimentary state. The interactive character of family processes makes it difficult to apply ordinary research paradigms, with their linear or straightforward assumptions about causality; however, approaches better suited to study of family interaction are still not well-developed. Applications of research perspectives and methods in case situations must deal with the complexities of both individual and family functioning and must cope with a volume of events and data that far exceeds anything produced in work with individuals.

One solution is to apply sharply focused techniques designed to alter limited aspects of family interaction. For example, one might use negotiation training to help a parent and child improve their skills in resolving conflicts between them. A practitioner can make a direct application of previous empirical work. (Robin 1981) By using a well-defined training method in a limited area (conflict within a single dyad) she is able to study processes of intervention and immediate change with about as much thoroughness as is possible in any examination of attempts to alter human functioning. This kind of unequivocally empirical approach, characteristic of many applications of behavioral methods to family treatment, is needed as a way of strengthening the scientific base of family treatment. But as yet it does not offer the diversity or scope needed for the range of situations that confront family therapists.

At the opposite end of the spectrum one can "solve" difficulties in applying the offerings of science by pretty much ignoring them, relying instead on global impressions, clinical experience and wisdom, intuition, gut reactions, speculative theory, expert opinion, and so forth. Much family practice can be characterized thus, which is not an indictment but rather a reflection of the state of the art.

As a field, family therapy has begun to move away from the second extreme, but progress has been slow. Much of the effort has consisted in evaluation of different family therapy approaches; since the early seventies, for example, a considerable number of controlled studies of such approaches has been conducted. Although some evidence has been accumulated that family therapy can be effective (Wells 1981; Gurman and Kniskern 1981), little empirical groundwork has been laid for specifying the kinds of therapy that may work best under varying circumstances of individual and family problems, family composition and structure, and so on. Moreover, tests of family therapy have generally involved complex and often poorly described amalgams of techniques, sometimes including nonfamily treatment approaches (Minuchin, Rosman, and Baker 1978). Even when outcomes have been favorable, it is usually not possible to trace the pattern of change from particular methods to particular outcomes.

Underlying limitations of knowledge at the intervention level is lack of scientifically based understanding of the dynamics of family conflict, of how and why problems originate and take the course they do. There are many theories—structural, Bowenian, psychodynamic, and so on—that proffer explanations, but there has been little empirical testing of predictions based on these theories. This is not to deny that practitioners do have a large fund of useful knowledge about family troubles based on their experiences as family members and clinicians. But knowing about families through these means is a far cry from reliable scientific knowledge. Against this background, it is not surprising that family therapy makes limited use of research. It must be acknowledged that there is an insufficient body of tested knowledge and methods to support any but the most limited models of intervention.

Two general aspects of the empirical base of the present model warrant further discussion. One has to do with existing research relating to task centered work with families. The other concerns the use made of case data in application of the approach.

Over twenty studies of the task-centered model have been conducted in this country and abroad. Most studies that focus on work with families have lacked control or comparison groups that would enable one to assert that treatment was responsible for observed changes. They have been limited largely to work with marital or parent-child dyads. These studies have found that families did realize an appreciable degree of problem alleviation (Ewalt 1977; Bass 1977; Reid 1977; Rooney 1978; Segal, 1983). In a study confined to treatment of marital problems (Reid 1977), the gains achieved appeared at least comparable to those reported in a large-scale survey of marital treatment in family agencies (Beck and Jones 1973).

Task-centered treatment of marital and relationship problems received a more extensive and rigorous test in a large-scale suicide prevention experiment conducted in England (Gibbons et al. 1978; Goldberg, Gibbons and Sinclair 1984). Four hundred patients who had taken drug overdoses in apparent suicide attempts were randomly allocated to experimental (task-centered) and control (routine service) groups. Difficulties in "continuing personal relationships," usually problems with a spouse, were reported in two-thirds of the cases. Research interviews were conducted with the patients four and eighteen months following termination of service. Measures of change in personal relationships favored the experimental group at both follow-ups, with statistically significant differences obtained at the second follow-up.

In another controlled study (Reid 1978), task-centered methods were tested with eighty-seven cases divided between adults from a psychiatric outpatient clinic (n = 38) and children and youth, mostly from a public school system (n = 49). About a third of the problems dealt with involved difficulties in family relations. Results showed that significantly more problem alleviation occurred under treatment than under control conditions. It is noteworthy that the adult cases, in which family relationship problems were more in evidence, were relatively more successful than the children's cases. Finally, a series of single-case studies, using multiple baseline controls, have provided evidence for the effectiveness of the model in treating communication problems of a marital pair (Tolson 1977), in helping parents with children in placement (Rzepnicki 1981, 1984), and in enabling a mother to improve communication with her young child (Wodarski, Saffir, and Frazer 1982).

These studies evaluated task-centered work with families at different points in the evolution of the model and prior to systematic incorporation of newer developments presented in this volume. Moreover, as noted, studies were limited largely to treatment of dyadic relationships. Nevertheless, this body of research gives evidence to the viability of the strategy of the model as a method of treating family problems. Brief, structured treatment focusing on specific client-perceived problems and stressing straightforward client tasks as a means of solving them did appear to be a reasonably effective approach for most families seen in the projects.

Research on related forms of practice have contributed findings to the empirical base of the model. A good deal of this research will be examined elsewhere in the volume in relation to particular types of tasks (chapters 6 and 7). Only certain aspects relating to basic features of the model will be considered here. Over the past two decades, a considerable amount of evidence has accumulated to support the proposition that planned short-term treatment (usually no more than twelve sessions) is as effective as treatment of longer duration for family problems. As far as I have been able to determine, all controlled evaluations that have compared brief and longer-term treatment (Reid and Shyne 1969; Wattie 1973; Fisher 1980, 1984) and all reviews of research (Butcher and Koss 1978; Gurman and Kniskern 1978, 1981; Wells 1981), support that hypothesis. Moreover, even when directional limits are absent, the great majority of cases involving work with families appear to be of relatively short duration (Beck and Jones 1973). Thus, a brief treatment structure, especially one with provisions for extensions, cannot be seen as depriving families of services they desire.

One general approach to family treatment, problem-centered therapy (Epstein and Bishop 1981), is similar to the task-centered model in many respects, including focus on specific problems, structured interventions, stress on family problem solving, and use of tasks. (The two models have evolved independently, although there has been some recent collaboration.) In the major evaluation of the problem-centered model reported to date (Santa-Barbara et al. 1979; Woodward et al. 1981), 297 families containing a child between the ages of six and twelve with academic or behavioral problems received problem-centered therapy. Outcome data generally were within the range obtained in task-centered projects. Although a control group was lacking, the large sample size and proportion of intact families treated strengthens and broadens the case for similar task-centered work with families. Moreover, results of a six-month follow-up, like the results of Gibbons et al. (1978) referred to above, suggested that gains from this form of intervention were reasonably durable.

Although the studies reviewed certainly offer a respectable base for task-centered practice, they also reveal considerable room for improvement and a host of unanswered questions. As is typical of studies of the outcomes of family treatment generally, outcomes for task-centered projects, while favorable in most cases, show a substantial proportion of cases falling in the slightly to moderately improved range. The picture also becomes more sobering if we assume that outcome ratings based on client self-report, heavily used in evaluation of task-centered methods as well as other forms of therapy, are probably biased in a positive direction (Reid and Smith 1981). Although treatment may be as effective as longer therapies, most of the studies mentioned here as well as others have identified problems of dissatisfaction with time limits on the part of an appreciable proportion of clients. (One recent study [O'Connor 1983] suggests, however, that dissatisfaction may be less of a problem in conjoint family treatment than in work with single clients.)

Since the "unknowns" far outnumber the "knowns" in the family treatment business, it would take pages to simply catalog what we need to be better informed about or need to do more effectively. Of priority concern are needs for knowledge and techniques in respect to the following: the relation between selected target problems and other difficulties faced by a family, methods of formulating and revising problems, the kinds of tasks best suited for particular kinds of problems and situations, the effectiveness of the use of straightforward tasks in cases involving high conflict or entrenched patterns of interaction, the effectiveness of the model with parents and children seen conjointly, the extent to which use of tasks focused on specific problems can bring about contextual change, and the durability of change in problems and contexts resulting from intervention. While most of these needs are at least addressed in the present volume, and additional research is presented in relation to some of them, they remain perennial areas for future work.

Use and generation of research is part of the empirical orientation of the model. Another part is found in the relation between theory and data. Some approaches, as well as the styles of many practitioners, are characterized by use of a priori theories about family problems and functioning. These theories provide high-level abstractions for understanding family phenomena—homeostasis, enmeshment, triangulation, and the like. Such concepts are used to construct explanations of the dynamics of these phenomena, often viewed in terms of covert processes. For example, a child's problem may be seen as a symptom of parental conflict. By having the problem the child maintains the homeostasis or balance of the family, the analysis goes, but how exactly the process works is not apparent from the data at hand. These theories, as noted, are based largely on conjecture, albeit informed by clinical work with families.

From a task-centered perspective, such theories are viewed as providing potentially useful insights into family processes and problems, but insights that must be applied with caution as well as openness to alternative possibilities. No one theoretical system or particular set of explanations is regarded as having sufficient empirical support to be applied in wholesale fashion to a case, or applied on the basis of small amounts of inferential evidence that might be found therein.

The task-centered model is more data-centered than most in its emphasis on spelling out problems and goals in terms of specific identifiable behaviors, beliefs, interactions, and the like. Following the rule of parsimony, these data are organized and analyzed with a minimum of assumptions. Simple, "obvious" explanations are favored over complex interpretations based on notions of hidden processes.

Practitioners are, of course, expected to come prepared with theories and knowledge about families, but this information is applied in close interaction with the data at hand. In some forms of practice the data, and subsequent pursuit of them, are guided by a particular theoretical framework. In task-centered practice the data themselves suggest which modes of understanding to apply. Generally one uses as a starting point the family's own formulations of the difficulty, if they are at all coherent, and tries to build upon them. In the process information may be revealed that may point to certain theoretical interpretations. The father of a predelinquent boy boasts of his own escapades as a youth, and one wonders if a psychodynamic theory of delinquency might apply—that the father might be receiving vicarious satisfaction from his son's misbehavior and thereby tacitly encouraging it (Johnson 1959).

Hypotheses of this kind are pursued by further inquiry. Data that might support or reject a hypothesis are sought and evaluated. While the amount and kind of data needed to accept a hypothesis is a matter of judgment, an evidential case must be made. If the theory to which a hypothesis relates has prior research support then less evidence is needed, since the prior research would increase the chances of the hypothesis being correct. The practitioner's prior experience or reported experiences of others with similar cases may also be used in this fashion, but with much greater caution. The practitioner, for example, may be inclined to select out from the case at hand evidence that might support her existing beliefs, while ignoring contradictory evidence. But in any event, evidence must be marshaled from the case at hand. It is not enough to say that this is a "psychosomatic family," hence X, Y, and Z must be going on. They may be, and it may make sense to look for them, but evidence must be found.

An important part of this evidencing process consists in spelling out theoretical constructs—systems boundary, homeostasis, coalition, resistance, and the like—in the form of specific indicators. Constructs of this order overpopulate the family therapy literature. In few instances have they been adequately operationalized, and the validity of some of the most important, such as homeostasis, have been challenged (Dell 1982). Despite their lack of empirical grounding, such ideas often are tossed about as if their meanings were crystal clear. In fact they often form a fog over the actual complexities of a case, obscuring rather than illuminating its realities.

In the task-centered framework, systems and other theoretical constructs need to be operationalized through case data in order to be taken seriously. For example, when the idea of restoring family homeostasis or balance is applied, there should be some description, even if crude, of the preexisting pattern of interaction and specification of the deviations that have occurred from this pattern.

Data requirements may be difficult to meet for hypotheses of covert processes and for high-order theoretical constructs, especially in complex cases. Consequently, practitioners may gravitate toward more obvious explanations and simpler ideas. In my view, this is as it should be: it is better to work with limited knowledge than with false knowledge that masks ignorance.

As one consequence, a practitioner using the model often proceeds on the basis of a very partial understanding of "what is really going on" in a case. She may have tentative hypotheses about the complex interactions surrounding a family problem but may not be able to obtain sufficient evidence for them. Practitioners find themselves making remarks like: "I don't know," "I am not sure yet," "It could be that but there may be other explanations." And supervisors just as often: "That's an interesting hunch, but what is your evidence for it?" "Could you give me some examples of how this coalition works?"

To illustrate some of the points just made, let us take a case of a sixteen-year-old girl who has serious conflicts with her parents. She sees them as harsh and rejecting and is aware of their marital troubles. Over her parents' protests she runs around with a wild crowd, experiments with drugs and sex, and gets involved with an older boy and becomes pregnant. According to her account, the pregnancy was an accident. She thought she was in a safe period of her menstrual cycle (but obviously wasn't), and her boyfriend did not have a condom. She normally insists that he use one.

There are theories that suggest that such a pregnancy is "no accident" but is rather the result of covert motivation on the girl's part that was reactive to her relationship with her parents. For example, it could be interpreted as an unconscious attempt to pay her parents back for their mistreatment of her or as an effort to save the parental marriage. Some practitioners, given the evidence at hand, would conclude that such processes were at work.

A task-centered perspective would suggest that the girl's explanation would be as good as any in light of the facts available. Psychodynamic or systems theories notwithstanding, errors of judgment do occur. The interpretation is the most parsimonious, since little evidence has appeared to support the more assumption-laden interpretation of covert processes at work. While there are theories that say such processes could provide an explanation, those theories, as far as I know, have never been rigorously tested. What kind of case evidence would be needed to indicate that the theory might apply? Suppose the girl told her boyfriend on several occasions not to bother to use a condom when he was prepared to do so, and after becoming pregnant made a point of blaming her parents for having driven her into seeking solace and sex from her boyfriend. Evidence of this kind would provide support for the interpretation that her pregnancy was in fact reactive to her relationship with her parents. The empirical orientation of the model does not automatically reject the notion of covert processes in family life. It does, however, insist on evidence for their existence in the case at hand.

A Multisystems Perspective

As has been repeatedly pointed out, systems concepts provide a useful way to think about the family. They offer a means of understanding the reciprocal influences present in family interaction, pressures toward stability (negative feedback, homeostasis) and change (positive feedback, morphogenesis), tendencies toward inclusion and exclusion (boundary making), the presence of rules governing interaction, and so on. My intent here is not to review those concepts in the abstract but rather to introduce them. Their meanings will be developed as they are put to use in understanding families.

At this point, I shall present a perspective about systems thinking that guides the use of these concepts and application of the model in general to work with families. The idea is simply this: the family is one of a configuration of systems that occupy the practitioner's attention. In work with families the practitioner needs to attend not just to the family as a system but to multiple systems.

A useful point of departure in considering multiple systems is Tomm's (1982) formulation of open hierarchical systems. As Tomm puts it, "Within this perspective each element or unit at a particular level of the hierarchy represents both a holistic system at that level and part of a larger system at the next higher level" (p. 72). To begin at the lower levels of the hierarchy, we can consider the various systems—circulatory, central nervous, cognitive, and so on—that make up the individual. The individual is a system at a higher level, and in turn usually is part of a family, a system at a still higher level. The family as a system is part of such systems as the community. Individual family members are parts of other systems—schools, employing organizations, and so on.

In this view, the family is no more a system than is an individual. They are both systems at different hierarchical levels. A given problem can be thought of at different levels, or as Tomm (1982) suggests, at different levels simultaneously. For example, at the individual level, Mrs. V's depression may be viewed as a result of a poor self-image, dating back to adolescence. At the family level, attention may be focused on how her poor self-image is accentuated by her husband's behavior, which in turn is provoked by her own depressed state. At the level of her employing organization, we might learn that her contributions are being depreciated by a male-dominated staff, another factor in her depression. As can be seen, explanations at the individual, family, and external levels overlap, but none alone may be sufficient. The family focus does not account for the history of her self-image or for the influence of work-related factors.

The notion of a systems hierarchy is a helpful way of seeing how systems fit, and is especially useful in conceptualizing the relation between the individual and family. That formulation does not account, however, for systems that family members or families relate to but are not part of, such as community organizations. Here the idea of a systems configuration or ecology is useful.

The interaction of systems gives rise to temporary "situational" systems. The idea is close to Siporin's (1975) conception of "social situation": "a combination of people and physical objects in time-space circumstances" which, as he points out, "may be understood as a form of social system" (p. 237).

In the present framework this idea has two major applications. First, it defines the actual grouping of family members and practitioner(s) who are interacting at a given point in time. A treatment session involving the parents, one of their children, and the practitioner creates a transient situational system. The patterns of interaction in this system may not be the same as the patterns that obtain in the family system at home. The presence of the practitioner and the selection of members present creates a novel system. Minuchin and Fishman (1981) refer to the therapist as "joining" the family system. It is more accurate to view the process as one of creating a different kind of system.

The second application, which incorporates the first, comes into play when the practitioner works with a grouping of family members and others or with a set of unrelated persons. A given case, for example, may involve a family and the daughter's boyfriend; or a foster parent, a child under care, his natural mother, and a child welfare worker. For many social workers such groupings are more the rule than the exception.

Finally, a multisystems perspective includes dimensions of individual and family functioning that may be important in assessment and intervention but cannot be adequately analyzed with the terms and concepts of systems theory. A good example is provided by the ethical dimension of family relationships (Boszormenyi-Nagy and Ulrich 1981; Karpel and Strauss 1984). Notions of loyalty, trust, indebtedness, obligation, entitlement, and the like are sources of powerful dynamics in family life. A daughter may feel loyal and indebted to her invalid father and hence may feel obliged to care for him. Her brother does not see himself as having such an obligation yet considers himself entitled to half of his father's estate. The father may trust his son but not his daughter. Conflicts and feelings expressed in this ethical dimension may dominate a family interview to plan for the father's care. In this instance one can think of an ethical system, which like any system consists of interconnected, mutually influential elements. Systems concepts may not, however, prove the most fruitful in pursuing the analysis.

In general, a multisystems perspective is a way of articulating the theoretical openness of the model. It alerts the practitioner to the many networks of elements that may be useful in understanding problems. It encourages a pragmatic style of analysis, one fitted to the system under consideration.

In working with a family, the practitioner repeatedly shifts attention from one system to another. Attention may focus on the internal dynamics of one family member, may shift to the interaction between that family member and another, may dwell upon the family as a unit, may move to the functioning of an organization to which the family is relating, and so on. These shifts in units of attention are determined by one central purpose: to understand target problems and their context as a basis for intervention. Problems are not defined by theoretical considerations, but rather collaboratively by family members and the practitioner, although theory may suggest to the practitioner problem areas that might be brought to the family's attention. Typically, understanding gained by attention to individual and external systems is related to the family system, which becomes the central point of reference.

This formulation is quite compatible with ecological and other points of view that stress interactions of people and their environments, although somewhat different concepts and terms are used (Meyer 1983a; Maluccio 1981; Germain and Gitterman 1979). In the present formulation, the environment is broken down into systems, and the notion of situational system is used to capture transient interactions between people and their environments. Because this book presents methods of family treatment, the family system naturally is center stage.

But occupying center stage is not the same as being the only actor. The multisystem perspective forces attention to the interpenetration of individual, family, and environmental concerns. Although family therapy approaches generally subscribe to systems viewpoints, they usually do not give much theoretical attention to the linkages between the family and other systems and tend to deal minimally with external systems in practice applications. As Pinsof (1983) observes, "Unfortunately in much of the family therapy literature 'system' has become virtually synonomous with family" (p. 20). In some instances looking beyond the family system is even discouraged (Haley 1980).

Family therapy may become too centered in the family system to the neglect of other systems. For example, family involvement may be indicated in work with a child who has problems of academic and social difficulties in school, but this involvement may not provide sufficient leverage for change. The necessary leverage may come from tasks carried out by the child at school and practitioner tasks directed at altering the school environment. The family's role may turn out to be subsidiary, although still important. If they look assiduously enough, therapists always can find explanations for problems within the intricacies of family systems, but may have a difficult time finding evidence to support them. Even if the explanations have validity, they may not provide the best basis for problem resolution. The multisystems perspective suggests that the practitioner examine a problem from the perspective of a variety of systems and intervene in the system where the best leverage for change can be found.

A Collaborative Relationship

In the present approach, families are seen as collaborators with practitioners in a joint problem-solving effort. However, in this relationship the family and the practitioners have different responsibilities. In the initial phase, the family ultimately is responsible for deciding which problems are to be worked on and which goals will represent an adequate solution of these problems. The practitioner's initial responsibility is to help the family define its problems and goals. In that capacity she may help family members perceive aspects of their behavior or situation of which they might have been unaware, provide new ideas or information, or challenge family members' initial conceptions of problems and goals. If family members cannot agree, then she assumes a mediational role and, if necessary, helps them as individuals define problems and goals they can "exchange" with one another.

Although practitioners may need to be relatively assertive in certain cases, particularly in work with disorganized or highly conflicted families, they are enjoined to stay within the family's conception of the problem. But this conception is not static; it evolves in response to the practitioner's contributions. Through these contributions, which may include negotiations with community agencies, families may accept the need to work on difficulties not originally acknowledged, such as mandated problems (chapter 2).

In any case, family members must agree to explicit statements of problems and goals. As a result the family is in a position to know what is being planned and to assent to the plan. From one point of view, the family is guaranteed a basic consumer right— to be aware of and approve what it is getting into. From another perspective, the family is given the opportunity to begin the first stage of the problem-solving process, defining the problems to be worked on. A structure is provided to enable the family to sort through, identify and articulate its problems, perhaps more systematically than it has ever done. The greater the responsibility the family can take in this process, the more it will learn about how it best can be done.

Collaboration between the practitioner and the family becomes more fully developed as problems are worked on. The structure of the model continues to support, stimulate, and strengthen the family's own problem-solving abilities. The practitioner attempts to generate and maintain the family's own initiative in developing problem solutions. An arresting example of success in this respect was achieved in one home visit. The family became so engrossed in working out the details of a solution that the practitioner, who finally had to leave for another appointment, simply encouraged the family to carry on and departed!

The gain for the family should be not only improved problem-solving skills but also better solutions than if the practitioner were to "direct the show." This is so because family members, despite their conflicts and distorted views of one another, have intimate and detailed knowledge of their interactions that the practitioner does not possess. They may know, often intuitively, what will or will not work and how it will work best. Moreover, the intricacies—the delicate balances—of a family system need to be respected. No amount of clinical perceptiveness, theoretical sophistication, or assessment activity can fully divine the complex ecology of family life. What is more, the practitioner's opportunities to gain knowledge about the family usually are quite limited, if not by the unwillingness of the family to undergo long periods of study, then by the imperatives of the problems it presents. Rather than pushing forward on the basis of partial and misleading knowledge or speculation about family dynamics, it may be better to let the family begin to work on its problems in its own way and to restrict intervention to the mobilization and guidance of its problem solving. Solutions may emerge that may not have occurred to practitioners. As Hoffman (1981) puts it, "Families can think up far more amazing solutions than we can" (p. 34).

If the family founders in its problem-solving efforts or does not hit upon solutions that seem obvious to the practitioner, the practitioner becomes more active in making suggestions or even assigning tasks. These more active maneuvers still are done, however, in an atmosphere of collaboration. To preserve this atmosphere, the practitioner provides the family with the reasons for her suggestions or assignments if their rationale is not apparent. If there is a compelling basis to withhold this information beforehand, she asks the family to trust her for the time being, indicates that an explanation will be forthcoming later, and then provides it at a subsequent point.

What becomes of "resistance" in this formulation? The usual conception of resistance, as covert processes within the client or the family system that oppose positive change, is replaced by the notion that forward movement on problems, goals, and tasks may be blocked by obstacles that may occur at any systems level—the individual, family, agency, or environment. Obstacles, like problems, arc identified and worked on cooperatively with the family. By presenting obstacles as barriers to the family's attainment of its own goals, the family's stake in their removal is made clear. Clarifications of obstacles include making explicit dysfunctional structural arrangements, such as patterns of alliance or coalition. (The kind of diagrams used in training films to depict relationships within the family may be used with family members as an aid in explanation.) Such forthrightness is intended not only to enlist the family's cooperation in working on the obstacle but also to serve the prior step of checking the practitioner's hypothesis against the family's own understanding of how it works.

While family members may not have articulated their patterns of interaction, it is reasonable to assume they have some awareness of them if in fact they are important in their lives. Often they will make reference to them. (My wife sides with the children. Mom is forever trying to keep peace in the family.) As Wile (1981) suggests, family members may not be entirely content with these patterns and can be engaged in working on them. If family members want to hold on to them for dear life, there is probably little the practitioner can do to change them.

The assumption is that the family is continually in the process of change and that its agreement with the practitioner to work toward specific goals is evidence that particular kinds of change is sought. The practitioner reinforces this "frame of expected change" by emphasizing the "what" and the "when" of change, not "if" change is going to occur (de Shazer 1984:15). If identified obstacles cannot be resolved, then the practitioner may suggest that the family does not wish to change in that way; other ways are considered. This process may lead to revision of goals and target problems if the family decides that certain kinds of change are not possible or desirable. In this formulation, clients do not "resist," they rather make choices about what kinds of change they want.

The position just outlined perhaps can be more sharply delineated if key aspects of it can be compared to alternative points of view. For most approaches it might be claimed that treatment is a collaborative enterprise between practitioners and family members, and in some sense that may be true. What, then, is distinctive about the kind of collaboration advocated here?

To begin with, in the task-centered approach definition of the family's problems, explanations of problems, and the treatment plan are developed through a dialogue with the family. In this dialogue the family members' opinions are taken seriously and mined by both family and practitioner for useful insights. The practitioner's contributions to this process, which may draw from a variety of theories, research, or her own clinical experience, are offered as possible ways to understand the situation or to deal with it. The practitioner shares her thinking with family members, modifying it in light of feedback she receives from them.

A rather different position is presented by Stanton (1981a), an exponent of the structural approach. "The therapist's plan is gauged against his knowledge of what is 'normal' for a couple or family at a given stage of development. His aim is to help a couple [or family] establish a developmentally appropriate structure with due consideration, of course, for their socio-economic, cultural, ethnic and religious context."

In this position the therapist has her own conception of what a "developmentally appropriate structure" might be, and presumably this conception guides her intervention. Although it is acknowledged that what is developmentally appropriate can vary according to cultural and other contexts, it is still up to the therapist to make decisions about these variations. The therapist emerges more as an expert who guides the family toward her conception of normative goals and less as a collaborator. In a similar vein Anderson and Stewart (1983) state: "It is not necessary or desirable that family members agree with all the therapist's goals for the family, particularly such general ones as 'less enmeshment'" (p. 61).

The structural perspective has a certain attractive simplicity. Diverse problems in individual and family functioning can be viewed as symptoms of basic structural flaws: a coalition between one parent and a child against the other parent, the use of a "parental" child to oversee other children, the failure of the parental subsystem to discharge its executive responsibilities, and so on. Although structural ideas have much to contribute to the understanding of family problems, and to the present model, they are less certain in application than in conception.

There may be general agreement in the abstract on the desirability of certain norms, but it may be difficult to agree on how these norms should apply in particular instances, and in work with families it is the "particular instance" that is invariably at issue. This agreement in the particular is often difficult to come by because general norms cannot be expressed in absolute terms. They are always relative to contrasting norms, their opposite numbers. Yes, parents should be in charge of their children, but children have need for a certain amount of independence from parental control. We want neither parents nor children to be servants to each other's whims.

At the case level, uncertainty about what a "developmentally appropriate structure" should be is more the rule than the exception. Is a father exerting reasonable authority when he prohibits his sixteen-year-old daughter from using birth control pills? Or is he being a tyrant? Or just foolish? Practitioner opinions, I am sure, would vary, perhaps with as much discordance as would be found in the general public. It is misleading to regard idiosyncratic decisions about such matters as expert judgments. The example provides a relatively simple case. Matters become much more complicated when family structure assumes "nonconventional" forms, such as "blended" families with children from previous marriages in which there may be even less of a standard defining what is "developmentally appropriate."

Even if there is an agreement that a pattern reflects some structural flaw, it still may not be clear if change is desirable or how it can be brought about. For example, a common pattern is an isolated, detached father and a mother who has formed a coalition with her children. The children satisfy her need for a close meaningful relationship that may be missing from the marital relationship; she in turn offers the children the kind of attentive care the father may not be able to provide and may in addition shield them from the father's punitiveness. Problems may flare up as the children move into adolescence and seek greater independence from a mother who is reluctant to let go. A structuralist solution would point toward restoring or strengthening the boundary around the marital subsystem—that is, bringing mom and dad closer together, or at least having them face issues between them in order to decrease mother's involvement with the children.

In some cases this strategy may make sense, but not in others. The family pattern may be too entrenched to change or may prove on balance to be a better arrangement than some half-realized shift toward a more "appropriate" structure. It may be more sensible, and quite possible, to help the family work out ways of handling the presenting problem without changing the theoretically "dysfunctional" pattern in any fundamental way.

Of course, it is recognized that a clinician with a structural orientation might well proceed in the manner suggested if it made sense to do so. But the clinician would be without specific guidance from the structural model. By contrast, in the task-centered model itself there are very few assumptions about what is "normal," "developmentally appropriate," "good," or "bad" about family life. The practitioner's starting position is that these are matters for the family to thrash out, perhaps with the practitioner's help. The practitioner is free, however, to introduce her own values, or community values, into the treatment process. But as she must so explicitly, identify their source, and present them within a collaborative framework as alternatives to consider or, in the case of community values, as realities that may need to be faced.

In true collaboration on problem solving, each participant has valid contributions to make toward devising a solution, but these contributions may spring from different sources. In task-centered family work, the practitioner provides some degree of expertise about families, helping skills, and acess to resources. Family members bring special knowledge of themselves, of one another, of their interactions, and of their social and environmental contexts. Both practitioners and clients have certain problem-solving abilities, as we all do. A good deal of weight is given to the family's own ability to solve its problems; the practitioner's initial job is in fact to help the family make the best use of that ability. Although practitioners may occasionally make some use of problem-solving techniques, such as paradoxical tasks, that may prove temporarily baffling to the family, the center of operations is collaborative problem solving within a framework that makes sense to the family members. In fact, the family is constantly encouraged to apply its collective ingenuity in the search of novel solutions.

A different point of view is reflected in strategic therapy, an approach good for purposes of contrast since it also focuses on resolution of specific problems and makes use of tasks. The problem, however, is seen as the product (or a part) of the family's unsuccessful problem-solving efforts (Fisch, Weakland, and Segal 1982). Rather than trying to help the family understand why its problem-solving attempts have failed and how they could be improved, the practitioner devises interventions that clients may find puzzling, such as advising them to "go slow" in their change efforts (p. 159), or warning them about the "dangers of improvement" (p. 162).

Directives (tasks) are devised by the therapist without consultation with the family. "Movement in a case can only come from action by the therapist, guided by his strategy of treatment. Effective strategies are likely to be ones opposite from the patient's basic thrust" (Fisch, Weakland and Segal 1982:115). It is assumed that reflective discussion with clients about what has not worked and what has can contribute little to the process. Bross and Benjamin (1982) describe a "confusion technique" to "neutralize resistance" in families that "tend to intellectualize everything." "Task prescription proves relatively fruitless as the client shoots down every suggestion with a variety of reasons why it won't work." Producing "intellectual confusion" through "complex pseudological explanations and other kinds of doubletalk" is the method proposed (p. 20). A more collaborative alternative would be to elicit suggestions from the family members about what they thought might work.

In this "therapeutic jujitsu," as Stanton (1981b) describes strategic techniques, the practitioner searches for leverage to change a recalcitrant system. She not only is the mastermind of the change effort but also must proceed with it single-handedly.

In theoretical terms, the rationale for discounting the family's problem-solving activities in various therapeutic approaches is that the family's problems result from systemic forces largely outside the awareness or control of the family members. Patterns of interaction that give rise to problems are maintained by homeostatic, or balance-preserving, mechanisms. These mechanisms exert pressure to hold onto the status quo. Presenting problems can, in fact, be seen as expressions of these mechanisms.

If problems are rooted in system dynamics that family members are unaware of, and in any case would be unwilling to disrupt, their families could not be expected to make much headway in a rational, problem-solving approach. It would run headlong into powerful resistance and would be bound to fail. The practitioner must attack the systemic basis of the problem, often by indirect or deceptive means. The family is not so much a help in this process as it is a source of resistance. As Wile (1981) suggests, such theorizing can lead to an unfortunate "assumption of an adversary relationship between therapist and family" (p. 28).

This theory of family problems and functioning doubtless applies to some problems in some families but there is little evidence to support its universal application, and there is research to suggest that families can make headway with distressful relationship problems through guided problem solving (Woodward et al. 1981; Jacobson 1977, 1979; Robin 1981). Moreover, it is reasonable to assume, as noted, that many problems families may want help with can be modified without altering underlying relationship patterns. A systems perspective does not mean acceptance of complete dependence of manifest problems on systemic patterns. Social systems vary considerably in the degree of interdependency among their different components. For example, how much a given type of problem can change without altering family structure is an empirical question that has not been satisfactorily answered.

Finally, the stress on therapist-initiated system change, and the consequent subordination of the family's participation in problem solving, is based on a *morphostatic* view of the family as a system. A system controlled by morphostatic processes is highly resistant to change. Stability is maintained by strong homeostatic mechanisms; change occurs only when the system is sufficiently challenged. The assumption that family systems, even disturbed ones, are generally governed by change-resistant morphostatic processes is open to question, however. *Morphogenic* processes, those that account for systems change, are always present, even in systems that appear to be stable. Profound change in family systems is a commonplace phenomenon, as we are reminded when we think of births, deaths, children leaving home (or being removed therefrom), or split-ups resulting from divorce and separation. Families in the throes of such changes are likely to be overrepresented in the case loads of social workers and other helping professionals. Moreover, the appearance of a family at the social worker's door (or vice versa) is evidence that forces for change have been set in motion in one relevant system or another—in individual family members, the family, or its environment. If change processes already are at work, then the argument that practitioners need to "unbalance the system" in order to produce change has less force. Rather, the question becomes one of identifying and utilizing change dynamics within the network of relevant systems.

The last element of collaboration I shall consider here concerns the practitioner's sharing with the family her assessment of the dynamics of the family's problem, her rationale for less obvious interventions, her intermediate goals, and other knowledge and impressions she may have that might be relevant to the family's problem-solving efforts. In a genuine collaborative effort, participants share information they think would advance their common purpose. In this process selectivity is exercised, since certain information such as stray thoughts, possible false impressions, or uncomprehensible messages might hamper the joint effort. At the same time, information could well be shared simply because it might prove helpful to others without knowing exactly how they might use it. To insure effective coordination, participants would reveal intermediate goals and provide reasons for trying to attain them. Further, if the enterprise were truly collaborative, a participant would not introduce deliberately misleading information. Hollis and Woods (1981) put the point more strongly: "We believe that when the therapist consistently withholds impressions, the treatment relationship degenerates into an 'expert-idiot' format in which the family is at the mercy of the manipulations of the worker—which the worker never explains" (p. 270).

This conception provides general guidelines for users of the task-centered model. The practitioner's style of communication with family members is open and forthright, but is restrained by considerations of what might be understandable or useful.

A rather different tack is taken by certain "systems based" therapies (for example, structural and strategic), in which the practitioner's communications often are guided by a current plan of overcoming systemic resistance to change. Thus, practitioners may give excessively negative prognoses, withhold information about intermediate goals, or give deceptive explanations for paradoxical directives.

These maneuvers are carried out, of course, with the purpose in mind of helping the family and may, at least in some cases, work as intended. But perhaps not enough attention has been paid to different meanings of these messages as they might be interpreted by family members. In another context, Gurman (1981) has criticized behavioral therapists for ignoring the multiple levels of meaning in their behavior-exchange contracts. A husband spends time with his children in exchange for a bottle of beer presented by his wife (Gurman's example). In the short run, Gurman notes, the wife may see her husband's behavior as an improvement but, at a different level of meaning, "may eventually conclude that husband sees her as a mobile, beer-dispensing machine" (p. 494).

The argument is well taken, but can also be applied to a practitioner's use of deceptive or paradoxical communication. It may be effective in the short run, but what of the long-run consequences? Many clients, at least those who catch on to the therapist's tactics, eventually conclude that the therapists view them as too inept or childlike to be dealt with in a straightforward way. Catching on may not even be necessary. Thus, clients may well "misread" paradoxical injunction as the sort of reverse psychology one uses with children, or evidence that the practitioner is not taking their difficulties seriously.

Clients may not read any particular meaning into the practtioner's moves but may simply be confused by them. Clients who do not comprehend what their therapists are up to soon begin to think of other ways to spend their time. This point has been made quite convincingly in follow-up studies of clients of individual psychodynamic treatment, another form of helping that sometimes proves more baffling than beneficial to its recipients (Mayer and Timms 1970; Silverman 1970).

The point certainly is not that these techniques have no place in the present model, but rather that they should be used only after more straightforward methods have been tried and found wanting. Also, they should be used sparingly, with appropriate explanations and debriefings. In other words, they should be fitted into a relationship that remains essentially collaborative.

Action Emphasis

It is almost a truism to say that family members must act (and interact) differently if family problems are to change. Thus, all schools of family therapy view their methods as helping their clients undertake new forms of action. But approaches vary in respect to the means by which that goal is reached. Some systems of therapy seek to generate new forms of action from the inside out. For example, psychodynamic and Bowenian approaches stress the importance of changes in the individual's psychological and emotional structure that underlie individual and interpersonal functioning. These approaches make considerable use of techniques that help family members express and become aware of underlying conflicts, feelings, and expectations. As these processes are worked through, changes in action will tend to follow.

Other schools of therapy place emphasis on bringing about change in action through more direct means, such as straightforward tasks, paradoxical injunctions, behavior exchange contracts, manipulation of interaction in the session, and training in problem-solving and communication skills. Interventions concerned with psychological and emotional processes may be used but are directly related to immediate action objectives. However, their use is more optional and supplementary than fundamental. Improvement in emotional or psychological well-being are assumed to follow or accompany constructive changes in action. Structural, strategic, behavioral, communications and problem-centered approaches fall into this grouping (Levant, 1984) as well as, of course, the task-centered model. The common thread identified here is general emphasis on direct methods of changing ways family members act and interact. The approaches differ in other important aspects, as well as in their precise strategies for bringing about changes in action.

On this dimension, the task-centered model can be distinguished by its focus on *problem-solving action* conceived of in a particular way. In the model, attention is centered on particular problems or obstacles and the action that may be taken to work them out. The question ever present in the practitioner's mind is: "What is the difficulty being worked on and what can be done to resolve it?" As a result, considerable emphasis is placed on problem specification, selecting and planning appropriate action, facilitating actions within and outside the session, addressing impediments to action, and reviewing actions that have been attempted.

In the task-centered approach, an attempt is made to help family members utilize a constructive, rational problem-solving response to family difficulties. This manner of problem solving is commonly used by families to resolve ordinary problems of living. A husband and wife identify a disagreement; compromises are negotiated and carried through. Academic difficulties a child is having at school are brought to the parents' attention. Different ways of handling the problem are considered: help with homework, less TV, a conference with the teacher, and so on. Action alternatives are selected and implemented. Often the problem-solving response is quick with its steps compressed into a few moments. A mother criticizes her teenage daughter's hairdo. Daughter sulks. Mother chides her about sulking. Daughter sulks more. Mother then thinks of something amusing to break the ice, and problem is resolved.

These problem-solving responses just illustrated are constructive in that they alleviate problems at hand and do so in a way that enhances the well-being of the participants and promotes cohesion. They are rational in that they involve such logical steps as reflective identification of the difficulty, consideration of alternative ways of solving it, use of negotiation and compromise, implementation of problem-solving action, and use of feedback to guide further action.

Problem-solving responses to family problems are frequently neither constructive nor rational, as we all know. Blaming and attacking one another, denying one's own responsibility for a difficulty, withdrawing, or using coercive tactics are familiar response patterns. They achieve short-term gains—protecting self-esteem, or forcing others to knuckle under—but in the longer term tend to make matters worse for all concerned.

No matter how constructive and rational, problem-solving action has its limits. It cannot resolve deeply entrenched conflicts (although it can make them easier to deal with). It may not work if conflict is too intense. It cannot knit together relationships devoid of respect or caring (but can facilitate a decent ending to those that have no future). In the task-centered model, an attempt is made to strengthen and extend the more constructive kinds of natural problem-solving responses that occur in families. This emphasis gives the model a distinctive cast, even though a variety of methods from other approaches also are used. It might be said that the task-centered practitioner places more stock in problem-solving action than practitioners based in other approaches. She is more inclined to start with it, stay with it, and return to it. As a result, a task-centered session is more likely to be concerned with the "how to's" of straightforward problem solving than with stragetic or structural approaches.

Although the task-centered model makes considerable use of methods identified with behavioral therapy, it places them within a framework that offers broader conceptions of action and includes a variety of "non behavioral" methods for reaching solutions. Whether done by an individual or by family members in concert, problem-solving action provides the main means of change in family problems. In addition, action provides a means of learning methods for solving a particular problem and for problem-solving in general. Reference here is primarily to learning through doing, or experiential learning that may be acquired through participating in session or home tasks. The participation may also involve learning by observing the actions of others in these tasks (modeling effects).

Action-generated learning can be facilitated by insight achieved through the practitioner's exploration and interpretation of individual and family dynamics or the family's situation. In the task-centered model, the main function of such understanding is to help people work through obstacles blocking actions or to make use of resources. For example, a family's realization that one member is being scapegoated obviously is useful in designing tasks to alter the scapegoating pattern. (However, in the absence of such tasks, the insight would not be counted on to have any lasting effect on the family's treatment of the scapegoated member.)

Although insight is seen primarily as a means of facilitating problem-solving action, efforts to carry out actions or tasks can themselves have powerful effects on the understanding we have of ourselves and our relationships. Success at tasks not only can inform clients about their abilities, but more importantly can also change the reality on which their judgments are based. If clients can achieve greater competence in performing family roles, they acquire a realistic basis for better self-concepts.

Failures, as the saying goes, can be instructive. Inability to carry out a task that seems reasonable and that one has agreed to do may stimulate an examination of self or intimate relationships. Mrs. Roberts agreed to do a simple task of rewarding her ten-year-old, Nick, with verbal praise and time together if Nick kept his room clean. Nick did his task but Mrs. Roberts found herself unable to live up to her part of the bargain. Work on this obstacle pushed her to acknowledge her punitiveness toward her son and her resentment of him as a burden, as well as feelings connected with her marriage and divorce. The understanding that resulted helped her to complete the task and be more responsive to her son in other ways. If she had discussed her problems in the session, her punitiveness and resentment could have remained buried under her projections and denials. Her inactions spoke louder than her words.

Insight, then, will be most productive if it is developed in conjunction with action efforts. Insight can lead to tasks which, if carried out, can reinforce and elaborate the understanding. Failure to perform tasks can prompt a useful examination of one's self and situation.

4. *Dimensions of Interaction*

To understand family problems one needs to comprehend the workings of the systems that make up their context. Included would be knowledge of individuals, families, and external systems, an area of knowledge that is encyclopedic in scope.

This chapter will focus on a central aspect of this knowledge domain—the dimensions of human interaction that characterize the functioning of social systems. These processes will be dealt with initially and primarily within the context of the family system. Their relevance to external systems then will be discussed, and their use in that context will be illustrated. Aspects of individual functioning will be taken up in the following chapter.

The exposition will be organized around key concepts, their meanings, and applications and research relating to them. In keeping with the theoretical openness of the model, I shall concentrate on presenting conceptual tools that can be used within different approaches, especially those within the structure/process group (Levant 1984) from which many of the ideas have been drawn.

COMMUNICATION

Communication is an essential part of interaction. When communicative aspects of interaction are at issue, attention is focused on exchange of *messages* that contain explicit or implicit meanings. Although communication is sometimes used almost as a synonym for interaction, it is viewed in the present framework as a component of interaction. Any interaction has a communicative element, but interaction is a broader concept that includes interior phenomena (cognitions and feelings) that may not be communicated as well as behavioral aspects that do more than convey meanings. A husband who beats his wife black and blue is not simply engaging in a form of body language.

Channels

Human communication, in the family and elsewhere, occurs largely in three channels. The language channel expresses meanings in symbols according to rules of syntax. Accompanying language is paralanguage, which conveys meaning not through the symbolism of words but rather through vocal behavior, such as tone of voice, loudness, pace, laughter, crying, and so on. The third channel is kinesic communication, or "body language," which includes facial expressions, gestures, body movements and posture.

Most communication uses the three channels simultaneously, usually in a complementary or at least congruent way. A verbal insult may be delivered in a loud voice and accompanied by an appropriate hand gesture. Clinicians learn to be on the alert for lack of congruence, which often is a sign that something interesting is involved. For example, in a dialogue between a mother and daughter about the latter's problems with her boyfriend, the mother may ask, "What do you plan to do?" with a smile and a slight vocal stress on "what." The smile suggests a supportive question, but the stress betrays her possible impatience. Mother is taken aback when daughter with a typical teenager's sensitivity to nuances of parental communication responds: "Don't rush me!"

Revealing clues from paralinguistic and kinesic sources often is interpreted at an intuitive level without much help from theories, concepts, or research. We sense an underlying hostile tone but we cannot articulate why we label it as such. The point is illustrated by a classroom exercise I have used for several years. Students listen to two tape-recorded versions of a husband and wife discussing a problem. One is an actual session task, the other is a reenactment by amateur actors using a script of the original dialogue. Students first are asked to identify the "real" couple, and the great majority of the class can do so without difficulty. They then are asked to give reasons for their identification, making use of paralinquistic concepts that they have just read about. The actual differences between the couples on the tape are entirely paralinguistic, since they use the same language. The students have great difficulty with the second task, usually doing little better than saying that the real couple sounds more "natural." Only after playbacks of selected passages from both tapes are the students able to put what they had correctly sensed into technical concepts. Communication in the genuine dialogue was characterized, for example, by a greater number of pauses and a more varied and more subdued stress pattern.

Careful attention to paralinguistic and kinesic clues over the course of work with a family can reveal patterns that might otherwise escape attention, particularly patterns that convey hidden motives or feelings. For example, a person's speech may exhibit certain qualities when the person is distressed, even though his language per se does not give a clear message. In one case a wife's speech took on a sing-song quality when she was upset; in another, a daughter's voice became quiet and lost its timbre when she was under stress; in still another, a husband would grip his chair when angry. The significance of nonverbal indicators is best established through observation of several incidents. The interpretation of isolated incidents often can prove erroneous, since they may reflect mannerisms that may not be connected to affective or other expressions in any straightforward way.

Metacommunication

Some communication is about other communication—*metacommunication*, as communication theorists call it (Watzlawick, Beavin, and Jackson 1967). In family treatment, metacommunication provides a principal means of explaining and clarifying communication issues, including possible discrepancies between different channels of communication. The mother, whose daughter interpreted her question as rushing her, might respond at a metacommunication level with "I was just asking a question," to which the daughter might retort with another metacommunication, "But your tone of voice made it sound like a nag."

Content and Process

Another fundamental distinction is between the "content" and "relationship" or "process" aspects of communication. The content of a message describes its substantive meaning. If a wife tells her husband, "It's time to take your medicine," the content is about her husband's medicine taking. Further exploration of this might concern what medicine he takes, what he takes it for, how often he takes it, and so on.

The same message can also be interpreted in quite a different way, as a statement about the relationship between the partners. In this situation, the wife takes a dominant position vis-à-vis her husband, assuming the role of a "good nurse." From this vantage point one might ask such questions as, "Does the wife attempt to be dominant in other aspects of their relationship?" "How does the husband react to the wife's control in this instance or in others?" Any message can be examined from these two perspectives.

Usually the content of a message is more apparent than its relationship implications, but the latter inevitably are present. Thus, a matter-of-fact exchange between two parents concerning what chores their young son is to do may indicate equality in their relationship. Should they carry on their communication with their son present and not involve him in it, their communication would define both of them in a superior relationship over the son and would indicate at that moment a boundary around the parental relationship that would exclude the son. Suppose the son breaks in to ask, "Do I have to do that?" and looks to the mother as he puts the question. This bit of kinesic communication might suggest that the son sees mother as having more influence over his activities than father. Isolated instances can be atypical or misinterpreted: as with paralinguistic clues, one looks for repeated instances.

RULES OF INTERACTION

Regularities in communication or interaction can be thought of as rules (Haley 1963; Wertheim 1975). The concept has been used in two ways in family theory. Rules sometimes refer to patterns of interaction that actually occur; for example, when father reprimands daughter, mother comes to her rescue. But the same term also is used to refer to desired norms or regularities. We should be able to talk without arguing, or Diana should be home by ten p.m.

In the present framework this ambiguity is dealt with by using the terms *descriptive rule* or *pattern* to refer to actual regularities, and the terms *prescriptive rules* or *norms* for desired regularities. Like a set of Russian dolls, rules of family life are fitted into one another. Father's yielding the floor to mother's interruptions when the children are being discussed is a descriptive rule we might observe in a single session. This "micro rule" may be a part of a larger rule that describes mother's dominance in respect to child-rearing matters. That rule in turn may be part of a pattern in which mother decides who shall be in charge of what.

These higher order rules are referred to as *metarules*, or rules about rules. Metarules may be either descriptive or prescriptive. The principle of reciprocity, or "fair exchange," is an example of a metarule that may describe a good deal of marital interaction. The rule also may be enunciated as a desired norm and used to decide rules for particular circumstances. If the husband cooks, the wife will clean up afterwards since, in light of the norm of reciprocity, the arrangement seems to be a fair way to divide up kitchen chores. Descriptive rules may themselves constitute target problems and almost always make up part of their contexts.

Viewing rules in both descriptive and prescriptive senses, we are interested in learning about the actual patterns of interaction as well as the desired norms that govern family life as a means of identifying obstacles and resources that bear on target problems. To reduce the chore to manageable size, we shall examine rules primarily in relation to four dimensions: *control*, *involvement*, *alliance*, and *flexibility*. An additional dimension, *conflict*, will be viewed as a pervasive element that will be dealt with as it affects each of the first four. These concepts serve to organize most of the theoretical, empirical, and clinical literature on interaction patterns that bear upon the assessment and resolution of family problems.

Control

Under the rubric of *control* can be included aspects of family life that relate to power, dominance, and hierarchy. Questions such as, "Who is in charge of or influences whom?" "How is control attempted and maintained?" "Where do power struggles occur?" are among those commonly raised in exploring this contextual area.

Like other dimensions of family life, control is best understood in relational terms. In analysis of face-to-face communication between family members, one observes the relationship-defining aspects of messages. As in the example presented above, a simple question asked by a wife,—"Have you taken your medicine"—is a move toward control. But the move itself does not define the relationship. The husband must be heard from. If he accepts her dominant position (Yes, I have taken it), then for the moment the relationship can be said to be dominant-submissive. If he responds in a way that suggests rejection of his wife's dominance (Don't nag about that) then a different relationship is suggested.

Concepts of complementarity and symmetry (Watzlawick, Beaven, and Jackson 1967; Ericson and Rogers 1973) are used to convey these relational distinctions. A complementary interaction refers to one characterized by differences between interactants, usually differences along a dominant-submissive axis. The person taking the dominant or superior position is said to be "one-up"; the person taking the submissive or inferior position is "one-down."

A husband and wife are planning a home improvement project:

WIFE: We'll need to do lots of things; wallpapering the kitchen and fixing up the basement and . . . .

HUSBAND: (*interrupting*): Yes, but let's concentrate on one project at a time.

WIFE: Well, we could do the wallpapering in the kitchen.

The interaction becomes complementary when the husband defines how they should proceed with home improvements ("One project at a time") *and* the wife, taking a one-down position, follows his lead.

In *symmetrical* interactions, on the other hand, a control pattern is lacking. Persons interact on a more or less equal basis, although they may do so with varying degrees of cooperation. In the example above, the exchanges would have been symmetrical either if partners had proceeded to generate ideas about possible home improvements or if the wife had rejected her husband's one-project-at-a-time proposal and continued with one of her own.

By describing interactions and relationships, the concepts of complementarity and symmetry avoid the fallacy of reducing interactional phenomena to individualistic terms, as in "controlling mother." If a mother is truly controlling, she needs children willing to be controlled. When observing family members interact, one usually finds shifts between complementary and symmetrical communication depending on subject matter, mood of the participants, and so on. And when communicaiton is complementary, one-up and one-down positions rotate for the same reasons. Changeability in dominance patterns extends to all aspects of family interaction and particularly to relationships between adults. In American marriages, for example, the question of who controls what normally cannot be simply answered. The wife may be in charge of the children, the husband in charge of the cooking, and both may share influence in a symmetrical fashion regarding large expenditures.

It is usually an overstatement, and often meaningless, to say that the husband or wife is the "dominant person" in the relationship. Although observations of face-to-face communication may give important clues about dominance patterns, information about interaction in the home is necessary in order to get a complete picture, if one is needed. One spouse, for example, may take responsibility for decisions in a certain area, but the apparently one-down partner may hold "veto power" or the right of the "final word," which, while seldom exercised, may influence decisions of the spouse apparently holding a one-up position. Selected types of complementary and symmetrical interaction are described below.

Cooperative Complementarity and Symmetry. In cooperative complementary and symmetrical relationships, partners interact without conflict; either the dominance of one partner is accepted by the other, or both see one another as having equal status. Metarules pertaining to obligations, equity, and reciprocity—what Boszormenyi-Nagy and Ulrich (1981) refer to as "relational ethics"—provide a normative framework. In stable complementary relationships, such as may be found between parents and children, older and younger siblings, and in traditional marriages, there is a perceived mutual obligation for one person to provide leadership and for the other to accept it. Obligations result in entitlements. Parents are entitled to respect from their children, who in return are entitled to financial and other support from their parents. Norms of reciprocity (fair exchange) and equity (fair treatment) serve to maintain balance in what family members expect from, and do for, one another.

In transactions that are cooperatively symmetrical, partners feel obliged to treat one another as equals and are entitled to be treated accordingly. Exchanges should be both reciprocal and equitable. Both types of interactions over time produce an implicit "ledger" which "carries a statement of entitlements and indebtedness for each individual in the family" (Boszormenyi-Nagy and Ulrich 1981:164). These ideas put in a larger framework a number of notions used to understand family life, including theories of social exchange, equity, and reciprocity (Gergen, Greenberg, and Willis 1980).

Their use here, of course, is as analytic concepts and not as value prescriptions. As analytic tools, they are employed to help us understand how family members perceive their relationships, and there is little doubt these perceptions, even if not always articulated, are of considerable importance. These norms permeate all family interaction, and we shall return to them in different contexts.

Cooperative complementary and symmetrical interactions (and attendant relationship ethics) provide important resources in family work. Even in severely distressed families we assume that there usually are elements of cooperative interaction that can be built upon, or reserves of obligation or indebtedness that can be tapped, in order to stimulate cooperative interactions. For example, a father in the midst of a lengthy tirade against his daughter remarked that he wanted "to do what was right for her" but her behavior made this impossible. Acknowledging his frustration, the practitioner focused on his sense of obligation to do "what was right." Could he say more about that? The resulting discussion brought out the father's hopes for the daughter's happiness. By pointing out that father and daughter had a common goal, her well-being, the practitioner was able to move into consideration of what they might do to attain it.

Coercive Complementarity and Symmetry. In a smoothly functioning complementary relationship, the one-up person's position is accepted as legitimate by the one-down partner. One-up can exercise influence because one-down gives him sanction to do so. When the sanction is missing, the relationship must be "enforced" through some type of coercion: threats, verbal and physical punishment, hostile silences, and so on (*coercive complementarity*). The person who feels coerced may present the relationship itself as a problem, or coercive complementarity may fuel other problems including striking back, passive noncompliance, fleeing the relationship, and somatic reactions.

As Patterson and Hops (1972) have pointed out, "as one member initiates the coercive process, another is likely to use it" (p. 130). When a relationship takes this turn it operates under a rule of *coercive symmetry*. Like other types of relations, it may escalate as each partner becomes progressively more coercive toward the other. The end result may be domestic violence. In most relationships, however, escalations are limited by homeostatic mechanisms that restore balance before violence occurs. A wife may punish her husband for spending money unwisely by not talking to him; the husband may retaliate by not repairing his spouse's car; the wife refuses to have sex; the husband storms out of the bedroom. At this point both realize that they are in danger of going "too far" in alienating one another, or perhaps they become weary of the fight. They make up or let things cool off. As Hoffman (1980) has sagely suggested, "the exercise of power tends to be self-limiting in families since power carried to an extreme defeats one of the overriding objectives of the family—to provide an orderly access to intimacy" (p. 191). Coercive strategies may bring about compliance, but in so doing they may disrupt the affectional bonds that are the essence of family life. We want others in our families to do our bidding but not at the expense of their hating us for it. This self-limiting principle is not completely benign, however. The relief experienced when the coercive spiral ends may reinforce a relationship that really is not working very well and deplete motivation for changing it.

For given problems, particularly those involving domestic violence, it may be important to know in detail how these rules operate. An act of violence does not necessarily mean that the limiting principle has broken down. Physical abuse may be another step in the coercive spiral, often one that triggers homeostatic reactions; the abuser becomes contrite, the abused becomes forgiving.

In explaining coercive spirals, the practitioner wishes to identify the interlocking coercive actions of the participants and mechanisms of control and rebalance. Of particular importance is the identification of triggers that result in rapid escalation. Often they are not obvious—for example, calling another a certain name, a derogatory reference to someone or something another is fond of, or even a look or gesture. In coercive symmetry a good deal of punishment may be exchanged and particular responses may be motivated by anger or desire for revenge. Still, the essential theme is a struggle to have another do what one wants.

"Oppressive" Complementarity. Some complementary relationships appear to be cooperative. They are free of conflict and coercion. One finds, however, that the person in the one-down position is paying a price for the surface harmony.

In one type, the one-down partner has negative or mixed feelings about being put in a subordinate position. He or she may feel put-upon, pushed around, and so on, but at the same time is unable or unwilling to be assertive, and often welcomes freedom from the decision making that his or her partner assumes. Often one-down's complaints about the relationship are vague and lack behavioral specifications: "He treats me like a child"; "I feel overwhelmed"; "She doesn't let me be myself." A common result is for one-down to become depressed or to develop somatic reactions. In a marriage the submissive partner may have been attracted to the dominant one because of the dominance but now wants less of it or something different than he or she did initially. In a parent-child relation, problems are likely to arise as children become adolescents and want more freedom. In exploring these relationships, the practitioner needs to be aware of the ambivalence of the submissive partner and the possible gratifications he or she derives from the subordinate role. This understanding must then be related to how the dominant partner exercises control and the gratification he or she receives from that role.

In the following example a dominant husband and submissive wife are working on a session task to explore ways in which the wife can be more assertive in her family relations.

WIFE: I do too much for everybody in the family, I know that.
HUSBAND: Yeah, like you wait on the children hand and foot.
WIFE: I know.
HUSBAND: Like at dinner when they ask for catsup and things not on the table. Don't jump up. Let them get the stuff.
WIFE: Yeah, I suppose so.

Although they are supposedly working on how the wife can be more assertive, the husband deftly controls the conversation by focusing on the children and away from him. He takes on the one-up role as an assertiveness trainer. Paradoxically the more he advises her on how to become assertive with the children the more he is able to keep her in a subordinate position with him—an excellent example of the content of communication being undone by the process. Observing this rule, the practitioner suggests that the task be restructured: the husband is to tell the wife what *he* can *do* to help her be more assertive.

A second variety of oppressive complementarity is structurally similar to the first except that the one-down participant accepts the arrangement. Since whoever is one-up is not likely to complain, the relationship usually is not presented as a target problem. It may, however, be a contributing factor to other problems. In this category falls the syndrome of the overprotective parent and the complaint, dependent child. The child is typically seen for a behavioral or health problem, and in addition may have some form of developmental disability that gives the parent(s) rationale for the overprotectiveness.

Parent-Child Relations. A generally accepted metarule in family structure is that parents should have authority over their children, that there should be a complementary relationship between parents and children with parents accorded the one-up position. Like any metarule, the norm of parental authority is subject to numerous qualifications and varied interpretations. Parents are to exercise authority, but excessive coercion in the form of harmful physical abuse is proscribed. As children become older, parental authority is expected to diminish until eventually a symmetrical relationship is reached. Much conflict between parents and adolescents concerns issues of control in the absence of generally accepted norms to guide particular kinds of decisions.

In the human services such values and ways of implementing them are marked by cross currents. For example, there has been a gradual movement toward greater public scrutiny of parents' use of physical coercion with children. Mandated reports of child abuse is one reflection of this trend. Children can now (and do) report possible abuse against themselves to practitioners who may be required to inform a child protection agency, which in turn may be required to conduct an investigation.

On the other hand the family treatment field has been witnessing its own parent power movement led by such theorists as Haley (1980) and Minuchin (1974), who stress "putting parents in charge" of their troublesome offspring. The trend is perhaps a reaction to earlier tendencies in one-to-one treatment for practitioners to identify with adolescents and to view their parents as excessively controlling or punitive. The notion of inadequate parental authority as a cause of deviant behavior in youth has well-established roots in both professional thought and popular views. Haley, Minuchin, and others, however, have extended the causal influences of this insufficiency to a range of other problems of youth, including mental illness and anorexia, and view it as part of a larger problem of family structure as shall be discussed below.

Although "putting parents in charge" is a laudable goal, problems of inadequate parental authority and the means of solving them have not been well conceptualized or adequately studied. Often "putting parents in charge" has been used as a slogan and applied rather simplistically to complex interactions.

Well-functioning parent-child relationships can be characterized as essentially complementary but with significant areas of cooperative symmetry that enlarge as children grow older. When children are young, symmetrical elements may be introduced by the parent in order to help the child develop autonomy. The symmetry may become competitive, particularly with adolescents, but when push comes to shove the children know who is boss.

This pattern of complementarity may give way to less functional forms which may dominate a relationship or significant parts of it. When children act up, parents may use coercion in increasing amounts (grounding, corporal punishment, and so on). The relationship remains in this complementary form but succeeds in exercising only sporadic control of the child's behavior.

Dysfunctional symmetry may be the next stage, in which children no longer respect the authority of their parents. Parents are unable to restore complementarity when they really want to. Several patterns are possible. A relationship may become competitively or coercively symmetrical as the parent and child fight like peers. It may become a form of disengaged symmetry: the parent and child may have only peripheral contact with one another. The ultimate stage in the degrading of parental power is a reversal of the usual complementary positions. The child takes in effect a one-up position which he maintains through coercion—tantrums, threats to run away, anti-social behavior in the community, and so on. The child is not out of control but rather in control.

Psuedocomplementary and Psuedosymmetrical Relationships.
Dominance, like any aspect of human interaction, can be manip-
ulated by family members in order to serve covert interests. A
husband repeatedly accepts blame for problems in the marriage
but at the same time conveys the message that he "can't help
himself"—that's the way he is. By taking an apparent one-down
position the husband really assumes control and can frustrate
efforts of wife (or therapist) to bring about change. Or a wife
insists her husband take responsibility for making an important
but risky decision affecting the family, on grounds that he is the
"head of the house." If a decision turn out well for the wife she
will enjoy its benefits; if it proves to be a mistake in her eyes, she
will blame her husband and will take some satisfaction from
that. In effect, the wife maneuvers the husband into a phony
one-up position. Or parents assure their daughter she can pick
the college of her choice but point out the shortcomings of her
choices (and the strong points of their own) on grounds that they
are helping her make up her mind. She has been placed in a false
symmetrical position.

The maneuvers illustrated in these examples are variations of
psuedocomplementary and psuedosymmetrical interactions
(Watzlawick, Beavin, and Jackson 1967). They are deceptive in
effect but not always deliberately so. Some people play such
games, as the transactional analysts would call them (Berne
1961), almost as second nature.

Empirical Basis. A considerable amount of research relating to
aspects of control in families has accumulated in the literatures
on such topics as family power and dominance, marital decision
making, methods of child-rearing, and parental influences on
the development of children. (Reviews may be found in Burr,
Hill, Nye, and Reiss 1979). However, the yield of empirically
based generalizations useful to practitioners has not been great.
Variations in definitions of key variables and populations studied, lack of adequate theoretical formulations, and shortcomings in research methodology have made the development of any
empirical generalizations difficult, and those that have appeared seldom approach the level of specificity needed in clinical work. Unfortunately, much the same statement can be made

about the remaining dimensions to be considered in the chapter.

In respect to the present dimension, perhaps the studies that have produced the most results of interest to clinicians concerns parent-child relations. My observations will be limited to that area. In their review of 235 studies, Rollins and Thomas (1979) examined the differential "effects" on social competence in children of several "parent variables." Not surprisingly they found positive relationships between presence of parental support (e.g., praising, approving, encouraging, affection) and various indices of social competence in children (cognitive development, moral behavior, self-esteem, and so on). On the other hand, parental reliance on coercive methods (punishment, threats, and so on) was found to be related to various problems, including aggression, learning disabilities, and schizophrenia. Parental use of methods of "firm control" (consistent, firm application of rules) has also been found to be related to desirable behavior in children (Coopersmith 1967; Baumrind 1973). Additional research (reviewed under *alliance* section, below) suggests that stable parental coalitions are associated with absence of problems in offspring.

Most of this body of findings has been produced, however, by investigations carried out within the framework of what Rollins and Thomas (1979, p. 317) called the "parent causation model," in which measured parental actions (parent variables) are assumed to be the causative agents of behavior in children. One obvious drawback to this model is the difficulty in ruling out the influences of other parental actions or characteristics. Another is failure to take into account interaction between parents and children. Without such interactive data it is difficult to extract the contribution to the process made by the children themselves. As a result of these limitations, it is hard to pinpoint the role of a given parent factor. For example, in her analysis of studies of firm control, Lewis (1981) convincingly argues that, since parents used reason to obtain compliance and respected their children's decisions, the children in the studies, if asked, might have seen themselves in control of the parents.

More generally, the association between parental "control" and "good behavior" of children might be simply a reflection of "disciplinary harmony" (Lewis 1981:562) between parent and child. The rules work because the child has a role in shaping and modifying them. Applying this kind of analysis to other studies, one might say that parental affection, encouragement, or support "works" in relationships in which children are themselves affectionate, encouraging, or supportive.

As a whole, research on parent-child relations may be useful in describing parental behaviors within functional parent-child systems, but it does not tell us much about how these systems work or about what can be done to repair those that do not. Thus, one would not necessarily expect parental control techniques that are fitted to responsive children to be effective with children who are rejecting parental authority.

Investigations of the intricacies of parent-child interaction are beginning to appear, however. Of particular interest has been the work of Patterson and his associates (Patterson 1976; Lorber and Patterson 1981) who have used observational methods to study moment-to-moment interactions between parents and children. Some of their findings conform to the systems perspective considered above. Certain parental techniques, such as punishment, can modify the behavior of "nonproblem" children but have little effect (or a deleterious effect) on the behavior of children out of control. With socially aggressive children, there appeared to be a pattern of "punishment acceleration" or mutual coercion in their observed interactions with parents. In fact, the matching exchanges of coercive behaviors between parents and children in their observational studies showed a degree of regularity that is usually found "solely in laboratory studies of monkeys and rats" (Lorber and Patterson 1981:74).

Translated into our framework, the research reviewed suggests that a relationship of cooperative complementarity between parents and children is likely to be associated with child behavior that we normally view as constructive. Patterns characterized by coercive complementarity or symmetry are likely to be linked to behavior regarded as dysfunctional. How these different patterns of interaction come into being, how they operate, and how they change (or can be changed) from one to the other has not yet been greatly illuminated by existing research. The studies do suggest, however, that trying to alter mutually coercive patterns by changing the behavior of only the parent or the child may prove to be a one-sided solution to a two-sided problem.

Involvement

A second major dimension of family interaction concerns what I choose to call "involvement" among family members, following Epstein and Bishop (1981). In simplest terms it refers roughly to the degree of "closeness" among family members in their interactions. Some family units appear to be "tightly knit"; others, to shift the metaphor somewhat, appear "loosely wrapped." Students of family life—indeed, but almost anyone with knowledge of families—are aware of such variations, which in many ways seem to depict the essence of family life. But of all aspects of family relations this one is perhaps the most difficult to unravel. To use Hoffman's (1980) understatement, it is a "hard-to-describe" phenomenon.

Involvement refers to a complex dimension that has been referred to by family theorists, researchers, and clinicians under a variety of rubrics: Enmeshment/disengagement (Minuchin et al. 1967); differentiation (Bowen 1978); cohesion (Olson, McCubbin, and Associates 1983); and centripetal/centrifugal (Stierlin 1972; Lewis et al. 1976).

These terms reflect a variety of meanings derived from differing definitions and theoretical perspectives. The amount of overlap is considerable, however, and to a large extent indeterminant because of lack of clear distinctions among the terms at an operational level. The collection can be seen as one of the numerous "concept clusters" in family theory. Involvement is an umbrella term that refers roughly to this cluster, and is used interchangeably with cohesion, differentiation, and related terms. Most writers view the involvement dimension (or its equivalent) as running from high to low degrees. Usually the optimum amount of involvement is thought to fall somewhere in mid-range.

Although difficult to operationalize, the notion of boundary provides a useful way of understanding concepts suggested by cohesion, involvement and related terms. As physical systems, individuals are bounded by their skins. In a more psychological and social sense, a person's boundaries can be thought of as rules that control what he expresses about himself, to others, or what he defines as belonging to himself as opposed to someone else. How "closed" or "open" these boundaries are usually depends on the persons one is relating to. With strangers our boundaries are relatively closed and controlled, like the boundary separating two countries. Behavior is governed by intricate rules about what is revealed, how much, about what, to whom. Between intimates boundaries are much more open, with freer and wider expression of thoughts and feelings. There is a less of a sense of separateness. Feelings not only are shared, but the feelings of one may be experienced by the other. Intimate relationships are sources of both happiness and peril, as we know. Rejections are more keenly felt, conflicts may be more intense, and autonomy may be sacrificed.

Within a family subsystem, boundary rules are those "defining who participates in its transactions and how" (Minuchin, Rosman, and Baker 1978:56). Just as the individual maintains his or her boundary by controlling his or her interactions with others, a subsystem preserves its boundary by processes of inclusion and exclusion. Parents (the parental subsystem) may exclude a child from certain kinds of talk, activities, and so on.

Similarly, the family as a whole has its boundary. For example, when boundaries are strong, members are more likely to turn to one another for support, consensual validation, and the like, than to the external environment. These structures have been referred to as "centripetal" (Stierlin 1972; Beavers 1977) and "consensus-sensitive" (Reiss 1971).

As noted, it is difficult to connect the concept of boundary to specific indicators. Minuchin, Rosman, and Baker (1978) give some arresting examples of boundary diffusion: the mother of the anorectic girl who describes her daughter's condition as, "We can't eat" (p. 62), or the daughter who asks, "Mother, I don't feel well. Am I going to throw up?" (p.66). When a husband declines to share his feelings about his mother's sickness with his wife, or when immigrant parents speak in their native tongue in front of their children who understand only English, it is clear that boundary-making activities are at work. But giving examples in clear-cut cases is not the same as developing measures to calibrate the many varieties and nuances of boundary phenomena. Interruptions, speaking for others, seating patterns, sharing of space, and independence in decision making and activities are among possible indicators that appear germane.

Another aspect of involvement, one perhaps even more difficult to operationalize, is the emotional connectedness among family members. It provides the force that shapes boundary phenomena. Its complexity presents formidable obstacles to study since emotional ties often are fraught with ambivalence. They defy straightforward measurement since they pertain to interior events that family members may not themselves fully comprehend or may not be willing to reveal. Again, the obvious case may be easily perceived, but we have not yet developed much to help us to discriminate beyond commonsensical or intuitive perceptions. These definitional issues will be pursued in the context of examination of different levels of involvement.

High Mutual Involvement. A high degree of mutual involvement among family members is most readily identified as a problem when it intensifies conflict. The large amount of interdependency among family members for meeting intimacy needs sets the stage for conflict. Perhaps because of the strength of these needs and the lack of other means of fulfilling them, family members place on one another demands that may be excessive and may upset the other's autonomy when these demands are not met. Patterns of escalating mutual frustration can ensue. The system becomes overreactive in the sense that a frustrating response triggers off chains of excessive reactions and counter reactions.

Mrs. Rogers and her twenty-year-old daughter, Nancy, quarreled incessantly over Nancy's boyfriends. None seemed to measure up to the mother's expectations of the "right" boy for Nancy. Why did she persist in dating "creeps" who would tend to be like her father, "a real bum" whom Mrs. Rogers had left when Nancy was an infant. Her daughter deserved better. Nancy kept no secrets about her liaisons from her mother, who seemed always hungry for details about them. Nancy would tell her about each one, sometimes hoping to win her approval at last, at other times as an act of defiance. When a relationship would break up, Nancy would blame her mother even though Mrs. Rogers might have had only minimal contact with the boyfriend.

At first glance only the mother appears to be overinvolved, given her unrelenting and unrestrained criticism of her daughter's choice of boyfriends. But we see that the overinvolvement goes two ways when we consider how the daughter responds. She feels it necessary to defend her boyfriends against her mother's attacks, wants her approval of them, tells mother all, and blames her when her relationships sour. Mother may have been driven by her need to control her daughter's love life, a need accentuated perhaps by her identification with her daughter. Nancy seemed to be reacting to a strong need for her mother's approval and to be using her mother as means of avoiding her own responsibility for difficulties in establishing satisfying relationships with men. The presence and strength of these interlocked needs might be inferred from client self-report data and constitute one kind of empirical indicator of mutual overinvolvement. Another indicator might be provided by the intensity, variety, and amount of interaction around the issue.

How might such a pattern be distinguished from any mother-daughter conflict concerning daughter's choice of boyfriend? Although a mother might object to daughter's choice, she usually would be more selective and less vehement in her criticism. Moreover, she would be constrained by the daughter's status as an adult with a right to manage her own affairs. A daughter less involved with her mother could be more selective about the information she would share, more likely to turn a deaf ear to mother's criticisms, less driven to seek mother's approval, and less likely to hold mother responsible for difficulties in her relationships with men.

It also should be noted that the interaction pattern in the example above might take the form of coercive symmetry. A given sequence may be described from different perspectives. The various rule categories being considered constitute a multi-dimensional classification of interaction.

High mutual involvement without conflict seldom is presented by the participants as a target problem, since the arrangement presents no immediate distress and may in addition
be a source of gratification and protection for both. This type of
overinvolvement may be part of the context of other difficulties,
however. It may create a mutually reinforcing subsystem that is
unable to adapt to the external world. Problem-solving actions
and exploration of useful alternatives may be blocked.

Harold, age ten, began to refuse to attend school, complaining
that older kids picked on him. His parents accepted his complaint, allowed him to stay home, and demanded that the school
do something about the older boys. Exploration by the school
social worker revealed that Harold was an unusually small child
with a mild visual handicap who was doing poorly in his studies. Although there was basis for his complaints about being
bullied, the situation did not appear nearly as bad as Harold
had made out. Also, there was evidence that he provoked some of
the aggressive behavior toward him by his taunts. His parents,
who always had been very protective of their son because of his
handicap, persisted in seeing Harold as the victim of a bad
school environment and saw as the only solution his placement
in a private school, which they would be able to do only at a
great financial sacrifice.

The example suggests a pattern of dysfunctional involvement
between Harold and his parents. Harold's retreat from probably
manageable problems at school is at least tacitly supported by
the parents. Harold's need for protection interlocks with the
parents need to protect. The parents' reactivity to Harold's complaints about the bullies reinforces his fears and avoidance reaction, which in turn makes the parents even more protective.
Caught up in this spiraling interaction, the family is unable to
consider alternative approaches to solving the problem.

The case also serves to make the point that mutual involvement without conflict raises some sticky theoretical and value
questions. Since the target problem is Harold's difficulties at
school and not the parent-child relationship, the pattern of
"overinvolvement" must be seen as contributing to the problem
or to obstacles to its solution. It is assumed that Harold's reaction to the bullies and his parents' response to it are excessive

and will close off exploration of a range of possibly viable alternatives to dealing with the difficulty. It is assumed as well that the solution selected is a "poor" one in terms of its consequences for the parents and Harold, and may help perpetuate a dysfunctional pattern.

The argument could be used as a basis for presenting the family with an alternative view of their situation. It is easy to see, however, that the assumptions may be questioned and challenged further by new information—for example, that Harold really was being victimized by older children, or that the child's visual impairment was worse than originally thought. The pattern of reactions displayed by Harold and his parents would take on a "healthier" look; we can easily imagine reaching a point at which "overinvolvement" would be discarded as an explanation and other causal factors such as the school or the child's handicap would move into focus. In fact, the family's tight cohesiveness might even be seen as a source of strength.

Extremely high levels of involvement, while creating problems in many situations, may be highly functional under certain circumstances, when the family is faced with an external threat and must make an immediate response. Moreover, in any consideration of involvement, a good deal depends on related family dynamics. Extreme involvement accompanied by a high degree of conflict among family members can create a pressure cooker of explosive forces. In the absence of conflict, the same level of involvement might result in a very stable family structure that may be quite functional for many purposes.

The general point is that a rule of interaction is not dysfunctional in any absolute sense but rather in respect to defined problems and their contexts. When the interaction rule is not a problem itself but is viewed as contributing to it, the links between the rule and problem must be thought through carefully, and the risk of loss in making false connections needs to be recognized.

Conflicts over Involvement. Up to now we have considered patterns of *mutual* involvement among family members. Another kind of difficulty arises when one family member demands more involvement from another than the other is able or willing to give. In Fogarty's terms one family member is the "pursuer," another "the distancer" (1976:226). When it occurs between marital partners, the conflict may take the form of one spouse feeling "ignored" or "put off" by the other, who in turn may resent demands the other presents for time, attention, closeness, love, and so on. One partner may be the pursuer in some aspects of the relationship and the distancer in other aspects, leading to contingent exchanges. The wife may want "attention"; the husband, more sex. If the husband responds to wife's needs, she will respond to his, and vice versa. With parents and children, children are more likely to be the pursuers when they are young (the well-known demandingness of children). As children get older and strive to become more autonomous, the reverse is likely to occur. The children begin to distance and the parents pursue, a pattern that may continue as children move into adulthood and parents into old age.

Conflicts over involvement may be directly presented as problems by either pursuers or distancers, or both. Each is likely to punctuate the problem as the fault of the other. Pursuers are likely to accuse distancers of being uncaring, aloof, detached, and the like, while distancers use such terms as demanding, insatiable, and oversensitive to label pursuers. Seldom do they jointly define a problem as disagreement over how close they want to be, though they may accept this definition as suggested by the practitioner.

Conflict over involvement may be a less obvious part of, or a contribution to, a range of difficulties, particularly those involving communication among family members. Complaints about "lack of communication" frequently involve one member's desire for more privacy or less interaction than the other member(s) wants. In one case, for example, a pattern of quarreling between husband and wife was attributed to his "irritability" by the wife. Closer analysis revealed that he was often depressed over his situation at work and would become irritable if his wife tried to initiate conversation at those times, particularly if she tried to query him about his mood. He would prefer just to be left alone. His desire for solitude and silence was interpreted by his wife, however, as a rejection of her, especially when he did not respond to her overtures. The task eventually developed was designed with sensitivity to their involvement. The husband was to attempt to share more with his wife about his work when not depressed about it and calmly explain to her when he was that he preferred not to talk about it. The wife agreed to respect his need to be by himself when he was moody.

Low Mutual Involvement. In this pattern, family members lack close connections with one another. Although they are not in conflict over the degree of involvement with one another, there may or may not be conflict around other issues. When conflict does occur, it is likely to be related to specific points of contention. For example, adult children who may have had little to do with one another for years may find themselves at odds over how to care for an aging parent. When conflict does occur in low-involvement relationships, it is likely to reactivate patterns established when involvement was greater. These old patterns may produce general conflict if the distancing was the result of an "emotional cut-off" (Bowen 1978). As Kerr (1981) suggests, a cut-off is a way of dealing with unresolved involvements in a relationship by withdrawing emotionally from it. When members who have solved previous difficulties by a pattern that has become one of mutual withdrawal are brought together around a crisis event, their unfinished business may intrude.

Two sisters, who had little to do with their family during the previous several years, were brought to a family conference by a medical social worker to participate in planning aftercare for their terminally ill father who was about to be discharged from the hospital. The conference soon erupted in a quarrel between the sisters and the father over his "mistreatment" of their now deceased mother some years ago.

A frequently encountered problem in social work, especially in child welfare practice, is lack of involvement between parents and young children. Extreme examples are child neglect and failure of parents to maintain contact with children placed in foster care. Less extreme examples involve parents who "emotionally neglect" their children through their coldness or relegating their care to others.

Empirical Basis. Studies of involvement (cohesion, enmeshment, and the like) do not lend themselves readily to summation. Conceptual and operational definitions of key terms as well as methodological rigor vary considerably across studies.

A number of investigations, however, bear upon what might be regarded as the central hypotheses relating involvement to family functioning and to problems of family members. The most general of these hypotheses asserts that mid-range levels of involvement are associated with "good" family functioning (as measured by other criteria) or the absence of difficulties among members, while extremes of involvement are likely to be found in families with relational difficulties or problems in functioning of members. This hypothesis has received support from a number of studies (Lewis et al. 1976; Russell 1979; Stedman et al. 1981; Olson and McCubbin 1983).

More specific hypotheses state that certain types of problems of members tend to be linked to extremes of high involvement, while other types are found when the level of involvement in families is extremely low. In general, problems linked to high involvement are presumed to be psychopathological or psychosomatic—schizophrenia and anorexia, for example (Beavers 1977; Minuchin, Rosman, and Baker 1978). Those found at the other extremes are thought to be associated with social deviance—delinquency for example (Beavers 1977; Olson, Russell and Sprenkle 1980). The theoretical justification for this distinction perhaps lies in the debilitating effect of excessive involvement on the development or maintenance of self-boundaries and autonomy in offspring, which may contribute to more internalized disorders. Lack of involvement, on the other hand, may result in failure to control children's behavior effectively and may cause them to turn to peers to meet emotional needs.

Evidence bearing on these hypotheses can be found in a number of investigations. Impressionistic data from clinical studies have suggested patterns of overinvolvement between schizophrenic offspring and their parents, usually the mother (Wynne et al. 1958; Bowen 1960; Lidz et al. 1965). Additional evidence of this connection emerged from a more rigorous recent study (Summers and Walsh 1977). Minuchin, Rosman, and Baker (1978) found enmeshment to be one of the main patterns in families with psychosomatic children but have provided largely clinical impressions to support their observation. At the other end of the scale the Gluecks (1950) discovered low cohesion to be much more prevalent in families of delinquents than nondelinquents. In a study of treatment of female delinquents, Druckman (1979) found that families moved from low levels of cohesion before treatment to more moderate levels at posttreatment assessment, a result in accord with the hypotheses above.

However, other studies do not clearly support, or at least limit, these hypotheses. In their study of families with delinquent children, Minuchin et al. (1967) observed (impressionistically) both patterns of enmeshment and disengagement in the families. Contrary to their prediction, Perosa and Perosa (1982) did not find a higher degree of enmeshment in families with learning-disabled children then in a group of comparison families. In addition, several studies suggest that patterns of overinvolvement may be found between mothers and problem offspring, but not fathers (Summers and Walsh 1977; Stedman and Gaines 1981; Perosa and Perosa 1982). The pattern of the overinvolved mother and detached father, which may also be a source of difficulty in children (Stedman and Gaines 1981), needs, in particular, to be distinguished from other patterns. Finally, a great deal of distinguishable types of interactions are lumped together under the terms considered. For example, in their use of the term enmeshment, Minuchin and his associates (1967, 1978, 1981) may be referring to lack of boundaries between individuals or between systems or to both. As Hoffman (1980) suggests, it is doubtful whether the many ideas in this broad area can be put on a single scale.

As a whole, the studies indicate some important connections between extremes of involvement and difficulties in family and individual functioning. Until additional and more rigorous research is brought to bear, these findings are best regarded as intriguing possibilities to be considered in work with families.

Alliance

As a general dimension of family life, *alliance* refers to the presence or absence of alignments or coalitions between family members to achieve a common purpose. Alliances convey the notion of joint goals and directed effort; they need to be connected to the purpose or functions for which they serve.

In the hypothetical normal family, certain alliances are seen as desirable—for example, the parental alliance for purposes of childrearing, a spousal alliance when partners are involved with the larger community, total family alliances when the family faces a crisis. Apart from such circumstances, it is assumed that family members, as Hoffman (1980) states, "are free to make alliances necessary to the operation of the moment." In fact, flexible, changing patterns of alliance are seen as one of the characteristics of the "healthy" family.

I use the term alliance to be equivalent to coalition, as do many writers in the field (for example, Beavers 1977), although others reserve "coalition" to mean an alliance against someone else (Haley 1977; Aponte and Van Deusen 1981). To simplify analysis and terminology, it is useful to view coalitions in terms of triads—the coalitional efforts of two persons in relation to a third. Probably most coalitions of concern to family therapists take this form. Much of what might be called coalitional theory uses the triadic unit (Caplow 1968; Haley 1977; Minuchin, Rosman, and Baker 1978; Hoffman 1980). Moreover, most observations about triads can be extended to include larger sets of persons or, conversely, larger coalitional sets can be analyzed in terms of a series of triads. Several common patterns will be examined.

Two for one. In this form of coalition, two family members are united *in support* of a third. Parents are allied in support of a child, or siblings unite in support of a parent. (As mentioned, the statement could be expanded to larger sets—parents joined in support of two children or, if triadic analysis were continued, one could say that in one triad, both parents support one of their children, and in the second, they support the other). This form of coalition generally is regarded as a desirable goal or resource in family work and is used to define "healthy" family functioning. It may contribute to the difficulties of a family member, however, if support is given to dysfunctional patterns either inside or outside the home. Family members who cannot do enough for a sick or disabled member, thereby depriving him of necessary self-reliance, provide a common example. Other dynamics, including overinvolvement, may be at work, but the coalitional aspect itself is important since it is more difficult to question or refuse support when presented by a united pair than by an individual.

This form of coalition can present an almost insurmountable obstacle when the dysfunctional pattern it supports also is accepted by the third party. In these cases the triad presents a completely united front—massive resistance, as the practitioner is apt to call it. There are greater opportunities for change if the third person is rebelling against or ambivalent about the support, which is often the case with an "overprotected" member. Leverage for change also may be found in differences between the allied partners. While searching for change possibilities, the practitioner still attempts to make use of the strengths provided by the supportive elements. In some cases, supportive coalitions are used entirely as resources when the target problem is located in an external system. In these cases the practitioner takes on a broker or advocate role in helping the family resolve the external difficulty.

In the type of supportive coalition discussed thus far, the allying partners are driven primarily by motives to help a third, even if these motives prove to be misguided or to have dysfunctional consequences. Whatever they are doing, they are doing it to promote the cause of another as they see it, rather than serving the needs of their own relationship. In another, more complex variant of the supportive coalition, the partners unite to support a third to serve the demands of their own relationship. Because the union is usually a means of avoiding conflict, this form of coalition has been referred to by structural theorists as "detouring-supportive" (Minuchin, Rosman, and Baker 1978). Coalitions of this kind are central in structural and strategic explanations of a range of individual problems, including anorexia (Minuchin, Rosman, and Baker 1978), addiction (Stanton, Todd et al. 1982) and schizophrenic-like behavior (Haley 1980). According to these formulations, the parents avoid marital conflict and find a basis for stabilizing their relationships through joint parental concern for the "problem child" (who often is a young adult). Stanton, Todd, et al. (1982) put it this way in the case of the drug addict: "By focusing on the problems of the addict, the parents choose a course that is apparently safer than dealing with long-standing marital conflicts" (p. 22). Because their problems—anorexia, addiction, or whatever—serve a stabilizing function for the parental relationship, offspring are under covert pressure to retain their problem behavior. According to the theory, when his or her situation improves, the parents' marital situation worsens. Only by becoming "symptomatic" can the child restore the equilibrium of his parents' marriage. In learning theory terms, problem "displays" are reinforced by parental concern and by improvement in the marital relationship. The child then, in effect, becomes the guardian of the parents' well-being. The triadic model can be extended to single-parent situations with a separated parent, male or female friends, a grandparent, and so on substituting for the "missing" parent (Stanton, Todd et al. 1982).

If we assume this theory does offer explanations for certain cases, the question in the present model is, "how do we know when it applies?" Confirming data are difficult to obtain since the processes presumably operate in a covert fashion and in a way to mask possible observable indicators, such as marital conflict. The applicability of the theory would gain support if there were evidence that a cyclical pattern was occuring—a rise and fall of conflict between the allied partners corresponding to increases and decreases in problem behavior of the child. Further support would be obtained if there were confirming self-report data from family members. For example, in the typescript of one reported case (Haley 1980), the "problem child" threatens suicide if her parents separate, evidence that the child may be acting to "protect" her parents' marriage. Also to be considered would be presence of alternative explanations. A disturbed marital relationship can be as well a consequence as cause of problem behavior in children and, even if a contributing factor, may not operate according to this particular theoretical model. Extrafamilial causes, particularly peer influences, need to be taken into account.

In this connection we note a curious passage from Haley (1980) who gives credence to peer group factors, then seems to deny their importance. "The peer culture has a powerful influence on young people and probably can generate enough social conflict to lead to behavior problems. However, for severe problems and for purposes of therapy, it is best to assume a simple explanation based on family relationships" (p. 166). Haley's subsequent explanation, which involves the kind of covert triadic processes just discussed, is by no means "simple," and why it is preferable to one that is complete is not at all clear. The passage provides an example of faith in a single theory that runs counter to the empirical orientation and multisystems perspective of the present model.

Two against one. When two family members are allied against a third, the coalition takes on an oppositional function. The variations that have received most attention in family therapy have been the *cross-generational* and *scapegoating* coalitions.

In the cross-generational two-against-one, the most common pattern is the alliance of a parent and a child against the other parent (parent-child coalition). The coalition may be acknowledged by the family or its existence may be denied or not even recognized by participants. Covert, cross-generational coalitions, or "perverse triangles" as Haley (1977) calls them, are seen as major contributors to problem behavior in children and to disruption of family systems. In this coalitional arrangement, the parents cannot function in a cooperative way in their child-rearing tasks and, what is more, the authority of each parent is compromised. The authority of the left-out parent may be opposed by the other. The authority of the parent allied with the child is, as Hoffman points out, "dependent on the child's support" (p. 108). In other words, the allied parent may not want to risk disrupting the coalition by discipline that may alienate the child, since presumably the parent has a need for the coalition. The parental need for the tie may also prevent the child from developing appropriate independence.

The most common source of the parent-child coalition is marital conflict. A parent may turn to a child to meet relationship needs lacking in the marriage or turn to a child as an ally in a marital conflict. Or a parent may feel the need to protect a child against harsh or capricious discipline from the other parent, which often is a way of continuing marital struggles around child discipline issues. Marital and family conflict may be exacerbated as resentment over the coalition, and its consequences, mount in the left-out parent. Another outcome is neutralization of conflict, but at the expense of a fulfilling marital relationship and adequate childrearing. In some families, however, the neutralization process may have gone on over a period of years and may be well entrenched. It may be risky, if not impossible, to alter the pattern of relationships, which may turn out to be the best the family can achieve. In still other families, a parent-child coalition may again be the best alternative available—for example, it may be the only way one parent can offer needed protection to a child who is being abused by the other. As is true of any problem-generating structural arrangement, the cross-generational coalition must be seen in relation to what change is possible and what the arrangement may be forestalling.

The second frequently cited variation of two-against-one is a scapegoating coalition. In a commonly encountered and especially damaging form, the allying partners are parents and the person "on the outside" is a child. Expansions of the triad usually take the form of adding to the alliance. Thus, a child may be scapegoated by parents, siblings, and other relatives. Scapegoating coalitions also can assume cross-generational forms, which are frequently seen in single parent families. A parent and a sibling ally against another sibling (chapter 8). In general, the scapegoated member occupies a subordinate role, at least to one of the allying partners, and exhibits characteristics or behavior that provokes the hostility of the scapegoaters. The distinguishing element of the process is an extra margin of hostility or blame heaped on the scapegoated member. This margin may result from conflict between the allying partners, a "detouring, attacking coalition" (Minuchin, Rosman, and Baker 1978). Or it may consist of blaming the scapegoated member for various frustrations which may or may not be related to his behavior.

When the alliance is largely reactive to a third party's behavior, a coalition is no longer scapegoating. It becomes simply oppositional. The payoff for the partners is mutual support against a troublesome third rather than benefits for their own relationship or opportunities to lay off surplus hostility. When the third becomes less troublesome, the coalition ceases to become oppositional. Probably most alliances against a third person contain some element of scapegoating, but it is usually difficult to determine its degree of influence. When scapegoating is a dominant theme, the partners are likely to exaggerate the difficulties in the third's behavior. Moreover, one or both partners may keep the pot boiling, for example, by failing or sabotaging problem-solving tasks. Like many cherished concepts in family therapy, the notion of scapegoating frequently is used loosely and without much empirical justification. Survival rather than scapegoating often is the key to parental alliances against "impossible" children.

Two After One. When two family members compete to form an alliance with a third, the result is a pattern of shifting, unstable coalitions. The process is commonly referred to as "triangulation" (Bowen 1978; Aponte and Van Deusen 1981; Hartman 1981). Common patterns are two parents competing for the allegiance of a child and siblings contesting to form a coalition with a parent. A child in the middle of parental triangulation efforts is exposed to conflicts of loyalty. Discipline between parents may be inconsistent and may be subordinated to parents' maneuvers to win the child's allegiance.

The practitioner often is "the person in the middle," as family members compete to win her allegiance. The family members may not necessarily proceed with the intent of triangulating the practitioner. They may simply present "their side of the story" and attribute to one another responsibility for the problem—behavior that might be seen as natural defensive-blaming responses. The function of such behavior, however, is to pull the practitioner to one side or the other. Successful triangulation occurs when the practitioner finds herself seeing things pretty much the way one family member sees them and attributing responsibility, like the allied family member, to another. The practitioner's use of clinical labels may disguise the process (the wife is struggling to cope with a passive-aggressive, obsessive husband). Triangulation of this kind is particularly difficult to avoid if the practitioner is seeing only one family member and must, of necessity, deal with information filtered through that person.

Empirical basis. Perhaps the most consistent finding concerning intrafamilial alliances is the greater frequency of parent-child coalitions in families labeled as distressed than in normal families (Doane 1978; Minuchin, Rosman, and Baker 1978; Beavers 1980; Stanton, Todd et al. 1982). The distressed families in the relevant research tend to be those in treatment and those who have at least one member with identified problem behavior, usually one of the children. The studies, therefore, provide some support for the notion that cross-generational coalitions are associated with problems in offspring. In a more specific test of this relationship Teyber (1984) found that college students with academic problems were more likely to report that the primary alliances in their families were "mother-child" than a matched group of academically successful students who were more likely to report the parental alliance as primary.

However, one could scarcely say that there is a convincing empirical basis for the widely held hypothesis that cross-generational coalitions are major sources of problems in children. Studies bearing specifically on this question have been few, measurements of coalitional behavior (e.g., eye contact, who talks to whom in structured tasks) tend to be indirect, and study designs usually do not control for alternative explanations. As is often the case in family life research, causal direction is difficult to determine. Suppose we do find a greater tendency for cross-generational coalitions in families with disturbed children than in families with normal children. In some cases the coalition may be contributory. In other cases, the parents may be reacting to the problem behavior: one parent may respond to the problem by imposing severe disciplinary measures on the child; the other parent may come to the child's support. Finally, there has been little systematic study of the mechanisms through which cross-generational coalitions affect or are affected by other parts of the family system, although one ingenious experiment

(Minuchin, Rosman, and Baker 1978) suggests how coalitional patterns may operate in an intervention situation.

Also, a fair amount of research evidence can be brought to bear on scapegoating coalitions, in which parents are allied against a child. In her review of relevant research, Rabin (1981) systematically builds an empirical case for this type of coalition. For example, parents that have labeled a child as a problem are more likely to experience marital discord than other families; parents with a child so labeled tend to exaggerate the severity of his behavior. As Rabin acknowledges, however, no study has yet established connections between these and other factors that make up the network of hypotheses in scapegoat theory. That is, as yet, we do not have adequate research evidence to show that maritally conflicted parents use a child to avoid or displace their conflicts, or to examine what processes might be operative in light of the research reviewed. Rabin reported that wives may tend to generalize hostility toward husbands to male children, who in turn invite such hostility by behaving, as a result of modeling effects, in an aggressive manner, like their fathers. Although children with behavior problems are more likely to be boys, and there is evidence that marital distress is more highly correlated with problems in boys than girls (Emery and O'Leary 1982), the formulation does not account for scapegoating pheonomena in girls, nor does it provide a more general explanation of the phenomenon.

One recent study on family coalitions will be examined in more detail because its methodology is of particular interest, and its findings bear on both parent-child and scapegoating coalitions; it also raises an important and rather typical issue. In this study, Bell and Bell (1982) compared two groups of approximately fifty families. The families were similar in demographic characteristics but differed in respect to the psychological adjustment of an adolescent daughter, as measured by a battery of standardized tests. "Better adjusted" (higher scoring) adolescents were found less likely to be involved in cross-generational and scapegoating coalitions than adolescents whose adjustment was poorer. The measures of coalitions were ingenious. All family members completed the

Moos (1974) Family Environment Scale, on which they agreed or disagreed that various statements about family life applied to their own families (We come and go as we want in our family). Coalitional scores were obtained through measures of agreement among the adolescents and their parents: the greater the adolescent's perceptions departed from the level of her parents' agreement, the greater the evidence for her being isolated or scapegoated; the closer her perceptions were to those of one parent in relation to her distance from the other parent, the greater the evidence for a cross-generational coalition. The measures provide quantitative indicators of coalitions based on standardized tests and were able to differentiate between levels of adjustment in the adolescents, all points in their favor. The measures of coalition, while indirect, have potential for use by practitioners in individual case assessments. On a substantive level, the findings provide additional support for the connection between coalitional patterns and problems in offspring.

An issue the study raises concerns the connection between data and theory. This study, like most that relate to family coalitions, deals with partial indexes of coalitions—in this instance, dissimilarity scores. Is an adolescent who diverges from her parents' impressions of family life being scapegoated? Possibly so, but the data obviously lend themselves to other interpretations. An adolescent who sees the family differently than her parents do, may be distressed but not necessarily scapegoated.

Flexibility

All aspects of rules considered thus far can be examined in relation to another dimension, their variability. At a gross level, some families can be characterized as relatively rigid—rules have a fixed quality showing little variation in response to changing or special conditions. At the other extreme, some families appear chaotic, with rules in a constant state of flux. This aspect has been referred to in different ways: as flexibility (Doane 1978), adaptability (Olson, Russell, and Sprenkle 1979; Olson, McCullin, and Associates 1983), and behavior-control (Epstein and Bishop 1981).

Flexibility can apply either to prescriptive rules (desired norms) or descriptive rules (actual patterns of interaction and behavior). Rigidity in prescriptive rules may not be matched at the behavioral level. Mr. and Mrs. Harris have a rule that their son Timmy should be in bed by 10 p.m., but Timmy devotes his evenings to finding ways to circumvent it and succeeds more often than not. The prescriptive rule remains constant but the descriptive rule turns out to be chaotic.

The question of how tight or loose these rules should be has long been of concern to family therapists. As with involvement, the usual position is that some mid-range level is optimal for most purposes. Excessive rigidity can pose constraints on the development of individual members and make it difficult for the family to change when change is needed. Excessive flexibility leads to a disorganization of family life in which the development of children and functioning of adults may be impaired.

The capacity of a family to alter its rules in light of changing circumstances—its adaptability, as Olson and his co-workers have put it—is particularly important in social work. Frequently, problems of primary concern arise from a change in the family's situation. A child moves into adolescence or out of the home, a family member becomes disabled, the breadwinner becomes unemployed, a family relocates, and so on. Old patterns of interaction may no longer suffice, even though they may persist. A useful prespective in such situations is to examine the problem in relation to the operation of old rules that have not been altered to meet the new conditions. Thus in one rural, impoverished family there was the implicit prescriptive rule that "everyone pulls his weight no matter what." The oldest daughter, who had developed arthritis, was struggling against expectations, subtly conveyed, that she do her share of the chores despite her disability. The practitioner often needs to help family members recognize the lack of fit between the accustomed rules and the demands of the moment, and to help them develop new modes of response.

In some families, areas of interaction seem to be continually in an unsettled state. There is little order or predictability. Rules may be devised at the spur of the moment and soon abandoned.

"They break 'em as fast as we make 'em," was the way one harassed father described his children's response to parental rules. The family may require assistance not only in constructing an adequate rule structure but in developing their rule-making processes.

Certain levels of flexibility may be better suited for some situations than others. For example, child care workers seeking to place disturbed, acting-out adolescents in foster care or adoptive homes are likely to give a close look at this dimension. A family may function well but may have fairly rigid rules that they expect a child to fit into. A child to be placed may do better in more flexible families with greater tolerance for "crazy" behavior but still able to enforce outside limits (Kagan and Reid 1984).

In addition to characterizing family units or patterns as having a certain level of flexibility, one can examine how fluctuations are managed. Interaction patterns in families tend to vary within a permissible range. When that range is exceeded, steps may be taken to restore the pattern to a range considered to be acceptable, as was noted earlier in respect to coercive symmetry. These restorative operations (homeostatic mechanisms) are most readily discerned when there is some knowledge of how the basic pattern operates and what deviations have occurred. For example, in the interactions between a given husband and wife, a certain level of hostility is tolerated. They can express irritation with one another's behavior without disrupting their normal, good-humored give-and-take. However, when hostile exchanges exceed certain limits, for instance, are too frequent, or touch on "sore points," the normal pattern of interaction is disrupted. Both feel angry and they stop talking. After a period, they may draw on one of several rebalancing devices that might include apologies, humor, undertaking an activity together, or "talking out" whatever problem has occurred. It is important to identify such devices since they reveal how problems of deviation within the system are resolved or could be.

In agreement with Dell (1982), I do not assume that a system is necessarily driven by some "homeostatic force" to maintain stability or "resist change." Systems are better viewed as constantly in the process of evolving and adapting, a process that brings about what Dell calls "coherence" among its parts. While it may be useful to examine rebalancing efforts in relation to specific patterns, it may be fruitless to try to divine whatever underlying homeostatic principles may be at work.

Empirical Basis. Like other dimensions of family interaction, flexibility has proved difficult to operationalize and study. Findings are largely in terms of its associations with other characteristics, problems, and so on.

Two quite different ways of operationalizing flexibility have emerged. One has to do with relatively objective indicators based on laboratory observations of free interaction or task performance. Indicators have included evidence of spontaneity in interaction (interruptions, laughter, simultaneous speech, and so on) and speaking order. The greater the spontaneity of speech and the randomness of sequences of who speaks after whom, the more flexible the interaction. The other method of measurement has relied on self-reports of family members pertaining to patterns of interaction at home. The latter measures tend to be more conceptually complex and may include other dimensions, such as control, discipline, and negotiation, as in the notion of "adaptability" developed by Olson, Sprenkle, and Russell (1979). It is, of course, difficult to be sure what findings from such diverse measures add up to.

Laboratory studies generally have suggested that nonclinic families show more flexibility than comparable groups of clinic families (Doane 1978; Olson, Russell and Sprenkle, 1980). There also is support for the hypothesis that moderate levels of flexibility in discipline (avoiding extremes of authoritarianism and permissiveness) are related to more desirable functioning in children (Rollins and Thomas 1975). Russell (1979) found that families who scored at a mid-level of flexibility in executing a laboratory task had less difficulty with an adolescent member than families with scores at either extreme.

As a whole, the existing research supports the notion that moderate flexibility in patterns of interaction provides families with a functional capacity to adjust to changing circumstances.

We need to learn much more than we know about components and indicators of flexibility, the lines that define optimal levels in given situations, and mechanisms that are used to maintain patterns within desired ranges of variation.

THE FAMILY AND EXTERNAL SYSTEMS

The concepts considered in relation to the family system can be extended to other social systems thay may be relevant in a case, as well as to situational systems (some combination of family members and other actors) that often constitute the primary unit of attention. Such applications help unify thinking in using a multisystems perspective, even though they may need to be elaborated and supplemented in different ways according to the system under consideration.

Thus, in helping families relate to social agencies, schools, hospitals, and the like, it is important to understand the processes of communication and rule structures that one may find in such organizations. Are family members getting conflicting messages from different staff members? For example, is one child care worker telling a child one thing about what will happen if he continues to get in trouble in the residential institution, and is the social worker telling the family something different? Is it an unspoken (descriptive) rule in a school system that black teenage boys will be punished more severely for infractions than other youth? Who makes the decision in a child protective agency whether or not to take a case to court or to have a child removed from the home? Is an adolescent's intense involvement with a drug-oriented peer group overriding her parents' efforts to control her behavior? Is there a coalition on the part of a family's neighbors to make things difficult for the family by continually calling the police or social agencies regarding their behavior? Would intervention with the neighbors run the risk of strengthening the coalition? How flexible are rules governing eligibility for a family to receive services from an agency, and who is in a position to modify the rules?

Such questions show how concepts for understanding family interaction can be generally applied in a multisystems perspective. The extension of the concepts beyond the family may be particularly useful in analysis of situational systems, as is illustrated in a case reported by Tavantzis et al. (in press). Two teenage children repeatedly ran away from home, complaining that they were being beaten by their stepfather. Aunts and uncles, teachers, the police, and a child protective worker became involved in one way or another in sheltering or supporting the children. The parents were virtually ignored. In this situational system, a community coalition was giving a message to the family that the parents were incompetent and that the children needed protection. Intervention by still another agency focused initially on getting the helpers to work through the parents rather than against them, which proved to be a critical factor in an eventually successful outcome.

5. *Contextual Analysis*

This chapter and the two following present the three major types of interventions used to help families move from problem definition to problem resolution: contextual analysis, session tasks, and home or environmental tasks. These interventions dominate the middle phase of treatment, which begins after problems have been formulated and initial tasks attempted. In most cases the three types are used in some combination, although one type may receive primary focus and all types are not necessarily used on all cases.

The order with which they are used also may vary, as discussed in chapter 2. A logical sequence for mid-phase interviews might be as follows: Following a review of problems and tasks, the practitioner might consider contextual factors, perhaps clarifying obstacles preventing progress. She then might make use of session tasks addressed to the obstacles; from this work would emerge ideas for home tasks which then would be planned. The next encounter with the family would start with a review of the home tasks. Although this logical staging may not be followed in practice, it gives a sense of how the pieces fit together and provides a framework for organizing our material on intervention.

Following this framework, we shall begin with contextual analysis. In general, the purposes of the analysis are to clarify obstacles and resources bearing upon problem-solving action and, if indicated, to suggest how the obstacles may be resolved or resources put to work. Contextual analysis is a "talking" method aimed at facilitating problem-solving action. The format is open discussion between practitioners and family members in which many of the techniques of conventional family therapy are used. The major difference is that the discussion is focused on *obstacles* or *resources* relating to the solution of *particular problems*. The first section of the chapter will be concerned with how shared *understanding* of obstacles and resources may be achieved. How the understanding can be used as a basis for change then will be considered. The chapter will conclude with a look at contextual analysis of intrapsychic factors, which will serve to give individual systems some of the attention they need in our multisystems framework.

DEVELOPING SHARED UNDERSTANDING

The primacy the model gives to action as a means of effecting change does not preclude use of methods to help family members enhance their understanding of their own functioning, their interactions with others, or their larger environments. Attempts to enable the family to achieve this understanding have special characteristics and functions in the model, however. First they are concentrated, as noted, on helping members gain insight into factors preventing or facilitating resolution of target problems. No attempt is made to develop understanding in areas not directly related to the problem, though the occurrence of such understanding may be welcomed as a by-product. Second, the insight achieved is intended to stimulate and guide action plans. Steps are immediately taken to convert insight into tasks. It is assumed that without such follow-through, the awareness will have only a transitory effect in most instances. Now and then, insight alone might produce significant changes, but this happy event is much more the exception than the rule. It is nothing to be counted on. Third, in helping family members develop awareness of obstacles or resources, the practitioner tries to encourage and structure the family members' own efforts at understanding. In this aspect of the model, as in others, she attempts to engage family members in a collaborative attempt to achieve understanding. Fourth, a broad conception of insight is used, pertaining not only to patterns of individual and family functioning not previously perceived but also to understanding the external environment—for example, awareness of the attitude and expectations of personnel in an organization to which the family is relating. Fifth, insight-oriented methods are used in variable degrees, depending on obstacles or resources encountered and the family's capacity to profit from these methods. Their use generally is not pursued when family members react resistively.

Finally, the practitioner's efforts to help family members develop understanding may be used indirectly, as is true of any intervention in the model, to affect patterns of relating among family members, if these patterns themselves constitute obstacles. In her choice of family members or events to focus on, in making one kind of interpretation rather than another, the practitioner's interventions may affect family structure. For example, an interpretation that justifies the behavior of a family member may serve to increase the power of that member vis-à-vis others. While insight-oriented methods are not routinely used with structural change objectives in mind, their use inevitably has some bearing on structural factors, a fact that always needs to be taken into account. In sum, to help people understand what is preventing them from taking problem-solving action or what can facilitate it is a very logical part of an action-oriented approach.

Techniques of Practitioner Communication

In contextual analysis the practitioner relies largely on use of two communication techniques, *exploration* and *explanation*. Communication techniques are ways of classifying practitioner responses in a session according to their apparent function (Reid 1978). Exploration consists of questions, requests for information, rephrasing comments, "echoes," encouragement to talk, and other means of facilitating communication by family members. While exploration is most commonly used to obtain factual data on the nature and occurrence of target problems, it also serves as the springboard for helping clients achieve understanding.

Exploration serves this function when the practitioner concentrates on actual or potential obstacles or resources through inquiry that becomes increasingly focused. As this "Socratic dialogue" takes on greater focus, family members may reveal things about themselves and their interactions that otherwise would not have occurred to them, and may be stimulated to think in new ways about these matters. Exploration with clients in family interviews takes on a dimension not found in one-to-one treatment; family members reveal themselves not only to the practitioner but to one another. Some of these revelations may lay the groundwork for new understanding.

Helen and Joe were working on their disagreements about disciplining their seven-year-old son, Tony. Obstacles appeared to be Helen's resentment over Joe's "lack of support" and Joe's belief that he must protect Tony from his wife's verbal onslaughts.

HELEN: Everytime I correct Tony, I get it from him (*indicating Joe*).

PRACTITIONER (*to Helen*): Can you give me a recent example?

HELEN: Yes, the other day while we were eating, I told Tony to stop making faces at his sister—getting her going—and Joe shouted at me to "calm down."

JOE: There was no need for her to scream at the top of her lungs.

PRACTITIONER (*to Joe*): It would have been O.K. with you if she had corrected him without screaming?

JOE: Yeah, he was getting out of line but she could have said, uh, could have made a joke out of it.

PRACTITIONER (*to Joe*): Had you thought of saying anything to him?

HELEN (*before Joe can answer*): You see he noticed what Tony was doing but waited for me—and he wonders why I screamed.

The excerpt illustrates use of focused exploration guided by a hypothesis. When the issue is raised, the practitioner asks for an example, a good way to bring the issue down to a concrete level where interactions can be seen more clearly. From previous discussion, the practitioner had formed the hypothesis that Helen's "overreaction" to Tony's misbehavior was due in part to her resentment at Joe for not taking a more active role in disciplining Tony. By getting Joe to look at what he might have done, the point is brought to the surface. A beginning is made at helping Joe see that his wife's behavior is not simply an excessive outburst at Tony but is a reaction as well to his giving her the responsibility for discipline. The structural implications of this beginning piece of insight development also can be identified. By calling Joe's attention to his parenting responsibility, the practitioner challenges, albeit slightly, the coalition between Joe and Tony and lays the basis for collaboration between the parents.

In use of explanation, the practitioner presents a hypothesis or data to the family about some aspect of the functioning or interactions of family members or about the family's situation. The technique is illustrated by the next practitioner response from the excerpt given above.

PRACTITIONER (*to Helen*): It seems as if you were reacting out of frustration with both Joe and Tony. (*to Joe*) And you only saw her anger at Tony.

As the example shows, the intent of explanation is to add to the client's awareness by providing new information. Usually what is formulated, at least in the present model, is fairly close to the client's awareness but still augments it. Explanation may achieve this purpose through articulating the client's partially perceived or once perceived thoughts and feelings, through presenting a new way of looking at the familiar, or by pointing out the obvious that has been overlooked. Its content has a wide range, from clarifying psychodynamics to conveying facts about the environment. In most uses it is roughly equivalent to interpretation, labeling (Kiesler et al. 1981), and person-situation reflection (Hollis and Woods 1981).

Although explanation usually takes the form of declarative sentences, it may be cast as a leading question. "Aren't you saying that you really felt angry?" In fact, there is a continuum between exploration and explanation. As questions become more focused and their underlying hypotheses become more apparent, they cross the line into explanatory formulations put as questions.

Although focused exploration can be effective by itself as a means of stimulating new understanding, particularly with insightful clients, it usually serves as a precursor to some form of explanation. Through explanation, the practitioner can present her ideas explicitly and with necessary elaboration. It can be seen, therefore, as the most important technique for developing the client's understanding. In subsequent sections, different facets of this technique will be examined.

Communicated Units of Attention

In chapter 3, the notion of units of attention has been used in relation to the practitioner's assessment of problems and contexts. The same idea can help describe the form and content of explanations.

The communicated unit of attention is identified by determining to whom the practitioner's response refers. The unit referred to, and the one addressed are often, but not always, the same. The references for different units of attention are presented and illustrated below in table 5.1:

Table 5.1. Units of Attention in Explanation

Unit	*Reference*	*Illustration*
Individual	Functioning of individual family members with no reference to others.	You look sad. He seems upset.
Interactive	Relation of two or more individuals in the family.	When you get angry, she withdraws. Do you think you may be too protective of him?
Collective	Functioning of two or more family members as a unit.	The two of you seem to be denying any problem. Those two are hard to figure out.
Interactive-Collective	The relation between a unit (as above) and other in the family.	I wonder if you and dad aren't ganging up on Phil.
Environment	Aspects of external environment.	Harold's teacher is unusually strict. It's hard to get into the housing project.

| Environment and Family | Relation between environment, including practitioner, and family members. | You and the hospital staff don't see eye to eye on this. |
| | | When Mike swears under his breath, the teacher becomes upset.
All of you seem angry at me today. |

The scheme above shows the range of explanations according to units of attention. Certain categories and distinctions are worth commenting on. Explanations in which the unit of attention is limited to the individual are not heavily used in conjoint family work, though they are by no means rare. In addition, many interactive explanations highlight one family member over others. Consider the following excerpt from a family therapy interview.

THERAPIST: You know it's interesting that Annabelle, in being so helpful to the family—one of the ways she does it is to centralize everything on to her. (Haley 1981:187).

This example of explanation occurred in a session involving the father, mother, and daughter (Annabelle). The unit of attention is both Annabelle and the family, hence would be "interactive-collective" in the scheme above. Still, the focus is on the daughter with the family in the background. The daughter is depicted as the moving force.

Contrast that with the following example:

THERAPIST (*to husband and wife*): When you (*pointing to wife*) complain (*now pointing to husband*) you withdraw, causing you (*now looking back to wife*) to have even more to complain about.

In this example, an interactive cycle is described in which the focus is spread between the partners. Still, the way the response is put, stress is on the wife whose behavior is considered first. "Punctuation effects" characterize most interactive explanations in family treatment; in fact they are almost unavoidable, given the structure of language.

All of this suggests that the units of attention advance from individual to interactive by degrees. In most explanations a given individual will occupy the spotlight, usually as the "initiator" of some interactive process. If a truly interactive focus is to emerge over the span of an interview, then the practitioner needs to switch the spotlight in explanations or other communications from one family member to another—in other words, to distribute the punctuation effects. If not, then the practitioner needs to realize that focusing more on one family member than another may have implications for how family members view the practitioner and themselves. A family member who has been seen more than others as the initiator may feel unfairly singled out, or that the practitioner is siding with other family members.

Here, again, one notes how interventions may convey messages about relationships. This theme can also be seen in explanations using a collective unit of attention. Family members included in the collectivity are being "put together" by the practitioner, thereby emphasizing their commonality or the boundary separating them from the rest of the family. For example, references to the parents as a unit ("you two," "the two of you," and so on), while a child is referred to in individual terms, conveys recognition of the parental boundary and to some degree strengthens it.

Content. In general, the content of an explanation can refer to almost any aspect of problems or context considered in preceding chapters. A systems perspective is useful in mapping this vast domain. With this perspective in mind it is possible to divide explanations into three classes. Explanations may: (1) *characterize* parts of the system or systems processes, (2) deal with *discrepancies* between parts of the system or between systems, or (3) make *causal formulations* of systems processes.

In simply characterizing different parts of the system, the practitioner brings into focus events that may be hidden or not previously considered, or she may explicate the latent meanings of events under discussion. The many possible forms such explanations can take become apparent if we make use of a multi-systems perspective and different units of attention. One may comment on the shared feelings of a marital system (Both of you look upset) or on perceptions or expectations of an individual (You see him as totally unreliable./You expect her to take care of the kids). Behaviors may be identified and defined (You seem to have a talent as a peacemaker). Instead of a "you focus," the explanation may concern others ("he/she focus") or some aspect of the environment (She appears to be angry./The hospital has no policy on this point). The main purpose of explanation at this level is to put things on the table. Although comments may concern characteristics of interactions as well as of individuals or units, formulations stop short of identifying discrepancies or making causal statements.

Explanations in the second category focus on discrepancies, inconsistencies or "incongruities," and the like between different parts of a system (or between different systems). Explanations may concern discrepancies within the functioning of an individual. For example, an incongruity may exist between an individual's self-perception and action (You say you're a cold mother but you just showed a lot of warmth just now toward Patty) or between linguistic and paralinguistic aspects of communication (Your voice sounds calm but you seem tense). Explanations of discrepancies between individuals may consist of any combination of these aspects. A common example is an interpretation of incongruity or conflict between the expectations of family members (Let's see, dad thinks that Tom should help out with the milk route while mom expects him to study). The same considerations can be applied to collectivities (The two of you are trying hard to make it sound as if things are O.K.—Are they?).

Pointing out discrepancies stimulates cognitive problem solving on the client's part and lays the basis for a resolution of the discrepancy that will lead to positive change. This intervention strategy incorporates techniques of cognitive restructuring (Beck 1976; Reid 1978). Thus, a husband and wife may be first made aware that their perceptions of one another do not match the reality of each other's behavior. They then may be helped to correct their distorted perceptions. The process may involve a sequence of explanations interwoven with focused inquiry.

Explanations concerning system dynamics may be addressed to psychodynamics (the internal functioning of the individual psychological system), to interactions between family members, or to the family's interaction with its environment. Because emphasis is on how one part of the system affects another, the explanations deal in some form of causation, although they may be expressed implicitly, for example, in terms of what precedes or follows what. Subtypes of greatest importance in work with families concern interactions among family members.

In one of these subtypes, stress is placed on the causes, reasons, motives and so on, for an individual's (or collective's) action in relation to another. Barton and Alexander's (1981) discussion of this kind of intervention is illuminating.

"A mother who reports, 'I'm just always mad at him,' leaves few options for change. The therapist can generate those options with the more complete view of the situation, 'When he doesn't respond to your questions, you get angry'" (p. 422). As the authors point out, the message tells the mother that "her anger is her reaction to a relatively specific circumstance which she has the option to change or avoid," and tells her son that "he has some influence on mother via a specific behavior of not answering" (p. 422). In addition to specifying the mother's response, the interpretation converts it to an interactional event and helps *both* mother and son understand their actions in relation to one another. In the example above, the causal sequence is implicit, though the punctuation of the intervention makes it clear that the mother is reacting to her son's not answering.

In another variation the purposes or functions of the action is made explicit. "Is your putting in all this extra time at work a way of seeing less of your wife?" Such "labeling of functionality," as Keisler et al. (1981) call it, stresses the rationale of a family member's actions. In effect the practitioner says: "You are doing this to achieve a certain result." By making clear the functions of the action, the practitioner hopes it can be examined critically. In the usual case the actions explained are seen as a reflection of some system malfunction: while they may achieve certain immediate purposes, they are in the long run misplaced and counterproductive.

Such latent functions of behavior assume considerable importance in a number of schools of family therapy. For example, in structural theory, anorexia may be viewed as a child's attempt, through not eating, to exert control over family interaction (Minuchin, Rosman, and Baker 1978). In strategic therapy, disturbed behavior of offspring is seen as stabilizing the family; its function is primarily protective (Haley 1980; Madanes 1981). In keeping with its designation, functional family therapy (Barton and Alexander 1981) stresses the functional significance of all family behavior. In therapies that use such models, these functional formulations are usually made explicit through the equivalent of explanations, and also guide other therapeutic strategies.

As noted above, the present model takes a more cautious position about explanations of this sort, given its empirical orientation and its openness to alternative theories. The functions served by different problems or behaviors are often difficult to clarify since they may involve hidden or unconscious motivations. When using the task-centered model, practitioners do not necessarily assume, for example, that disturbed behavior in a child is best understood as serving some protective or other function for the family system. Such behavior often can be more effectively explained in relation to other systems, or an explanation may not be necessary in order to change it. The practitioner then looks for evidence from the client's verbalizations or from repetitive patterns of interaction. If some evidence is present, the practitioner may make a tentative explanation as a way of testing it against the family's own perceptions and as a means of engaging the family in further examination of it.

In one case, for example, a single working mother and her daughter, Lori, age ten, were being seen concerning problems in their interaction. One day, Lori forged, in a very obvious way, a "note" from her mother asking that she be excused from school for the day. When she presented the note to her teacher, the forgery was immediately detected and the mother was called.

The mother was furious at Lori, whose trick note she saw as just another piece of troublesome behavior. The practitioner saw and explained it differently. Lori had previously complained that she did not see enough of her mother; the obviously forged note was perhaps meant to dramatize this message. The combination of Lori's complaints and the transparency of the forgery gave the practitioner evidence for the interpretation. While the correctness of the explanation can be argued, and should be, the example illustrates the kind and amount of evidence used in making inferences about latent functions of behavior (see also chapters 2 and 3).

Thus far, an event under consideration has been explained in terms of its causes, reasons, functions, and the like. Explanation also may focus on the *consequences* of an event for some other part of the systems. (Your downplaying his job seems to make him defensive.) This kind of punctuation puts responsibility on the actor for causing something to happen and suggests a direction for change if the consequences are negative. In using this form of explanation, practitioners should be aware that it may be seen as implying criticism of the actor (see section following).

Finally, an explanation may be concerned with an interactive spiral, in which actions are both causes and consequences. "When you don't call, she gets upset and lets you have it when you get home, and a quarrel results." Although some punctuation effects are inevitable, as noted, these formulations present a fuller picture of systems operations than more partial statements that stress either cause or consequence.

The Critical-Positive Dimension. Some explanations add up to overt or implicit criticism of behavior. Others put behavior in a decidedly positive light. In between are those that either are neutral or contain both critical and positive elements. As the previous discussion has suggested, many explanations tend to be concerned with problem aspects of interaction and hence may be interpreted (not unreasonably) by family members as criticisms of their behavior. Most clients expect some criticism and can accept it if it appears related to therapeutic goals, has a basis in fact, and is equitably distributed. But there is consider-

able variation on this score. Some family members may not accept practitioner formulations that attribute responsibility for
the problem to them, particularly if the person in the spotlight
is sensitive to being "exposed" in front of other family members.
For these reasons, interpretations that convey criticism are used
cautiously by family therapists.

In regard to this dimension, the general principle of trying to
develop understanding through a collaborative process applies
with full force: the practitioner attempts to build on and extend
the client's own awareness of dysfunctional behavior and avoids
sudden confrontative explanations. Recognizing the criticism
that may be inherent in an explanation, she is careful not to
concentrate explanations on one family member, even if that
person appears to be receptive.

Because of the risk of mobilizing resistance by appearing critical, many therapists, particularly those from the strategic
school, make considerable use of "positive interpretation" (positive explanation) (Stanton 1981b). In this technique, the client's
motives or behavior are put clearly in a positive context. For
example, what might be regarded as parental interference in the
lives of their children may be interpreted as expressions of parental concern, or an adolescent's acting out may be explained
as his attempt to keep the family together.

By stressing constructive aspects, positive explanations give
family members a legitimate rationale for their actions, thus
enhancing self-esteem. At the same time, the technique provides
family members with the sense of "being understood," hence,
may make them more tolerant of other interventions, including
less positive explanations. For example, a practitioner who interprets a mother's punitive behavior toward her daughter as an
outgrowth of her desire to have her child "learn how to act properly" might help the mother to see that sometimes her treatment
of her daughter does not always obtain the best result. She then
may be willing to modify her behavior in a less punitive direction so that she can help her daughter learn with less resentment.

In the task-centered approach, positive explanation is used
primarily as a means of maintaining or reaching a collaborative

relationship with family members. It is a way of connecting with the strengths of the family and identifying its resources.

Ned, age fifteen, and his parents were being seen for a combination of problems involving Ned's school behavior and his relationships at home. The school problems consisted of Ned's aggressive behavior with teachers, cursing, threatening, making faces, and so on. As a result, he was in continual difficulty, with frequent suspensions. Tasks designed to help Ned develop better ways of expressing his aggression were developed and worked on. Ned did begin to learn to be less overtly provocative in his interactions with teachers, but was caught in a class one day assiduously and skillfully embroidering the margins of a school text with pictures of his teachers engaging in various kinds of sexual activities. This incident led to another suspension and another family crisis. The episode could have been seen as another outcropping of underlying and unresolved hostilities at his teachers, his parents, or authority figures, but this formulation and others that were thought of seemed to provide little basis for effective intervention with this highly defensive adolescent. Pointing out possible consequences for his behavior had already been used to the hilt by principals and parents. Rather, a positive explanation was decided upon. The practitioner acknowledged progress Ned had made in learning how to express his anger toward his teachers. His "sexual" drawings were another step in this learning process, but in trying new ways it was easy to make mistakes at the beginning. From this interpretation a task evolved; Ned was to draw (at home) caricatures of these teachers (with their clothes on).

Explanation with positive connotations can provide an effective means of accrediting and making use of the client's resources. But, as with any kind of explanation, it is used most effectively to further change goals. Sometimes positive interpretations are employed without any follow-through in mind, or, one suspects, without even much thought. Because they tend to support the current modes of adaptation, they do not in themselves provide much stimulus or direction for change. Excessive use—overkilling with kindness—might actually reinforce problem behavior, and in the process weaken the practitioner's credibility. The family is not in treatment because things are going well, and may become skeptical of a practitioner who sounds too much like Pollyanna.

In Vivo or Referent. Some explanations may refer to *in vivo* events, that is, those occurring in the session (I have noticed that you have been speaking a lot for your husband). Others may relate to "referent" events, occurring outside the session (It sounds as if the two of you quarrel more about money than anything else). Explanations of in vivo events are used in the task-centered approach, as in most, to help family members become aware of their behavior and interactions virtually as they are occurring. Because the explanations relate to immediate realities, they have a kind of potency and precision that is difficult to equal in interpretations of events outside the session. At the same time, they are based on limited and possibly atypical samples of behavior. For this reason, the explanations are perhaps most valid when they are restricted to commenting on what is transpiring in the here-and-now rather than put in form of general statements about behavior or interaction. For example, a couple may be describing a conflict in a rather detached, abstract manner. To say, "It seems hard for the two of you to talk about feelings," subtly implies a generality that may not be correct. It would be preferable to say, "It seems hard for the two of you to bring feelings into your discussion." Whether or not the events occur more generally can be explored by a follow-up inquiry, "Is it something that happens often when you discuss things."

In many family therapy approaches, explanations of in vivo events are based on interaction as it occurs in free-flowing conversation among family members and practitioners. In the task-centered model, they also are used to provide feedback on client performance in session tasks. In this context an explanation may be very response-specific—for example, "I thought I heard a little sarcasm in that compliment"—and may be combined with encouragement, direction, modeling, and other techniques in what is generally referred to as "coaching" (see chapter 6).

Explanations of referent events can be based on wide-ranging data reported by family members. The accuracy and precision of the information are limitations, however. Family members may give differing accounts of pivotal occurrences or, on occasion, may present similar but distorted pictures of their interactions. Moreover, there is always the challenge of pinning down critical details when dealing with masses of recalled information. Complex patterns of interaction derived from reports of family members always remain foggy, even if everyone is trying to be truthful and accurate. Often a clarifying function is served by session tasks or "enactments" (Minuchin and Fishman 1981) in which family members are put in positions to reproduce referent events in the session. In general, practitioners attempt to obtain corroborative and amplifying data about reported patterns from in vivo interactions among family members.

UNDERSTANDING AND CHANGE

Although a client's understanding of obstacles or resources may lead to change without further intervention on the practitioner's part, it is assumed that some follow-through usually is needed. Completing session and home tasks provides a basic way of putting the insight to work and of demonstrating that it did make a difference. Tasks then can pick up where the analysis ends.

Prior to using tasks, the practitioner may try to advance the change process by combining insight-oriented methods with more action-oriented techniques, such as *encouragement* and *direction*. When used in this way, such techniques can be considered to be an extension of contextual analysis.

Encouragement expresses verbal or nonverbal approval of what clients have done or intend to do. It is similar in conception to "reinforcement" as that term is used to describe practitioner intervention in behavioral therapy ("That sounds like a good move. I like that.").

In direction, the practitioner takes an advising role. Direction may take the form of giving family members explicit or implicit suggestions for actions, or it may take the form of stating a position that differs from the family members (a concurring position is a form of encouragement). The position should have implications for how the family member should think, feel, or act ("Perhaps the two of you can visit her together," "I don't think that would solve anything").

In both encouragement and direction, the practitioner's authority and relationship with family members are used to stimulate change. The main difference between them is that in encouragement the practitioner follows the client's lead, and in direction the practitioner leads the client. In contextual analysis they usually are used to activate understanding that has been attained through focused exploration and through explanation.

The process is illustrated by an excerpt from an interview with a couple where the husband, Ed, recently lost function of both legs as a result of a spinal cord injury. The target problem under discussion was his depression. A cause of the depression (as well as an obstacle to overcoming it) was his feelings of loss and inadequacy associated with his disability.

PRACTITIONER: (*summarizing*): As you said, you feel depressed because you've had to give up a lot of things that were important to you—like physical activity. That's natural but, you know, you are doing other things—like spending more time with Rob [*his son*].

JOAN (*the wife*): And you've been lifting weights.

PRACTITIONER: Hey, I didn't know about that. That's great.

ED: Yeah, I've got to take care of what's left.

PRACTITIONER: That's important. It will take time but it's important to, as you said, to build on what you have—to look for new outlets—new things you can do. (*To both*) What else has he been doing?

The clarification of Ed's feeling of loss is followed by focus on development of new activities. The practitioner's encouragement is combined with direction about searching for new outlets, which she pursues with focused exploration. We also note Joan's role as a resource. As might be expected, activity tasks were developed for Ed to do at home. The encouragement and direction at this point helped to prepare the way for the tasks by reorienting the interview toward new activities. These interventions also provided a test of Ed's readiness for tasks of this type. Had he responded negatively, the practitioner might not have pushed toward tasks at this point. Finally, the combinations of explanation, direction, and encouragement might be expected to have an effect on the obstacle even if home tasks were used for other purposes.

To achieve effective concentration of effort, however, one attempts to relate contextual analysis to work on tasks. This principle applies especially when the analysis ends with encouraging or suggesting some behavior. One does not want to give the family too many messages that may compete with tasks. When encouragement and direction are used during the interview to promote certain actions, tasks should be extensions of these interventions. It is good to recall here that encouraging or suggesting some action during the course of a session is quite different from putting that action in the form of a task. Unlike a task, these interventions do not require an agreement from the client that the action will be attempted.

WANTS, FEELINGS, AND BELIEFS

In the final section we shall examine in more detail contextual analysis of certain psychological factors as they play themselves out in family situations. These factors merit special attention because they influence the development of obstacles and resources at interactional and behavioral levels.

In the task-centered framework, these factors are viewed as consisting primarily of wants, feelings, and beliefs (cognitions) (Reid 1978). Wants refer to felt needs and self-perceived motives. Unsatisfied wants give rise to problems as the person perceives them. Emotions or feelings consist of the usual range of affects— love, anger, depression, anxiety, and so on. Beliefs are either evaluative or knowledge-oriented in nature. The former generate values and expectations; the latter, perceptions. Although the components mutually affect one another, the belief system or cognitive realm is paramount. How we perceive and evaluate ourselves and the world determines largely what we want and how we feel (Beck 1976; Reid 1978). Wants, feelings, and beliefs in concert control our actions and hence our contribution to interactional phenomena. Actions and interactions in turn provide feedback that affect what we want, feel, and believe. Thus, actions that produce what we want strengthen our belief in their efficacy and are likely to be repeated, lending positive reinforcement in behavioral terms.

Wants

In the present formulation, the key component of an individual's motivation is his or her *wants*—a term usually used to denote conscious desires and wishes. But it may be extended to refer to wants of which the person is unaware. Wants that relate to target problems usually are clarified in the process of problem and goal formulation. (I want Jody to be home by a reasonable hour; I want mom to be nice to my boyfriend.) A host of other wants may impinge upon the target problem, however. Of particular importance are unexpressed wants that may undercut efforts to resolve target problems. These wishes make up the hidden agendas so often seen in family treatment.

For example, a family member may be involved in tinkering with a relationship that he wants to alter in a fundamental way. A husband wants to separate but cannot bring himself to make the move. Instead he brings himself to marital therapy, where he is confronted with a difficult paradox: the more successful he is in resolving the relationship problems, the less rationale he has for terminating the marriage. A wife really wants to discontinue weekly visits to her mother-in-law's home but fears her husband's anger. A white liberal father wishes that his daughter would break off her relationship with her black boyfriend but doesn't want to appear hypocritical. Unexpressed motives of this sort often run counter to apparent solutions to particular problems.

The possible presence of unexpressed wants necessarily must be inferred. Inability to move forward in problem solving, rejection of reasonable proposals, or lack of investment in tasks are among the signs.

When revelation of hidden agendas would immediately facilitate family problem solving, the agendas can be explored and interpreted in the session or discussed by family members in session tasks (chapter 6). When there is reason to believe that

revealing the hidden agendas would have a disruptive effect—
for example, in the case of a spouse who hasn't revealed his
desire to end the marriage—one may wish to investigate the
possibility in an individual session.

Because unsatisfied wants define problems as individuals perceive them (Reid 1978), it is often useful to refocus on what family members want if the problem focus becomes hazy or appears
to have shifted from what was originally agreed upon. In some
cases expressions of what family members want of one another
can help reframe problems in a positive light. For example, it
may be helpful for a husband, who interprets his wife's coldness
when they meet after work as a rejection of him, to hear that she
wants him just to be more expressive and tactful at those times,
not to be a different person. Conflicts over particular issues
sometimes can be put into a more soluble form if it can be established that the participants want similar things in a larger
sense. Working parents embroiled in arguments about particulars of child rearing may find themselves in agreement if they
focus on what kind of person they want the child to become.
Agreement at this level can help bring about a cooperative orientation toward resolving specific issues.

Feelings

Whereas unsatisfied wants define the content of a problem, feelings define the kind of pain experienced by the problem ac-
knowledger. Most feelings associated with the problem—anger,
depression, guilt, frustration, and so on—usually are revealed,
though maybe not labeled, as the problem is discussed. Some
feelings that are part of the problem may not be expressed; also
not expressed, or withheld, may be other feelings that are part of
the problem context. John acknowledged his distress about his
daughter's decision to move out of the family home to live with
her boyfriend. While his anger at the boyfriend and daughter
are revealed, his resentment over what he has interpreted as his
wife's lack of support for his position is not expressed, but only
hinted at. These feelings, whether expressed or not, are part of
the problem. In addition, accumulated feelings of hostility to-

ward his wife for having sided with his children against him in the past—part of the problem context—are not verbalized.

An important issue in this model, as well as in any form of family treatment, concerns the desirability of exploring hidden feelings that are part of the problem or related to it. In the present approach, a conservative stance is taken: Exploration directed at helping clients express feelings close to the surface generally is encouraged. These are feelings that are fairly obvious and would be likely to emerge in any case. Intensive probing of possibly deeper feelings is, as a rule, avoided. When feelings are revealed, an effort is made to help clients express them in ways that other family members would find understandable.

Although ventilation of feelings has its undeniable values, these values may be more easily realized in one-to-one treatment than in family therapy. A client expressing suppressed feelings to a practitioner can be reasonably assured of a sympathetic, accepting ear and can have confidence that his revelations will be used only to help him. When feelings are expressed in a family session, they are heard by other family members, whose reactions are less predictable. The other family members may react negatively and suffer inwardly or strike back at the ventilating member. On the other hand they may find the revelations illuminating and, even if painful to hear, may find them helpful.

Because expression of emotion is a normal and desirable part of family life, as well as therapy, the practitioner certainly does not take a repressive position. The questions are how far to go, and for what purposes, in eliciting expressions of feelings. In the present model, the purpose of helping a client reveal his feelings should not be simply to encourage ventilating as such, but rather to enable family members to understand one another better. In accord with Stuart (1980), the goal is one of "measured honesty" in which family members can learn "to develop the listening, expressive, request-making, feedback and clarifying skills they need for achieving genuine agreements" (p. 220). An effort should be made to help clients identify and express in nonthreatening ways distressing feelings that other family members may not be aware of. The helping effort should not be overdone, however. A family member's reluctance to reveal hidden feelings should be respected.

The function that expression of feelings appears to be serving in the session is an important determinant of how the practitioner proceeds. If feelings are adding to the understanding of other family members in helpful ways, the practitioner may facilitate continued expression. A husband may not have realized the sense of loss his wife felt when they separated. It may be therapeutic for both partners to have these feelings aired. On the other hand there usually is little to be gained by continued ventilation of hostility that appears to be increasing the anger and defensiveness of other family members. Once the client has made his emotional point, he should be helped to move on.

Values and Expectations

The role of values in family life scarcely can be overestimated. What is valued, and to what extent, influences all aspects of family functioning, from the importance awarded education to how often the bathroom is cleaned. To function smoothly together, family members need to draw upon a common set of values. A divergence in values is likely to give rise to conflict.

To add flesh to this notion, I shall turn to two schemes for understanding the role of values in family interaction. One is the value-orientation theory of Kluckhohn (Kluckhohn and Strodtbeck 1961) that has been applied to family therapy by Spiegel (1981). According to this formulation, the value orientations of cultures, families, and individuals vary according to how they solve a set of common human problems found in all cultures. For example, one such problem is orientation to time. Here one can value the future (as most middle-class Americans tend to do), the present, or the past. Comparable variations are developed for other basic dimensions, pertaining to the nature of human activity, human relations, man's relations to nature, and how man is viewed.

The ideas of variation and order of preference are central to this formulation. Within a family or individual, different variations in values regarding these basic questions coexist; certain variations may be preferred under some circumstances, other variations under others. Subtle differences can be a source of conflict.

For example, in respect to time orientation, a husband and wife who are generally future-oriented may both subscribe to the importance of saving for their children's college educations or for unanticipated expenses. They may differ, however, in respect to such issues as how much should be saved. The wife may be more "present" oriented, in this respect, than her husband. She may think it is time that they use some of their resources to get some "fun out of life" and may propose an expensive trip abroad. The husband might see the wife's plan as frivolous, considering their responsibilities. If the situation is changed, we may find different preferences and other conflicts emerging. The husband may see social gatherings in a more present-oriented way, as a time to have fun. The wife may have a more future-oriented view of such functions and show more concern over the impression they may be making on people she hopes will include them in their social circle.

Zuk (1978) has identified two broad value clusters which he sees as central to value conflicts in families. The "continuity" cluster comprises values which emphasize empathy, warmth, idealism, anticonformism, and intuition. In the "discontinuity" cluster, greater value is placed on distance and coolness in relationships, on rules, a pragmatic approach, an analytic orientation, achieving, and structuring.

Zuk hypothesizes that, in conflicts between husbands and wives, husbands are more likely to express discontinuity values and wives, continuity values. Familiar arguments in which husbands accuse wives of being "overemotional," while wives complain that their husbands are "distant" and "detached," provide common illustrations. Parents are more likely to express discontinuity values, such as the importance of rules, than children who are more likely to espouse continuity values—for example, the anticonformist complaint that the parents are too concerned about rules. Finally, in conflicts between the family and its external world, continuity values are more likely to be held by the family; discontinuity values, by the external world. The clash between families with nonconformist life styles and community attitudes illustrate the point. More generally, Zuk argues, "those who take the continuity' position in conflict situations tend to think of themselves and be thought of as less powerful than those who take the discontinuity position" (p. 52).

It is important to keep in mind that the values discussed and illustrated above are beliefs that have been legitimated in the minds of the believer and are not simply expressions of sentiment, behavior, and so forth. Two husbands may be "distant" from their wives. One husband may value closeness but is incapable of attaining it. The second may regard his aloofness as proper behavior. It is the element of self-justification that makes values resistant to change. Opportunities for change arise, however, when we apply the notion that a person may hold competing values which vary according to circumstances and whose order of preference may fluctuate. Further, most values do not take the form of hard and fast rules but rather are complex organizations of beliefs, a reason why the term "value orientation" is particularly a propos. Beliefs within these orientations are continually modified as part of the normal business of living.

When values are applied to making judgments on what is right or proper in respect to particular actions or situations, they can be thought of as *expectations*. An expectation usually refers to what one family member thinks another ought to do or what he should do himself (a husband expects his wife to defer to his wishes and expects himself to be protective of her in return). Expectations usually cover a spectrum of behavior ranging from what is acceptable (minimal expectations) to what is regarded as ideal, or *really* what one should do. (Note that the term often is used to describe what one thinks *will* happen, as in "I expect her to come in anytime." I use the term "anticipation" to refer to these future possibilities.)

Expectations are related to different family roles—father, mother, parent, son, daughter, and so on. Family roles are laden with expectations derived from past and current cultural influences. The trend probably has been toward increasing diversity in expectations with the growth of newer family forms such as the equalitarian marriage, the single-parent family, the reconstituted family, and cohabiting couples. These cultural influences combine with the personal natures and personalities of family members to produce the unique expectations that each member has of himself and other members. For example, a husband who has little tolerance for being put down by a woman may expect his wife to phrase any criticism of his behavior in the gentlest terms possible, and reacts with irritation if she does not. From a range of culturally permissible ways of expressing criticism, from the blunt to the sugarcoated, the husband allocates to his wife one that meets his personal needs. He still may regard his expectation as normative, and may have all sorts of justifications for it as well as for his anger when his wife does not behave accordingly. His wife, who tends to be outspoken, expects her husband to be tolerant of her bluntness and may justify her position in a similar manner. The practitioner may find herself with a position on the issue, perhaps one falling somewhere in the middle but probably leaning toward either the husband's or wife's. Her position, like the clients', can be traced back through her own cultural and familial influences, although it is likely to be justified in terms of what might be considered disturbed, healthy, functional, and so on.

Values and expectations vary in respect to degree of modifiability. Some are well entrenched, particularly those that reflect invariant and strongly sanctioned cultural norms. For example, American parents as a rule expect their adolescent children to eschew any use of drugs, and would not be willing to alter their position even though they may be forced to accept violations of it. But other values and expectations, particularly those where a variety of permissible positions exist within the culture, can be altered by new information or by reflecting on experience.

In exploring the context of a problem, the practitioner is particularly interested in the client's values and expectations that relate to the problem, how they are justified, how fixed they appear to be. Selected data are collected in the course of what clients reveal in their presentations of their problems and what they say to one another in the session. Focused inquiry on particular values and expectations is used when there is reason to suppose that clarification and discussion of them might facilitate progress toward problem reduction. There is little point in detailed examination of positions that appear to be unmodifiable. In any case the practitioner tries to avoid inquiry that would tend to make clients defensive about what they value. A session task called for clients to explain their positions to one another is often a fruitful way to gain preliminary clarification (chapter 6).

A person's values or expectations, like other cognitions, often exist in an inarticulated form without much attention having been given to them. They may be what Beck (1976) has identified as automatic thoughts. In the process of putting these thoughts into words, a family member, perhaps with some help from other family members or the practitioner, may realize that his expectations are unclear, contradictory, unrealistic, or actually different from what he thought they were. Thus, Gail, who has recently remarried, is incessantly critical of her son's behavior around the home, picking on minor indiscretions that she had overlooked when the two of them had been living alone. In verbalizing what kind of behavior she now expects from her son at home, she discovers that she is probably expecting him to be the "perfect child" so that he will prove acceptable to her new husband.

As Spiegel (1981) points out, practitioners tend to "pathologize" values that are seen as dysfunctional, that is, to attribute them to some unhealthy process in the person or the family. A strongly held value or expectation that forms an obstacle to the solution of a problem is often seen that way. In the present approach it is regarded as a position that may need not only to be understood but also to be respected. But to respect a value does not preclude efforts to bring about an alteration of it. The idea of "imposing" values on clients has long been anathema to most social workers, but that notion grossly oversimplifies matters.

Practitioners often find themselves in the position of trying to alter their clients' values, even though their efforts are seldom identified in this way. Consider a mother who thinks it's all right to leave her infant in the care of an eight-year-old, or the older person who no longer values life and refuses to take medication. To these extreme examples one could add such humdrum instances as the parent who expects that an older child should sacrifice his or her interests to help with younger siblings, or the husband who places a higher value on his work than his family life. In such cases practitioners are likely to act on positions counter to the value, although they may not deal directly with the underlying value orientation. They may label the client's behavior or the system as dysfunctional, point out possible adverse consequences of it, suggest preferable ways of responding, and so on. But these practitioner operations are, in effect, ways of advancing positions that run counter to the client's value orientation. If the practitioner is successful in bringing about desired changes, the client's orientation will have undergone modifications in the direction of the practitioner's position. The question is not one of imposing or not imposing values, but rather of when and how the practitioner should attempt to challenge the client's value position.

In the task-centered model, a basic requirement for initiating a challenge is that the value constitutes an obstacle to an agreed-upon problem. The service contract provides the practitioner with sanction to question clients' values in limited areas. As the process unfolds, the client is presented with a legitimate value conflict to be resolved. Presumably the goal to which problem solving is directed reflects certain values of importance to the client. If so, the client is faced with a choice, which the practitioner may clarify. Moreover, the case can be made that the value in question conflicts with other important goals or values or may have dysfunctional consequences which can be pointed out. When the value clashes with community standards, as in the case of mandated problems, this conflict can be brought to light. At any point, the practitioner can introduce her own opinion about what position seems to make sense.

Essentially then, the practitioner engages the client in a process of examining his or her values in which conflicts may be identified, alternatives offered, and resolutions suggested. The task-centered practitioner is more likely than is customary in practice to give explicit recognition to the client's value position, and to credit it as a difference in point of view rather than implying that something pathological is afoot.

The practitioner's own counterposition needs to be justified in terms of how it fits into a larger scheme of values and the extent of its societal acceptance, and she should be prepared to share her justification with the family. She is mindful throughout that value orientations are complex structures in which change is possible through reordering of value preferences for given circumstances. She deals with more modifiable pieces of these orientations, rather than deeply entrenched core positions.

For example, in treatment of dual-worker couples, a frequent obstacle to problem solution is disagreement over the extent of the husband's involvement in domestic and child care responsibilities. Wives usually want their husbands to do more. Husbands may argue in one form or another that such duties should be the wife's responsibility. The practitioner who subscribes to equalitarian values (Smith and Reid 1985) is likely to support the wife's position. If so, the practitioner may challenge the husband's position on grounds that the unequal division of labor in the home does not fit with newer notions of equity as a guiding principle for allocating responsibilities between spouses. If the wife works outside the home, the husband should share domestic tasks. The husband's position and its traditions are respected, and his arguments are taken seriously. All of this is brought out in a conversational manner. A light touch and some humor are helpful. One does not expect a dramatic reversal of the husband's position, but one hopes that new awareness, and with it some change in both value orientation and behavior, will take place. If only the latter occurs, it is likely to be tokenistic and transient.

In using this kind of direct approach, the practitioner usually forms a temporary issue-oriented alliance with one family member. She needs to make sure that it does not become (or is not understood as) a general siding with one member against another. Less commonly the practitioner may challenge the shared values of a family unit.

This method may prove fruitless if the client has arrived at a firm, well-defined value position. Some initial probing is used to determine if it makes sense to continue. A session task involving direct negotiation between family members is an alternative that in most cases should be tried first. Although a full-scale engagement of clients in discussions of their values may not be frequently employed, the exposition suggests how practitioners can take value positions with clients.

Perceptions

Our actions toward others are guided not by what others are "really" like but rather by our images of what they are like. These images or *perceptions* tell us how to interpret and predict their behavior, and we respond accordingly. Perceptions provide an approximation of reality, but in fact the approximation may be quite poor since it may be biased by our own wants, feelings, and values. Presumably, perceptions can be checked against reality, but the checking process may be influenced by the same bias. As a result certain pieces of data about another's behavior may be singled out and incorrect inferences made about its meaning. Evidence that does not fit the picture may be minimized or ignored. Intimate contact with another, of the kind that characterizes family life, can produce many richly detailed and accurate perceptions of that person. But it also can lead to perceptions that are not only highly inaccurate but also deeply entrenched. If the checking process has gone awry, one receives only repeated confirmations of preconceived images that may become progressively distorted. The process may culminate in labels—lazy, unresponsive, and so on. Usually the perceptions and labels have some basis in fact, and their creators can always point to behavioral evidence to support their view. The fault is more often the absence of balance and differentiation in how a person is pictured.

Distortions can be accentuated and cemented by gaining support for them from others in the family or outside of it, a process usually furthered by giving others selected evidence that would support the distortion. Counselors who have worked with family members in one-to-one relationships know how much of their clients' communications are taken up with trying to build cases that others in the family are at fault.

Often distortions are shared by family members. The extreme example in families is the shared delusional system in the folie à deux. Shared distortions are mutually reinforcing as participants both contribute evidence to support the common belief and obtain consensual validation from one another. The shared perception may cover the external world or another family member. In the latter case it may provide the rationale or even stimulus for an alliance between two family members against a third: Mr. and Mrs. B thus become convinced that Mrs. B's mother really is not able to live independently, despite her wish to do so and evidence that she can. Or such a belief may take the form of ignoring limitations or problems of a family member, a phenomenon well described by Haley (1980) in parents of "eccentric" young adults.

As has been observed, family members can reinforce one another's distortions or shared perceptions. Distortions also can be magnified through the interaction of different perceptions. Betty sees her husband John as "withholding"; John sees Betty as "prying." As a result they each may misinterpret the other's behavior in light of these cognitive frames. John's quietness (because he is tired) is seen by Betty as "hiding his feelings"; Betty's questions (to make conversation) about John's job may be viewed by John as an invasion of his private domain. Each may then respond in ways that appear to confirm their perceptions, Betty by interrogating her husband, in the first instance; John by becoming defensive, in the second. Each may in fact begin to conform to the other's perceptions, making them somewhat self-fulfilling. Labeling theory, which suggests that people tend to conform to images that others have of them, applies as much to family life as to other social situations.

As suggested in the previous chapter, distorted perceptions serve the interests of family coalitions. In both supportive and attacking coalitions, the allied partners may view a third in a highly selective manner—as sick or bad—in order to meet their own needs. Here the two partners reinforce one another's distortions, and the object of the coalition may respond to their perceptions in ways to reinforce them.

In applying methods of contextual analysis, the practitioner attempts first through focused exploration to gain a sense of the nature and extent of the distortions forming an obstacle. Through further exploration and subsequent explanation, the practitioner helps the family members to develop more functional views. As Minuchin and Fishman (1981) suggest, the purpose is not necessarily "to search for the truth but rather to construct a therapeutic reality in accordance with the therapeutic goal" (p. 214). In structural therapy this may amount to constructing a new "world view" that fits the aims of structural change. In the present approach the goal is usually more limited—to modify particular perceptions. An effort is made to correct obstructive aspects of the images that family members have of each other. Because these perceptions tend to be negative stereotypes or caricatures, the emphasis usually is on achieving a better balanced, better differentiated, and on the whole more positive picture.

For example, a mother may see her daughter as having completely failed a task, and the daughter reacts defensively. The mother's reaction may be highlighting the parts not done to the neglect of what was accomplished, perhaps part of a pattern of seeing the daughter's behavior primarily in a negative light. What the daughter did in fact is gently pointed out to the mother. A husband who does freelance repair work views his wife as controlling because she wants to know where he is going and when he will be back every time he leaves on a job. The accurate explanation is offered that his wife simply gains reassurance from knowing the whereabouts of people important in her life. As the examples suggest, explanations may not only involve filling in missing pieces of another's behavior but also offer a different way of understanding the behavior. The practitioner helps the client focus attention on those aspects of reality that would serve the goal of problem reduction.

Segraves (1982) refers to this process as a form of discrimination training that can be used to correct perceptions created in transference reactions. A wife may incorrectly perceive mild expressions of irritation by her husband as an attempt to intimidate her through anger, because that is how her father controlled her as she saw it. Pointing out the distinction between her husband's and her father's reaction can alter her view of her husband.

As Segraves further observes, timing of interventions and sensitivity to the client's perceptual frames are critical. It does little good and may, in fact, be counterproductive to abruptly introduce a piece of reality that sharply contradicts a family member's perception of another, no matter how distorted the perception and how obvious the reality. An enraged family member hurling insults at another will not be receptive to that kind of intervention, to say the least. While validating aspects of the client's perception, the practitioner initially attempts to add to it or raise questions about some part of it.

6. Session Tasks

In this chapter are described some types of tasks that are employed in joint sessions in task-centered and other forms of family practice. At this point the presentation is designed to set forth some of the more important types of tasks and to illustrate the range and variety that session tasks can take. As developmental work continues, additional types will be identified. Also, tasks actually used in sessions may be tailor-made to the situation at hand and may not necessarily conform to any given category.

DEFINITION, STRUCTURE, AND FUNCTIONS

A session task is a well-demarcated and sustained unit of work devised by the practitioner to accomplish specific purposes. The task has a definite structure: an introduction, a duration of normally several minutes, a clear end point, and often a follow-up discussion. A session task requires that at least two persons communicate face-to-face in the presence of at least one other. The communicators, usually family members, are referred to as "task participants." Practitioners may be selective about which family members participate in a given task. During client-to-client tasks the practitioner, for the most part, takes the role of an observer, facilitator, or coach. Whatever interventions are made during the task are directed at specific aspects of client-to-client communication. A lengthy interruption by the practitioner, particularly one leading to dialogue with the participants, would normally signify an end to the task.

Some tasks may involve dialogue between the practitioner and *one* client. Like any session task, practitioner-client tasks are set up to accomplish a particular purpose and have continuity and structure. If a practitioner asks Mrs. W to say how she felt when her husband (who is present in the interview) left her, the practitioner is carrying out a particular intervention, not setting up a task. A practitioner-client task in this situation might be structured by explaining to the couple that it might be important for the husband to hear how Mrs. W felt when he left her and that the practitioner would attempt over the next few minutes to help Mrs. W reveal her feelings about that event. The task would be controlled by this purpose.

Any task involving family members has multiple functions. The manifest, and usually primary function, of a task is captured in its announced purpose—to resolve a problem, to learn a communication skill, and so on. Other functions, often latent, arise from the fact that at least two family members are engaged in some form of cooperative, communicative activity. In session tasks, the way the task is set up and plays itself out has implications for roles of interaction in the family. Thus, the relationship between a father and son might be one in which the father is dominating and coercive (coercive complementarity). A session task in which they attempt to negotiate a difference might be set up to require them to work together. The father may still dominate, but their interaction is steered in a cooperative direction. Further, the practitioner might well intervene to keep their interaction on a cooperative course. Regardless of the issue being discussed or the outcome of the discussion, the pattern of interaction would have undergone a brief "restructuring." The new pattern can be brought to the attention of the participants and verbally reinforced by the practitioner.

Once a latent function has been made overt, it may be built into subsequent tasks as an additional purpose. In some instances, identifying the purpose of a function may impair its effectiveness. As long as the function is creating change in the direction of a previously agreed-upon goal, the practitioner may want to defer such identification until it can be used to augment the family's change efforts.

Another layer of function in the use of session tasks involves the relation between families and practitioners. Regardless of their content, tasks requiring family members to communicate with one another give the practitioner opportunity to withdraw from interaction with the family and become an observer. Moving to the sidelines can be a way of avoiding triangulation or other kinds of entrapment in the family system. For example, one practitioner found herself the object of "two after one" coaltion efforts on the part of a father and mother in the second family session. The parents had different styles of disciplining their "problem child," and each was trying to win over the practitioner. She had the impression that the parents were acting out with her the same kind of triangulation struggle that characterized their relationship with their children and, like one of their children, she was feeling increasingly helpless. Unsure about whether or not to confront them early in treatment with a pattern still shadowy in her mind, she identified one of the issues they had brought up and asked the parents to discuss it between themselves for a few moments. The session task blocked the triangulation effort for the time being and gave the practitioner an opportunity for further observation of their interaction.

Preparation.

A session task normally is suggested and structured by the practitioner. Setting-up operations include describing the nature and purpose of the task, designating the participants, and providing whatever instructions or guidelines are appropriate to the task. Certain communication ground rules can be set forth in advance: "stick to the topic," "avoid name calling," and so on. We have found it preferable to tailor whatever rules are needed to the particular task or participants. Whatever rules are developed, it is better to present only one or two of the more important ones as part of the intervention and to bring in others as needed. In general, the preparation should be kept brief and simple (see the sections on skill development and generic problem-solving tasks, below).

Practitioner's Activity During the Task.

As the task proceeds, the practitioner may enter to provide reinforcement, to keep communication on topic, to do on-the-spot coaching, and so on. Care is taken, however, to keep such interruptions from dominating the task or destroying the flow of communication between clients. It is better to allow clients to make some mistakes than to overwhelm them. Since the tasks usually are brief, important points can be withheld until the post-task discussion. Audiotape recordings of the task, which can be played back prior to the discussion, are useful as a means of recapturing details of the communication process.

If family members begin to communicate with the practitioner, she should direct them to speak to one another. Otherwise the structure of the task soon crumbles as the practitioner finds herself in the midst of an open discussion with the family. Having task participants sit facing one another often is a useful way of keeping talk moving in the right direction.

Post-Task Discussion.

The post-task discussion, which may range from a question or comment to an involved examination of what transpired, makes use of the basic communication techniques considered in the preceding chapter. The techniques are applied, however, to interaction that has just transpired. Although aspects of post-task discussions unique to different types of tasks will be taken up subsequently, some general observations can be made.

Focused exploration is used to elicit participants' feelings and expectations, as well as to center attention on aspects of their behavioral interactions. Exploration may also be directed at similarities or differences between any of these facets as they emerged in the task and how they play themselves out in other situations. Encouragement is used to show approval for positive aspects of performance. Explanation serves to share the practitioner's impressions of characteristics or dynamics of interaction, and direction usually is employed to suggest how performance might be improved. When explanation and direction are combined to point out deficiencies and suggest improvements, it is equivalent to what is sometimes called "feedback and correction" (Thomas 1976). For example, "It seems that the two of you were finding it hard to acknowledge the contributions of the other. Maybe on the next round you could try to do more acknowledging."

DEVELOPING SKILL IN PROBLEM SOLVING COMMUNICATION

A widely used form of structured interaction among clients in family treatment consists of programs designed to help family members improve their skills in communication and problem solving. Excellent reviews of work in this broad area are provided by L'Abate (1981) and Birchler (1979). In the present model, skill training is carried out through a series of session tasks.

Earlier in its history, the skill development movement emphasized enhancing skills of nonclinical populations, particularly marital couples in "marital enrichment" programs. In recent years skill development approaches have been applied increasingly to distressed families (Jacobson 1977, 1979; Gant et al. 1981; Baucom 1982).

As a result of these efforts, a large number of discrete programs have been spawned. Programs tend to be designed for particular types of family dyads, usually marital pairs, but with a growing interest in parent-adolescent dyads. They also tend to be specialized according to type of skill: communication, problem solving, decision making, and so on, although an examination of the specific training procedures reveals a considerable amount of overlap between them. In his review of such programs, Birchler (1979) found few "which did not include both basic communication and problem-solving components" (p. 290). Also, a certain hierarchy emerges. Some programs stress the fundamentals of communication processes (attentive listening, avoiding attacking or blaming statements, etc.) and no more. Those dealing with more specialized skills, such as problem solving or decision making, tend to incorporate some of the basic communication skills, on the reasonable assumption that these more specialized activities require some level of competence in communication. Programs of this more specialized variety can be thought of as providing training in problem solving, including decision making and conflict negotiation.

A training approach is a logical choice when the target problem is defined as deficits in communication, problem-solving, or other skills. Problems of this type may be presented by clients in such forms as, "We can't communicate." "Every time we discuss a problem, we end up in a fight." Such complaints do not necessarily translate into skill deficit programs, however. For example, the "we-can't-communicate" complaint may lead in any number of directions, including conflict over substantive issues that may constitute the core of the difficulty. Participants may be unable to communicate not because of lack of skill but because of specific conflicts. Session tasks may be used to help them resolve the conflicts, but without a training emphasis.

In many situations, however, concern with communication and problem-solving activities may offer a valid base for problem definition. The family may not be able to isolate particular substantive issues of major concern or, if such issues are present, may not be able to resolve them, either because the issues are too well-entrenched or because family members are unable to communicate with one another about them. For example, one family turned an initial interview into a nonstop quarrel about numerous marital and parent-child problems without being able to achieve agreement on anything. They were able to agree, however, with the practitioner's suggestion that they had a problem in being able to talk about their problems and were receptive to her proposal that training in problem-solving communication might be helpful.

As this example suggests, training formats not only are applicable to mildly distressed families who want to improve their communication and problem-solving skills, but also may be appropriate for families too conflicted to discuss their problems. In addition, training approaches can serve as useful adjuncts to more broadly based courses of therapy. In one situation (Mallon-Wenzel et al. 1982), negotiation training proved helpful to a father-and-son dyad who were involved in family therapy with another practitioner. Because training can be highly structured and focused, as it was in this case, it can be used adjunctively without creating conflicts of purpose between the "training" and "therapy" practitioners. Further, training can be used for skill deficit problems that may be of second priority. An advantage of a training format in this respect is that it provides a focus for work during periods when attention to the main problem becomes unproductive—for example, the couple whose problems have temporarily abated during a "good week." As this usage suggests, training programs can be used for parts of the treatment program. Stuart (1980), for example, begins marital treatment with behavioral exchanges that are followed by communications training.

Finally, a training format can be employed as a means of helping families work on substantive problems. Two controlled single-case studies in which the author participated (Knopf and Reid, in press) were treated in this way with positive results. With each, substantive target problems were identified, and a decision-making skills training program adapted from Thomas (1976) provided the means of working on the problems. Treatment goals in each case consisted of *both* reduction of the target problems and improvement of decision-making skills.

When training approaches are used in the present model, emphasis is placed on developing skills in *problem-solving communication*. This emphasis follows the problem orientation of the model. Moreover, it is assumed that the essentials of communication training can be incorporated into a format that provides training in more specific skills in problem solving. Finally, with the typically distressed families seen by social workers, communication difficulties per se are generally of less concern than inability to communicate effectively to solve problems.

The development of training goals and procedures was guided by several considerations. Skill training procedures may be followed obediently in the session but have little carry-over outside it. As a rule, the more the skill departs from the usual norms of conversation, the more difficult it will be to achieve generalization. "Artificial" skills, such as paraphrasing, may be useful as beginning exercises, but an attempt should be made to stress whatever parts of them may be used in ordinary discussions.

Another consideration was particularization. Many training programs come in structured, standardized packages. Not all components may be useful in a given situation, and those that are may need to be adapted to its unique circumstances. A third consideration has to do with the nature of problem-solving communication in family life. It generally does not follow the typical paradigm outlined in usual training format: define the problem, generate alternatives, select the best solution, and implement it. Although this paradigm may be useful in organizing and presenting a training format, it is unrealistic, and sometimes dysfunctional, to insist that family members closely adhere to it, or to use it as the sole basis for training. Problem solving often occurs in a "nonstepwise" manner and in "fragments," to use Thomas, (1976) terminology. For example, participants may work from partial definitions of the problem to possible solutions, then back to defining the problem again—not necessarily an illogical progression, since examining unworkable solutions is one way of defining the dimensions of the problem. Most problem solving in family life does not take place through extended discussions but rather through brief interchanges of reminding, requests, apologies, explanations, and so on. Large problems may be worked on in pieces extending over periods of time. A broad, flexible view of problem-solving communication is needed to encompass this variety.

Finally, how much of this business can be identified as teachable, generally useful skills is open to question. Certainly the notion of skill cannot be divorced from purpose and situation. Communications that deviate from the usual criteria of skill can be quite advantageous in certain circumstances. An ambiguous sidetracking comment may be just the thing to exit gracefully from a touchy interaction with one's spouse. Perhaps the ultimate skill in family communication is knowing precisely when to be clear, when to be obtuse, when to express feelings, when not to, and so on. Unfortunately, skill of this sort—perhaps "art" would be a better term—is beyond our ability to formulate or teach. What is possible is to capture and transmit certain ways of communicating that probably are improvements over the average ways of exchanging meanings in most families, particularly troubled ones.

Comprehending the multitude of family communication skills that have been identified in the literature can be simplified considerably if we keep in mind that most of them simply articulate characteristics of what most people would identify as constructive communication between intimates: that is, one should avoid attacking or blaming comments, express criticism in a tactful way, stick to the topic, let the other have a chance to speak, and so on. Most people have these skills or know what they involve. What they need to learn is how to use them to best advantage in their immediate family situations.

I shall present an outline of skills that may be drawn on in constructing an individualized program of training in problem-solving communication. I shall then take up considerations relating to format and technique in skill training.

Problem Identification. An initial step in problem-solving communication is identifying the problem to be solved, although, as noted, the step need not be necessarily carried to completion before possible solutions are considered. Also, problems may be recognized and noted without further problem-solving action being taken.

Listening. Although listening is a skill basic to all communication, it will be introduced as a part of problem identification, where it serves the critical function of enabling a person to learn what another sees as a problem. Half-listening is a phenomenon as common in families as in the lecture hall. At best we tend to listen selectively, taking in parts of what others are saying and interpreting these messages according to our own frames of reference. As a skill, listening requires being attentive to the other's messages. To facilitate attentiveness, family members may be instructed to face one another and maintain eye contact. These devices, like any of the skills under consideration, need to be used selectively, however. (Some people can listen quite attentively while looking out the window.) A more important part of listening is an effort to achieve accurate understanding of what a speaker is communicating. In addition to being attentive, the listener needs to "hear the speaker out," that is, not allow his or her own biases or emotional reactions to block out or blur the content of the message.

More sensitive listening calls for an empathic orientation toward the speaker (Guerney 1982). At this level, the listener attempts to understand what is being said from the speaker's point of view. Suppose Kim tells her husband, Brian, that she is tired of doing most of the domestic chores on top of her full-time job and wants Brian to take on a greater share of the housework. Brian feels his job is more demanding than his wife's and that he is doing enough around the house as it is. If he were to evaluate Kim's communication from his own frame of reference, he would be likely to experience resentment at her demands. If he were instructed to listen from her perspective, and perhaps after some practice, he might sense her feeling that her job was as demanding for her as his was for him. As a result, he might view her "demand" as not an unreasonable request, especially if she were listening and responding under similar instructions.

Acknowledging. An explicit acknowledgement for the other's problem statement provides assurance that the message has been received and understood. Replies consisting of paraphrases of the other's preceding communication are commonly used for this purpose (Jacobson and Margolin 1979). More elaborate is the use of "clarification" (Stuart 1980) or validation (Gottman et al. 1976) in which speakers, at the listener's request, may restate their communications, which the listener may paraphrase. When empathic communication is being emphasized, participants are instructed to reflect back the meanings of what each has said from the other's perspective. Such exercises, which may be tedious and artificial, ensure an awareness of the other's meanings that is probably rarely achieved, and certainly never sustained, in family communication.

Expressing Problems. Listening and acknowledging are ways of comprehending and clarifying what others view as problems. Expressing problems involves stating what one sees as difficulties. The focus will be on disclosing problems seen in the behavior of another participant, the most common and difficult type of problem expression. The skill here is in stating something undesirable in another person, in a manner that conveys one's feelings and perceptions but that minimizes angry or defensive reactions on the part of the other. Being specific about what is undesirable provides a way both of being clear and of keeping angry reactions in check. The practitioner stresses the importance of limiting problem statements to particular behaviors while avoiding pejorative labels or sweeping accusations. "I don't like it when you shut me up if I want to talk about something on my mind," as opposed to, "You're only concerned about yourself," or "You never want to listen to me." In addition, the problem discloser should make reference to his or her own sources of discomfort, as in the example above. "I" statements (Gordon 1970) or "owning up to your feelings" (Liberman et al. 1980) help locate part of the problem in the person making the disclosure, and avoid focusing simply on what the other is doing wrong. Beginning problem statements in the first person, followed by a specific indication of what one is upset about and an illustrative example, is a good way of disclosing problems. "It makes me angry when you're going to be late and don't call. Like last Tuesday when you came home at 7 o'clock." Direct statements of the problem are preferable to indirect "hints" that leave the other person guessing. Finally, problem statements should be limited to a single concern rather than a "gunnysack" of complaints.

Problem Exploration. Exploration of the problem begins when participants begin to discuss an identified difficulty. In exploration, detail is added, positions are clarified, feelings are expressed. Contextual factors are examined in a search for the factors responsible. Skills previously presented continue to apply, and additional ones may be brought to bear. Problem solving is helped considerably if each participant takes some responsibility for contributing to the problem. An admission of responsibility by one participant should, if possible, be matched by an admission by the other. This not only opens up additional solution possibilities and reduces defensiveness, but maintains symmetry between participants in respect to "who is to blame." Particularly to be avoided is one participant's using the admission of another to "prove the case" that the other actually is at fault. Nothing will succeed quite as quickly as discouraging further admissions from the "guilty" party. More usual than admitting responsibility are persistent efforts to justify one's own position while blaming the other for the problem, or introducing additional complaints about the other. The blame or complaints often may be based on assumptions about the other's intentions or motives (mind reading) which are likely to be viewed in the worst possible light.

This kind of quarrelsome communication is inevitable in work with families with conflict, and should be allowed to continue if it appears that in the process additional facets of the problem or its causes are being clarified. If the cross-blaming becomes repetitive or excessively attacking, the interaction should be interrupted and feedback provided (see section following). Discussion should be present-focused and kept away from remote or historical causes of the difficulty; however, immediate causes (obstacles) preventing solution should be explored (Jacobson and Margolin 1979).

As a problem is discussed in any depth, a typical occurence is for the participants to branch off into related concerns. "Sidetracking" or "target shifting" usually is better understood as a systems phenomenon than as behaviors of individuals. Usually one participant does not abruptly change the subject. One will move slightly off topic, the other will take the conversation still further in the same direction, and so on. Corrective feedback is more appropriately addressed to the system rather than to individuals. "The two of you seem to be getting off the track."

Generating, Evaluating, and Selecting Solutions. As indicated, this phase may begin once a problem has been identified or at any point in exploration of a problem. Participants may move into it of their own accord, or the practitioner may introduce it following a summary of the problem. Whether or not to allow participants to jump ahead to the solution phase is a matter of judgment. If suggested solutions appear to be viable ways of resolving the problem, participants usually should be permitted to pursue them even if there is need further along to return to earlier phases.

Usually solutions take the form of actions or tasks to be done by the participants. Generally the procedures used in planning home tasks apply (chapter 7), though they are adapted, of course, to helping participants plan their own tasks. Action alternatives can be generated through brainstorming (discussed later) or through a more natural discussion process. In any case, participants are encouraged to propose possible solutions.

Three specific training guidelines apply here. The first is to request that each participant offer to take some action on his or her own to alleviate the problem, although understandably their proposals will tend to call for actions others should take. The second guideline requests that participants make an effort to acknowledge positive elements in one another's proposals, or if they cannot, to respond neutrally rather than negatively. The third guideline asks participants to adapt a "spirit of compromise" in searching for solutions; each should be prepared to make concessions. In helping participants evaluate proposals, a useful procedure, adapted from Kifer et al. (1974), is to ask for statements of possible consequences of suggested alternatives. Selection and planning of the alternative chosen is the final step of the process.

Format and Training Techniques

Practitioners can develop individualized training programs addressed to some combination of skills outlined above, depending on their appraisal of what clients can best utilize. The usual format consists of sequences of session tasks involving family members. As a general rule, it is preferable to begin with problems that are less conflictual and to proceed gradually toward more difficult problems.

The practitioner initially explains the general purpose and structure of training, then focuses on skills for the problem identification or problem exploration stage, depending on whether or not problems have been previously identified. If training begins with problem exploration, listening and acknowledging skills may be incorporated into it. In addition to explaining what participants need to do to carry out a skill, the practitioner may model the skill in a role play with one of the participants, or each in turn. As Liberman et al. (1980) suggest, the participant with whom the role play is done can take on the role of another family member present, which has the advantage of allowing family members to see how they are being perceived by others, while avoiding "a too personal situation" (p. 145).

During session tasks the practitioner may make use of certain procedures to provide on-the-spot input. *Prompting*, which may take the form of whispered instructions to a participant, provides specific instructions to a participant about what to say or do next. In *doubling*, the practitioner speaks for a participant, a sort of mini-role-play; or a practitioner may take the role of a participant through a series of interchanges. Encouragement provides immediate approval for good problem solving. Corrective feedback calls the participant's attention to faulty performance and suggests how it could be improved.

In the present model the practitioner avoids "overtraining" by limiting interventions during the session task. A crucial practitioner skill here is tolerance of "mistakes" or deviations from the practitioner's conception of appropriate problem-solving communication. As Wells and Figurel (1979) suggest, the majority of the practitioner's interventions should be positive and reinforcing in tone. Whether complimentary or critical, the practitioner's interruptions should not be so frequent that the participants' interaction loses continuity and no longer retains the shape of a unit of work or task.

In training formats, task discussions are used to provide feedback on performance, summarize accomplishments, structure subsequent tasks, and provide instructions for carrying them out. Summarizing accomplishments may include listing problems identified, alternatives generated, or tasks agreed on, depending on the phase being worked on. Because emphasis is on training rather than the resolution of particular problems, the practitioner generally does not suggest solutions.

The guidelines to be used for training in problem-solving communication can be drawn on in other types of session tasks that do not have training as their primary focus. The guidelines may be used to introduce a skill-training theme into the tasks, to provide rules to facilitate more effective communication, or simply to inform the practitioner about the occurence of difficulties in the participants' communication.

The approach just presented can be augmented by use of available programs. The following citations give sources which describe programs for training families in problem solving, communication, decision making, and negotiation skills: marital partners, Gottman et al. (1976), Jacobson and Margolin (1979), Liberman et al. (1980), Thomas (1976); marital groups, Miller, Nunnally, and Wackman (1975); parent and adolescent, Kifer et al. (1974), Robin (1980).

Outcome Research

There have been only a small number of controlled evaluations of communication and problem-solving training as a method of intervention with distressed families.* Several of these studies (Baucom 1982; O'Leary and Turkewitz 1981; Gant et al. 1981; Jacobson 1977, 1979) also involved evaluations of use of home tasks and are reviewed in some detail in the following chapter. Although, as will be discussed, the effects of communication or problem-solving training often have been difficult to isolate from the effects of the home tasks, these studies provide some evidence that the kind of training format just presented can contribute to resolution of problems and improvement in family relations. In all these studies, programs that made substantial or exclusive use of communication/problem-solving training had significantly better results than control programs. Clients were distressed marital couples, and in one study (Gant et al. 1981) court-referred youth and their families.

An additional study (Robin 1981) compared problem-solving communication training against "alternative family therapy" (which varied in orientation according to therapist) and a wait-list control. Families ($n = 33$) experiencing parent-adolescent conflict were randomly assigned to the three conditions. The main experimental program consisted of a training model along the lines of the one presented above, supplemented by "cogni-

---

*Reviews of outcome research in this chapter and the next will be limited to studies in which control groups or equivalent procedures are used to isolate the effects of interventions.

tive restructuring" when "unreasonable beliefs interfered with the resolution of specific disputes" (p. 597). On essentially self-report measures, the problem-solving communication program did as well as the alternative family therapy but did better on observational measures of parent-adolescent interaction. In both programs gains were maintained over a three-month follow-up period. The study is of particular interest because it compared training against what appeared to be a creditable family therapy alternative.

These studies were selected because of their rigor as well as their relevance to the present model. A much larger body of controlled and uncontrolled research on communication training, done primarily in the context of marital enrichment and behavioral marital therapy programs, provides additional evidence that a skills-training approach can be effective in improving family relations (see, for example, review by Birchler [1981]). The empirical basis for training approaches still is quite limited, however. We have only a small amount of evidence, most of which is reviewed here and in the following chapter, that they are effective with the kinds of families customarily seen by social workers. Moreover, this evidence does not provide much of a basis for isolating effects of skills training from related components, such as home tasks, or for comparing these effects against those produced by contrasting forms of therapy.

GENERIC PROBLEM-SOLVING TASK

In the task sequences just considered, the problems worked on are subordinated to the development of skill in problem solving. The solution of immediate problems is considered to be a by-product. In the generic problem-solving task, the main objective is to resolve the issue on the table. Enhancement of problem-solving or communication skills is viewed as a secondary benefit.

The generic problem-solving task is designed for a wide range of situations, from resolving a specific dispute to developing strategies for coping with a family crisis. It is often used in beginning work with families. As obstacles to family problem-solving are encountered, or as specific situations arise, more specialized tasks may be employed. It is the task of choice when family members are able to engage in constructive, face-to-face problem-solving and when the focus is on the resolution of particular substantive problems rather than in enhancing problem-solving skills. This kind of family problem-solving was pioneered by Bell (1975, 1981) and is a central feature of the problem-centered model of family therapy (Epstein and Bishop 1981) and the electic approach of Janzen and Harris (1979).

Essentially family members are asked to work collaboratively toward resolution of a problem of mutual concern. Usually this consists of efforts to develop a plan for solving or alleviating the problem, a plan that they will try to implement following the session.

The task is set up after the problem has been defined through prior discussion with the practitioner. The following guidelines or ground rules (adapted from the skill development module presented earlier) may be introduced.

1. Participants should focus on the problem itself and solutions for it, rather than on each other's personal qualities.
2. In the case of disagreement, participants should attempt to make some concessions, that is, they should be prepared to accept something less than (or different from) their conception of the ideal solution to the problem.
3. Participants should try to see positive elements in each other's proposals, acknowledge the positives, and try to build on them.
4. Each participant should offer to take some constructive action to help resolve the problem.
5. Problem behaviors or possible problem-solving actions should be spelled out as specifically as possible.

Which of these guidelines are emphasized, how they are phrased, and whether they are presented at the beginning or introduced more gradually over several tasks will depend on a variety of factors, including the family's apparent problem-solving capacity and style, the amount of overt conflict among family members, the nature of the problem being worked on, and the amount of emphasis to be given to skills training.

As the session proceeds, the focus in the tasks may become more specific. Subsequent tasks may involve work on some aspect of the problem, deciding among alternative solutions emerging from preceding tasks, or planning home tasks from solutions decided upon.

Post-task discussions concentrate on various means of facilitating the family's problem-solving work. Family members can be helped to understand and adhere to the guidelines, to focus on key aspects of the problem, or to clarify and firm up potential solutions. The practitioner herself can suggest possible solutions in order to provide a stimulus for the family's problem-solving work or to present good alternatives the family might not have considered.

Use of the generic problem-solving task and its role in the model is nicely illustrated by work with Paul and Stella, a couple in their late forties who were seen in a medical setting concerning relationship problems associated with Paul's painful and incapacitating back condition. One of the target problems concerned their conflict over John, twenty-two, one of their adult children who lived in a nearby community. Stella felt that Paul was driving John away with his unwillingness to communicate with him and his inability to understand his problems. Paul acknowledged that he had given up on John. There had been little communication between them in recent weeks. Paul could no longer stand John's drug taking, drinking, and inability to hold down a job. He resented John's coming to their home high and his wife's protective attitude toward their son. Stella admitted that she bent over backwards with John to make up for Paul's coldness.

The estrangement between Paul and John, with the related coalition between mother and son, were identified as obstacles to the couple's efforts to resolve their conflict. A problem-solving task involving John was set up to work on the obstacle. In the task, Paul and John tried to come up with ways to solve their communication difficulties. Taking the initiative, John indicated how he wanted to become closer to his father, and in the ensuing discussion John acknowledged that coming home high was not the way to do this but that he had always felt left out when at home. The conversation touched on some of John's problems with his girlfriend. Paul, pleased at John's initiative, responded supportively and indicated his own difficulty in understanding the values of the younger generation. He would like to talk to John more about these things. John agreed to come home "dry" the next time.

When they had finished, the practitioners (two therapists were treating the family) made explicit the home tasks that they had agreed on: John would come for a visit next weekend and would stay straight. Paul and John would talk further and do something together. These tasks were successfully carried out and appeared to be an important factor in a subsequent improvement in the parents' relationship.

Not all session tasks flow this smoothly or have such productive results, but the example illustrates what can be accomplished through the client's own problem solving in what might appear to be an entrenched situation. The major ingredient here was the family members' readiness to move toward resolutions. This potential surfaced dramatically in the face-to-face encounter. It might not have otherwise. Although the practitioners' contribution appeared modest, it provided critical ingredients—for example, in structuring the discussion between John and Paul, and in formulating the home tasks. These interventions helped alter a triangle—mother and son against father—that had proven to be a major part of the obstacle in the way of an improved marital relationship.

Obstacles encountered in the generic problem-solving task—impasses in negotiations, inability to maintain focus, argumentativeness, distortions in perception, differing expectations, and so on—are dealt with initially through reference to the guidelines, through methods employed in skills training (presented earlier), or through focusing discussion on trouble spots. Supplementary use may be made of more specialized session tasks, such as "clarifying positions," or "exploring hidden agendas (see below)." One useful focusing technique, "fractionization of the conflict," has been described by Robin (1981). Impasses often result from participants becoming ensnarled in a set of interconnected issues at the same time, with the danger of the discussion sprawling to additional, and perhaps even more troublesome, areas. The procedure suggested by Robin involves a dismantling of the identified conflict into smaller units which then may be negotiated separately. The units most amenable to negotiation are settled initially to establish a pattern of compromise.

An example given in Robin (1981:181) involves an instance where a mother discovered marijuana cigarettes in her son's dresser drawer. The son was outraged at the invasion of his privacy and declared he would not stop using marijuana. His mother, equally outraged, declared her opposition to the boy's use of the drug in the house or outside the home and "grounded him indefinitely" (p. 182). The therapist "fractionated" the conflict into three components which would be dealt with separately: (1) the boy's use of the drug in the home, (2) the boy's use of the drug outside the home, and (3) the mother's invasion of her son's privacy. After lengthy discussion, the following were arrived at: the mother came to realize that it would be difficult for her to stop the boy from using marijuana outside the home. Mother made clear to son that she opposed his usage of marijuana but would not continue to bring up the issue for argument. Son in turn assured his mother that he was very careful as to where and when he used the drug, and agreed to cease using or storing marijuana in the home. Finally, both parties "agreed to communicate suspicions (mother had suspected that son was using pot which prompted her to search his room) directly rather than to obtain the information surreptitiously" (p. 182).

When these methods do not succeed, more intensive focus on particular obstacles may be necessary. The practitioner may forsake the session task format, at least temporarily, and make use of the methods of contextual analysis discussed in the previous chapter.

TASKS FOR SPECIAL PURPOSES

This section brings together a variety of additional kinds of tasks that are used in the session. Some of these tasks are commonly used in family therapy; others have been contributed by particular approaches, including our own. In the present framework, these tasks are designed to accomplish special purposes, such as locating or clarifying difficulties to work on, or resolving specific types of obstacles and problems.

Problem Search and Definition

Although target problems normally are located and defined through a dialogue in which family members and practitioners are co-participants, there may be occasions to have family members do this on their own. The usual problem formulation process may reach an impasse. The family may show a greater willingness or facility to explore their difficulties with one another than with the practitioner. Or, for whatever reason, the practitioner may simply reach a dead end in her attempts to formulate a problem with the family, and may decide that giving the family a try at it without her assistance may "shake things loose" or at least provide additional data on family interaction.

Another reason for use of this task is to give the family a structured experience in identifying and defining problems. A practitioner who wishes to emphasize the development of problem-solving capacity with a family may use this kind of task as an option during the initial problem-formulation phase. More generally, practitioners may use it as a means of targeting new problems during the course of treatment.

The task is set up by stating the general area of concern and whatever may have emerged as possible issues. The family then is instructed to try to identify a problem to be worked on. Following the task, the practitioner attempts to identify areas of agreement (or disagreement) among family members. She may reflect back to the family its definition of the problem, if it has arrived at one, or may suggest a way of formulating a problem based on what has emerged from the family's efforts. A problem may be suggested by how the family interacts in attempting to formulate a problem.

Enactments

Widely used in structural therapy, enactments call for family members to reproduce problem interactions in the session. Enactments have both diagnostic and therapeutic functions. Diagnostically they provide live re-creations of interactions that may be causing difficulty, thus giving the practitioner a firsthand view of the problem. Their therapeutic function evolves from the fact that they are structured by the practitioner rather than occurring spontaneously. Because family members are required to produce the interactions in the session, they must think about what they will do and how. The interactions may not involve the same emotional intensity, so members can be somewhat more reflective about their own and others' behavior. Moreover, an enactment usually does not duplicate the interaction but rather presents a variation of it, one that may be more studied and controlled. This aspect may demonstrate to the family how the interaction might be carried out more successfully. The practitioner can accentuate this process by deliberately introducing a variation.

A major point of contention between Marge and Fred was Marge's smoking. In recent months Fred's objections had increased in intensity. He often would leave the room if she lit up, and would accuse her of fouling the air and of threatening his health as well as the health of their two children. Marge had failed in several attempts to quit and was now becoming resistive to Fred's demands that she stop. Repeated discussion of the problem had failed to accomplish much.

The couple had presented the problem as their main concern in the initial interview and continued to do so in the second session. The practitioner, who wondered if the problem was not a disguise for deeper issues, structured an enactment task. Marge and Fred were instructed to have one of their "discussions" about the problem—to add intensity Marge was asked to smoke, which she was happy to do.

Fred took the initiative. He quickly repeated the various reasons why he did not want Marge to smoke, but added one that had not been brought out—that he hated to see someone he loved destroying herself. Marge, who had been responding defensively, became tearful at this point. When asked why later, she said she was responding to the realization that there might be some concern for her in Fred's problems with the smoking.

Although the couple had discussed this issue on numerous occasions, this time their interaction took a somewhat different turn. Fred's subdued presentation of his case, his expression of concern for his wife, his wife's "hearing" the concern were all parts of the difference. The practitioner's presence and the paradoxical stimulus added by Marge's smoking at the practitioner's request may have contributed to the difference. In addition to giving Marge, and possibly Fred, a new perspective on the conflict, the task demonstrated that the problem had considerable importance in its own right. Rather than a smoke screen (figuratively speaking), it seemed a "representative problem" (chapter 2), one that reflected issues of control and closeness in the relationship.

Brainstorming

Problem solving may reach an impasse because participants become "locked into" particular proposed solutions that are not mutually acceptable. It may be apparent that a wider range of possible solutions could be brought to bear. Under these circumstances, a brainstorming task may be useful. As a problem-solving method, brainstorming requires that participants generate as many possible solutions as they can without regard to how "good" or acceptable they might be (Osborne 1963; Jacobson and Margolin 1979). By design, criticism of any particular proposal is suspended as a means of encouraging creativity and innovative solutions. Once a list of possibilities has been generated, an effort is made to select the better ones for more serious consideration.

Because of its artificiality, and also because it may be unnecessary or counterproductive in many situations, brainstorming was not incorporated as part of skills training or generic problem-solving tasks. Often the most promising solutions to a problem are rather obvious. A concentrated discussion of them by the family may be more useful than throwing out ideas without much thought.

A brainstorming task is done in two segments. In the first part, participants are asked to concentrate on possible solutions, which the practitioner records. Once each participant has been heard from and several possibilities have been recorded, the participants then select the most promising solution(s) for further discussion.

Negotiating Rules

Conflict over rules frequently is dealt with in family work and often is a dominant issue when difficulties involve parent-child interaction. Moreover, problems that may be expressed in other forms, such as a child's misbehavior or a parent's inconsistency in disciplining, often can be conveniently formulated as problems about rules. To do so puts the problem in an interactional context and appeals to a common understanding shared by most people—that rules of some form are necessary in family life.

In putting a problem in "rule form," the practitioner can keep in mind that any recurring interaction among family members is an expression of a descriptive rule (chapter 4). "When Tim comes home late mom yells at him and threatens him with all sorts of punishments but nothing further happens," states a pattern or rule of interaction the way it is. Identification of such patterns sets the stage for suggesting to the family that it may be worthwhile to see if better rules can be developed. Family members may view rules rather narrowly, largely as prescriptions for the behavior of their children. They may need to be shown that rules apply to any patterned interaction among family members.

In helping the family negotiate rules, the practitioner may wish to ask participants each to state what his or her conception of what a desired (prescriptive) rule should be. Family members are thus stimulated to think about—and articulate—how things could be different. Novel situations, or at least promising directions for negotiation, may emerge from this process. In guiding negotiations in the post-task discussions, the practitioner helps participants clarify as specifically as possible what behavior each expects from the other and whether or not what is expected by one is regarded as fair by the other. When rules do concern matters of discipline, consequences (rewards and sanctions) for following or breaking proposed rules should be spelled out, as well as who will be responsible for seeing that the consequences happen.

When there are differences between parents about desired rules for a child, the parents can be asked to reach an understanding between themselves. The child (or children) can be put in the role of observers or be excluded from that portion of the session. If conflict between participants blocks a discussion, a technique that sometimes proves useful is to have the participants write out proposed rules—a technique that also can interrupt an escalating quarrel and give the practitioner a probably much-needed, quiet moment of reflection.

When family members negotiate rules, they are engaging in a way of rule making that most likely differs from their usual methods of developing rules. Usually rules are made without negotiation and often without much thought. Rarely are they made explicit. Although only a minor rule may be discussed, a different process of rule making is occurring. By calling their attention to how the process works, the practitioner can help the family members apply it to other situations.

In some cases an aspect of the rule-making process itself may be identified as an issue. Are some rules made as angry reactions to the children's behavior? Does a wife object that her husband tries to set rules for her behavior? Such *aspects* of the rule-making process can be dealt with through negotiation aimed at clarifying the problems and developing solutions. As tempting as it may be in some situations, one would probably want to avoid tackling a family's rule-making process as a whole.

Clarifying Positions

Efforts to resolve a problem may falter because participants fail to perceive, or misunderstand, one another's perceptions, feelings, motives, or expectations. The discussion may have become so highly charged as a result of trading of accusations that participants are unable to explain fully how they see an issue, why they feel the way they do about it, the reasons for their actions, or what they actually expect from one another. In short, each does not comprehend the other's "positions," seeing only pieces of behavior that are interpreted in a negative light. Often an opportunity to let each explain his or her position to the other will cast the problem in a new light and suggest new possibilities for solutions.

During the session task Harold and his father, George, became embroiled in an argument over Harold's work on a home-improvement project. Harold had agreed to do the work (insulating the garage), but he wanted to do it in his own way and to space the job out so it wouldn't interfere with basketball practice. George kept harping about his son's "sloppy" work and "lack of responsibility." Harold responded defensively, maintaining that he was doing the best he could and would get the job done eventually. His father, he remarked, was a perfectionist. There was nothing he could do to please him.

The practitioner ended the session task at this point and structured another. His father was to explain to Harold his reason for wanting certain things done in a certain way as if he were talking to a tradesperson. Harold was to listen without interrupting. Harold in turn was to tell his father, without being interrupted, why basketball practice was so important to him. The structured exchange that followed was an example of explaining positions. The task helped each to gain additional perspectives. Although the father's explanation was a somewhat dry recitation of the technical ins-and-outs of home insulation, it was done in a coherent, logical way so that Harold could at least get some idea of what was expected. In his turn Harold made the point, which his father apparently had not realized, that missing practice sessions could mean getting cut from the squad no matter how good a player you were. Following this task, the two were able to move toward a compromise plan.

The task can be set up to focus on certain aspects of the participant's positions, depending on what appears to be most useful. The exchange need not by symmetrical. A wife may clarify her expectations of the domestic responsibilities of her husband; the husband may be asked to explain more fully his references to be being "treated like a child" around the house. The explanations should be brief, focused, and nonaccusative. Participants should talk directly to one another, with prompting as needed from the practitioner. Constructive dialogue between the participants may develop and, if so, should be encouraged. Following the task, the practitioner can highlight revelations that might facilitate problem solving, or ask each participant to comment on what he or she learned from the exchange.

Role Play Tasks

The use of role play has been considered in relation to training in problem-solving communication. In that context, role play served a specific and adjunctive function. It provided a means of facilitating learning of particular problem-solving skills.

Role play can also serve as a general approach to helping family members work directly on target problems or obstacles. In this application, family members acquire and practice new ways of responding to (and understanding) given situations, and of gaining insight into their own reactions and the reactions of others. Role plays are similar to enactments, in the sense that behavior in the session is structured by the practitioner, but they differ in key respects. In an enactment, participants produce variations of their own behavior in an actual situation, that is, the session. In role plays, participants may be requested to engage in "as if" behavior—to take on roles of others or to enact roles in "imagined situations" (Shaw et al. 1980).

A sense of the role play possibilities that may be considered in a family session is illustrated in table 6-1, based on an actual case.

Table 6.1

Participants in Session	Roles			
	Father	Son	Practitioner	Teacher
Father		1, 3		2
Son	3	2	4	1
Practitioner		4		

Four role plays are illustrated. The numbers in the figure indicate who took what roles. For example, in the first role play (1), the father assumes the role of the (adolescent) son, and the son takes the role of his teacher, who has been giving the son a hard time. In the role of teacher, the son vigorously reprimands the father (in the son's role) about some minor infraction of a rule. The father tries to show how he would handle the situation, thus modeling appropriate coping behavior for the son. In the second task, the father takes the role of the teacher, with the son playing himself. The father now attempts to provoke the son, who is instructed to try out some of the behavior his father had modeled. The third task is a role reversal, with father and son exchanging roles in a discussion of the school problem to give each a sense of where the other is "coming from." The fourth task, another role reversal, was used to give the practitioner insight into how the son was perceiving him. As the practitioner, the son provided a nice caricature of the practitioner's interrogative style.

The example illustrates the many learning situations that are possible through role play: modeling, rehearsal, insight into another's and one's own behavior, as well as the use of the technique to take advantage of the learning resources that one family member (the father in this case) can provide another (the son) (see chapter 2). The grid displayed in the table is itself a useful device for laying out the role play possibilities in a case. As can be seen, only a fraction of the possible combinations were utilized, and, of course, three-person role plays involving all the participants could also have been used. The grid also is helpful in locating another important element in a role play, the observer. Who is observing and what that person may be learning becomes increasingly important as the number of family members attending a session increases.

In the post-task discussion, an attempt is made to augment experiential learning by calling attention to aspects of the interaction that might help illuminate the problem or that might suggest steps toward solving it. The clients' thoughts or feelings attendant upon carrying out the roles of another may be explained as a way of helping them gain awareness of what it is like to be in those positions. The following example illustrates the use of discussion following role play as well as additional facets of the techniques as a whole.

Because some unexpected company dropped by, Mrs. Albert felt she could not keep her prior commitment to take her four-teen-year-old daughter, Katie, shopping for jeans. Expecting that Katie should realize that their plans could not be carried out, the mother grew increasingly annoyed at her daughter's nagging about when they were to leave. Finally, Mrs. Albert told Katie to get out, which she preceded to do, slamming doors on the way.

When they began to discuss the incident a few days later in the session, the practitioner asked them to role play what happened, which they did. In the post-task discussion they were able to identify obstacles that had prevented resolution of their con-flict. To the practitioner's questions, Mrs. Albert acknowledged that she had unwittingly expected her daughter to "read her mind," and that she had been vague about if they could go. Both saw that they could have explored the possibility of going an-other time.

They then role-played the scene again. Mrs. Albert stated her position more clearly and suggested another time. Katie ac-cepted her mother's position, and they negotiated an alternative date. The post-task discussion focused on identifying skills dis-played during the role play—for example, making positions clear and exploring alternatives. In the process Mrs. Albert com-mented she often expected her kids to "know what I'm thinking." The example also illustrates the use of successive role plays, with the second used to correct problems suggested by the first.

Family Sculpting

Like role play, family sculpting involves an imaginative leave-taking from the immediate realities of the session. If role play-ing reminds us of acting in a play, then sculpting suggests panto-mime or perhaps ballet. Essentially, the technique requires family members to use nonverbal means to express their thoughts and feelings about family members or family relations

(Simon 1972; Duhl, Kantor, and Duhl 1973; Papp, Silverstein, and Carter 1973; Papp 1976; Constantine 1978; Jefferson 1978). A family member (the sculptor) is asked to construct "a live family portrait placing members together in terms of posture and spatial relationships representing actions and feelings" (Papp, Silverstein, and Carter 1973:202). As Simon (1972) has pointed out, sculpting is an extension of what the family members do naturally when they distribute themselves in a seating pattern at the beginning of the session.

The literature on family sculpting presents dramatic examples of this technique. In one case, a father spatialized his position in the family by arranging himself, wife, and children on the floor and demonstrating how he was "swimming upstream in the mud" with the rest of the family in tow (Papp, Silverstein, and Carter 1973). In another case, a mother surrounded herself with physical objects representing children, husband, dogs, school, job, etc. and had them shout at her: "Give me this! Give me that! Take care of me!" (Jefferson 1978:74).

Family sculpting may serve both diagnostic and therapeutic functions, often simultaneously. Although it may be used as the primary means of conducting treatment, in the present approach it is offered as a type of session task for use in certain situations. It is probably most helpful as an alternative means of communication when language fails. The communication function of language may be impaired for any number of reasons: language may be used as a weapon in hostile interchanges; as a means of defense, denial, or obfuscation; or simply not used very much or very well, as in the case of children or taciturn members. When words seem to be failing, it may make sense to shift to a more kinesic (physical) form of communication. By putting communication in a new channel, new opportunities for expression may be opened up and new insights gained. Even if the sculpture itself is relatively unproductive, it may seem to break up a verbal impasse.

The sculpture may take the form of a single task involving one family member as sculptor, or of a task sequence in which different family members take the role of sculptor in turn. Paradoxically, shifting to the physical may provide more meaningful discussion among family members than had taken place before

the sculpting began. If it appears to be productive, verbal interaction can be encouraged. Following conclusion of the task or
task sequence, the practitioner can elicit insights family members may have gained and can offer her own comments.

Although an action-oriented technique, a major function of
sculpting is to provide family members with a fresh perspective
on their relationships. In the hands of one skilled in its use,
sculpting may be able to achieve breakthroughs that even good
verbal communication cannot attain. For practitioners lacking
such skills, a more conservative application is suggested, though
the technique may be considered when verbal communication
appears to be getting nowhere. Language (together with paralanguage) is a powerful, efficient, and versatile means of communicating thoughts and feelings. If a mother can readily put
into words her feeling that she is being pulled in opposite directions by her husband and child, little is gained by having husband yanking at one arm and her child at the other. If she
cannot, the physical expression may be extremely valuable.

Positive Exchange

In this task, which may be quite brief, each participant is asked,
in turn, to describe things about the other that he or she likes or
considers to be positive. The practitioner should prompt until
two or three attributes are mentioned by a participant. A
positive exchange task is a useful means of "breaking up" long
runs of mutual derogation that may be blocking constructive
work on problems, if not exacerbating conflict.

In the follow-up, the practitioner attempts to relate positive
attributes expressed to the problem at hand. If this is not possible, she simply makes the point that it is good for family members to look at positives in one another when dealing with
problems.

Planning Exchanges of Positive Actions

This task grows out of a sizable amount of research and clinical
experience in behavioral approaches to marital and family therapy (Jacobson and Margolin 1979; Stuart 1980). In the present

adaptation, participants are asked in turn to request a number of specific changes from one another. The requests sould involve actions that can be done immediately and should be stated in specific matter-of-fact terms. As Stuart (1980) suggests, they should not be the "subject of recent intense conflict" (p. 191). In structuring the task, the practitioner asks participants to agree to do accepted requests before the next session, or regularly until then if they involve recurrent actions. She gives examples of requests that might be appropriate, pointing out that they should be at about the same level of difficulty (I would appreciate it if Doug could use his headset when listening to music," or "I would like Dad to fix my bike.").

The participant of whom the requests are made may ask for clarification if necessary, and then indicate whether or not there are any that he or she would not be willing to do. Rejected requests can be replaced until each participant has agreed to at least two.

The practitioner serves as a recorder. In the follow-up the practitioner may ask for further specification herself, to make sure that requests and agreements are clearly understood, or may suggest that certain requests be modified, usually scaled down, to help ensure that they actually will be done.

In behavioral approaches, procedures of this type are part of a larger intervention strategy—for example, love days (Weiss 1975) or caring days (Stuart 1980)—which often are used at the beginning of therapy to promote quick positive change. In the present model, which is directed at defined problems, positive action exchange has a more specialized role. It may provide a useful initial task in situations where it has not been possible to come to closure on specific target problems but where there is agreement that general relationship difficulties are an issue. The task also may fit interpersonal problems that remain defined at a fairly global level or that take on a more general shape as treatment proceeds, particularly if work on specific conflicts becomes stalled. (See also "Reciprocal Tasks," chapter 7.)

Planning Mutually Enjoyable Activities

A problem may consist in part of a lack of mutually satisfying interactions between family members. Typical situations are spouses in ruts of child care, home projects, or career interests that somehow have squeezed the fun out of their lives or parents (increasingly mothers as well as fathers) who are too busy with their work to spend time with their children. Sometimes the problem is not defined in this way but there is a need to bring about satisfying, constructive interaction as a means of resolving other issues. For example, a father and his teenage son may be embarked in conflict about such staples as the son's use of the car, drinking, and choice of friends. Exploration reveals that they engage in no recreational activities together, although they once did and still have these common interests. A renewal of some shared activities might help strengthen their relationship bonds, which in turn might make it easier for them to handle conflict.

The task should be set at a point in the session when the atmosphere is relatively free of tension. The practitioner gives a rationale for the task and some examples of what might be developed, and sees if the participants are interested in giving it a try.

Following the task, the practitioner helps the clients plan whatever home tasks are required to carry out the activities agreed upon. If the clients fail to agree on an activity, the session task is terminated before tension develops between the participants. The practitioner attempts to elicit possible activities of common interest and, if any are found, structures another planning task. (See also "Shared Tasks," chapter 7.)

Modifying Communication Problems

Specific difficulties in face-to-face communication may be target problems, or may arise as obstacles to problem solving. For example, participants may continually interrupt one another: one may tend to monopolize the conversation while the other responds with "put downs," and so on. For various reasons, such as the press of substantive problems, skills training may not be indicated. A remedial effort can be made by first identifying the difficulty, and then structuring a task in which participants are instructed to communicate without engaging in the interactions identified. If the communication difficulty is a target problem, the content of what the participants communicate about is secondary as long as it involves an issue likely to give rise to the difficulty. In structuring the task, it is usually good practice to identify the difficulty as interactional (interrupting one another) or as two-fold (he monopolizes, she is accusatory) in order to preserve a balance of responsibility in the task.

In the follow-up the practitioner can critique the participants' task implementation, giving emphasis to positive aspects of their performance and suggesting, if needed, how it might be improved. Other techniques such as modeling and role play, discussed earlier in conjunction with skills training, can be used. A case example conducted within a task-centered framework can be found in Tolson (1977).

Tasks Affecting Alliances

When the interview involves at least three family members, session tasks can be used to affect alliances or triangles that may be interfering with work on problems, or that may be targeted as problems in their own right. For example, work on a generic problem-solving task involving parents and their adolescent daughter, concerning her educational plans, may reveal a tendency for the mother to "speak for the daughter" and to be subtly critical of any suggestions the father might make. The apparent mother/daughter coalition may be blocking progress on the problem and may, in addition, be causing the father to feel left out, hence likely to sabotage whatever plan might be arrived at.

In such situations the family member "left out" can be "brought in" through tasks in which he or she works with one member of the coalition. In the example given father and daughter could be asked to work on the problem themselves, with the mother put in the role of an observer. The task could be set up on the basis of giving the father and daughter a chance to exchange views directly for a while, since this seems too difficult for them to do with the three of them talking. Or the parents could be asked to work out an agreement on some aspect of the problem with the daughter playing the role of an observer. An alternative approach is to continue with the same participants but to structure the next task in ways that weaken coalitional patterns.

Thus, the mother might be instructed to let her daughter speak for herself, with the practitioner providing corrective feedback if this instruction is not followed.

Shifts in seating arrangements can be used to accentuate boundaries that are part of the process of developing alliances. For example, the father and mother might be asked to sit next to one another to carry out the task mentioned in the illustration above. Or the practitioner can physically suggest a boundary by shifting her seat between two task participants and an observing third.

These tasks generally involve multiple functions. In the example given, problem solving is carried on at one level; at another, the patterns of alliance are being affected. As noted, if a change in patterns of alliance had been previously clarified as a goal, these multiple functions need not be taken up. They can be if their clarification would help family members proceed more effectively with the task or learn more from its results.

Exploring Hidden Agendas

Joint problem-solving efforts may become stalled because of a participant's "hidden agenda"—that is, perceptions, feelings, beliefs, and the like that are not expressed but are nevertheless influential. The result is often a form of pseudo-problem-solving that leads nowhere, because logical solutions are foreclosed by the hidden agenda.

Susan had promised her mother to bring her new boyfriend over to meet her. In a session task to plan the visit, the two could not seem to agree on how this should be done—when, where, how long, under what circumstances, etc. For every suggestion the mother had, Susan had a reason why it wouldn't work. Suspecting a hidden agenda on Susan's part, the practitioner terminated the task and suggested that the two of them (the practitioner and Susan) explore the situation a bit while the mother listened. Knowing some of Susan's past difficulty with her mother around boyfriends, the practitioner explored Susan's feelings about what might happen on the visit. Susan acknowledged her fears that her mother would be critical of her choice and revealed some details about the young man that she had withheld from her mother. It was now possible to have Susan and her mother discuss Susan's apprehensions about her mother's reactions.

The practitioner-client session task just illustrated was suggested by Birchler and Spinks (1981) as a means of exploring hidden agendas that may impede problem solving. In some cases, hidden agendas can be revealed by clarifying positions or by the practitioner's inquiry during post-task intervention. When the agenda items are well hidden, however, more sustained exploration may be necessary.

7. *Home and Environmental Tasks*

Actions planned in the treatment session to be carried out between sessions are widely used in family therapy. They appear under many labels: tasks, homework, directives, behavioral assignments, exchanges, and contracts, to name some of them. In many therapy models, they take on the critical function of translating contemplated changes growing out of the treatment session into realities in the lives of family members. In the present model, all these out-of-session actions are referred to as home and environmental tasks. In this chapter, I shall consider varieties of such tasks, their functions and limitations in treatment, and methods of planning and implementing them.

HOME TASKS

Home tasks are actions usually carried out by family members in the home setting. Although these tasks may involve the environment, emphasis is on what one family member does vis-à-vis other family members (so that others can use the phone, Sarah will limit her calls to her boyfriend to fifteen minutes). In an environmental task, on the other hand, an attempt is made to change (or extract something from) the environment of the family. (Mr. J will contact the school principal to request that Rick's homeroom be changed. Mrs. A will try to obtain a part-time job.) Tasks involving family members and others close to the family, such as friends and relatives, fall in a gray area and can be referred to by either designation.

Classification of Home Tasks

The most important way of categorizing home tasks is in terms of the interrelations among tasks of different family members. Tasks can be put on a continuum ranging from high to low degrees of interconnectedness. At the high end are tasks so closely interwoven that they can be seen as single, *shared* tasks undertaken by all members of a family or by certain family members working together. For example, a family will go on an outing; a husband and wife will work out a budget. Although it is understood that each family member will have a part to play in the task, individual actions are not specified. At a middle level of interrelationship are *reciprocal* tasks, in which actions of family members are reciprocated or exchanged. They may take the form of a balanced or symmetrical exchange of comparable actions (Gary will take care of the children on Saturday afternoons; Marcy will accompany Gary on a visit to his family on Sunday). Or they may involve an unbalanced or complementary exchange of actions, generally between parents and children. Usually the behavior of the child is matched by rewards or sanctions (Sarah will come home promptly after school; each day she does she will be credited with fifty cents toward purchase of a personal stereo set; each day she fails to she will not be allowed to watch TV in the evening). In either case, reciprocal tasks are tied together through an explicit bargain: If you do this, I will do that.

At the lowest level of interrelationship are *individual tasks*, which have no explicit connection with tasks undertaken by other family members. For example, a mother and daughter may do a set of reciprocal tasks to help resolve a conflict between them. Father may undertake an independent task related to another problem. Notions of reciprocity, or each contributing fairly to work on family problems, still apply to individual tasks, as shall be made clear subsequently. Each of these central types of home tasks will be examined in detail.

Shared Tasks

The most obvious use of shared tasks in the model is to provide a means for carrying out at-home problem-solving and communication tasks worked on in the session. Such session tasks, which are also shared, can be continued at home. A simple continuation can be used to complete a task begun in the session. For example, in an initial session task, a mother and her teenage son began to work out what the son might be reasonably expected to do to care for his handicapped younger brother after school. They agreed to finish the task at home. Or shared tasks can be structured to enable participants to work on an additional aspect of a problem, or to practice new ways of communicating that they have begun to work on in the session. Generally an agreement is reached to devote a certain amount of time to the task. What the participants are to try to accomplish is worked out; exactly when and where the task is to be done may be set. The participants may be asked to tape-record the task and bring the tape to the following session. A replay of the tape in the session can serve as a task review and a point of departure for further work.

Shared tasks also may be used to help family members work on practical problems or projects in which joint efforts make sense—house repairs or improvements, looking for a new car or residence, helping a child with homework. Tasks of this kind can be planned in the session, but unlike problem-solving and communication tasks, cannot be undertaken there. The intent here is to use a shared task simply as the most sensible way of getting a job done. Emphasis in this function is on the content of the task.

Finally, shared tasks can be used to affect relationships between family members. Emphasis here is not so much on the content of the task but rather on the process and its implications for the interaction between participants. A shared task, particularly if it is mutually meaningful or enjoyable to both, can serve as a way of bringing family members closer together or of increasing their involvement with each other. Marital partners, for example, may be interested in lessening distance between them, but each is reluctant to make the first move. A shared task instigated by the practitioner but shaped by the couple into concrete form—a trip together, an evening out, and so on—may provide the necessary bridge. The form of the task may resemble the kind of project discussed above, but the purpose differs. A father and son might work together to repair the son's bike. The goal is not bike repair—quite possibly the father, or son, could do the job more efficiently by himself—but rather to give them an opportunity to interact.

Bringing family members closer together through shared tasks can be done with the purpose of affecting family coalitions and boundaries. Suppose Mrs. L's overinvolvement with her handicapped daughter Nancy is an obstacle to Nancy's successful participation in a rehabilitation program. Shared tasks might be used to involve the mother with her husband, and the daughter with an older sibling who might be a source of helpful support. Sister, rather than mother, might help Nancy with her physical therapy exercise while Mr. and Mrs. L work on a yard project.

Finally, shared tasks can be addressed simultaneously to target problems and contextual change. As Mills (1985) has demonstrated in a thoughtful analysis of task-centered work with a marital couple, home tasks involving structured discussions, learning how to "fight fairly" (Bach and Wyden 1981), and "dating" can be used both to alleviate specific target problems, such as quarreling and lack of mutually enjoyable activities, as well as to bring about changes in basic rules (metarules) governing the couple's relationships.

Reciprocal Tasks

The first type of reciprocal task, involving a balanced or symmetrical exchange of actions, is equivalent to the quid pro quo contract that has been used extensively in behavioral marital treatment. *Symmetrical tasks* are generally used between adults who have claim to more or less equal status in a relationship. The actions exchanged need not be equal, but each participant needs to feel that he or she is receiving an adequate payoff under the circumstances.

A wife resentful at having carried what she thinks has been an excessive load of domestic and child care responsibilities has become increasingly less affectionate and more withdrawn toward her husband, who now is anxious to bring about a thaw in their relationship. He begins to see some justice in his wife's complaints. Under these circumstances the wife, who feels more wronged than the husband, may demand and get more in the exchange. The exchange may still be thought of as "psychologically balanced," in that the wife is getting repaid for past debts. Thus the husband happily may agree to take over a major household chore in exchange for his wife's agreement to resume their habit of having a predinner cocktail together. Exchanges then need to be framed within the context of the participants' perceived obligations and entitlements (chapter 4), not simply in terms of what might seem to be "fair" on the surface. As Tsoi-Hammond (1976) has suggested, in some situations participants may demand too much or have too little commitment to the relationship to permit meaningful exchanges of any kind to occur. Individual rather than reciprocal tasks may need to be used, at least until some basis for a task exchange has been established.

Questions of who goes first, or what happens when one participant does not do his or her part, inevitably arise in setting up or carrying out reciprocal tasks. These issues take on added importance when participants are mistrustful of one another, as is often the case. The question of "who starts" can be settled in the session in which the task is planned. In some cases, the issue of initiation is built into the task: a wife agrees to accompany her husband on a visit to his relatives if he will finish a house repair project. Often, however, the initiation process is not clear from the basic exchange. Joanne agrees to pick up the kids' toys in the living room and on the front porch if Kirk will agree to have a conversation with her about his "day" as soon as he comes home. In this example, it would be important to determine, by flipping a coin if necessary, who makes the first move and when this is to happen.

The problem of possible failure of one participant to live up to his or her part of the bargain can be addressed by encouraging each to give the other at least a second chance, or both partners can agree as part of the bargain that they will try the exchange a second time, perhaps with the time specified, if the first "cycle" does not work for any reason (Lester, Beckham, and Baucom 1980).

Reciprocal tasks often involve expressive actions whose value can be undercut if carried out in a perfunctory or subtly hostile manner. The husband in the example above could make a travesty of his conversational task in any number of ways. If this kind of reaction seems to be a possibility, it may be useful to employ a procedure suggested by Azrin, Naster, and Jones (1973)—to suggest that each participant do the task in a way that he or she thinks would please the other person. This method offers a simpler and probably better guideline, given the knowledge family members usually have about one another's likes and dislikes, than trying to work out specific "performance criteria," which also can be undermined. This task structure assumes that participants' intentions toward one another will be good enough to make the task work. Not a great deal can be done in the planning process to insure this (see Task Planning, below).

Thus far in our discussion, reciprocal tasks have been limited to exchange of one specified action for another. Making use of Stuart's ideas of "caring days" and the "holistic contract" (1980), it is possible to design reciprocal task plans involving exchanges of a larger number of actions. In the present adaptation, participants are asked in turn to request a number of specific changes from one another. The participant of whom the request is made may ask for clarification and then indicate whether or not there are any that he or she would not be willing to do. Rejected requests can be replaced until each partner agrees to do several. The practitioner may ask for further specification to make sure that requests and agreements are clearly understood, or may suggest that certain requests be modified, usually scaled down, to make sure that they actually will be done. She then records the final task lists, giving copies to the participants. The following lists were generated by Sally and Harriet, two women living together, each with children from former marriages.

Sally's Tasks	*Harriet's Tasks*
1. To keep Kevin (her son) from hitting Debbie (Harriet's daughter).	1. To tell Sally when Kevin is doing something wrong rather than yelling at him.

2. To pick up Kevin's toys at night.

2. To put her own breakfast dishes in the dishwasher before she leaves for work.

3. To get the second TV set repaired.

3. To tell Laurie, her daughter, to get off the phone when Sally needs to make a business call.

Enough task possibilities should be generated to permit flexibility and avoid focus on any one. Stuart (1980) recommends as many as eighteen for each partner. The participants attempt to do as many of the tasks as they can. Planning can also be done through a session task format—planning exchanges of positive actions (Chapter 6).

This kind of plan, as Stuart suggests, avoids some of the problems that have been considered in relation to single-task requirements for each participant. Because both participants agree to do as many tasks as they can, issues of who goes first and what happens when a task is not done, or not done "correctly," are less likely to arise. Multiple-task exchanges may be indicated in situations where it has not been possible to come to closure on specific target problems, but where there is agreement that a variety of relationship difficulties or problems of living together are at issue. Or the plan may be useful when progress on specific problems becomes stalled. Obviously, one sacrifices whatever advantages there may be in focusing on single problems and tasks, which include opportunity to make more progress in areas of greatest concern, as well as greater clarity and specificity in respect to problems and related tasks.

Although symmetrical exchanges are generally used with adults, as the examples have suggested, they can be applied with little modification to sibling relationships within a family or to relationships between parents and adult children. Their use is more limited as a means of alleviating conflict between parents and adolescents or younger children. Understandably, parents are reluctant to enter into exchanges with children as if everyone were of equal status and, moreover, this task structure may complicate goals of attempting to reinforce parental authority.

However, under certain circumstances, balanced exchanges between parents and children can be used to advantage. One occasion is when a parent and child, often an adolescent, are involved in a coercively symmetrical struggle, and efforts to bring about a benign complementary relationship have failed or appear futile. The very idea of parental authority may have become a red flag for the child, and the parent may be locked into a pattern of increasingly punitive reactions. It may make sense to step out of an authority framework and have parents and children negotiate changes in each other's behaviors. To parents who may be reluctant to trade such exchanges with their children, it can be pointed out that they no longer have any effective control over them, and perhaps this may be a step toward getting some back. Such situations fit well the observation of Morawetz and Walker (1984) that "the establishment of reciprocal tasks helps the therapist create order out of chaos" (p. 100).

In one project, for example (Bass 1977), children who had run away from home were encouraged to present to their parents the changes they wanted as a condition of staying at home. Parents in turn presented to their children what they wanted changed. Negotiations produced reciprocal tasks, which often led to children agreeing to obey rules in exchange for parent's agreements to change their behavior toward them (Daughter to mother: "You have to tell me what you want yourself, not let others do it," Mother to daughter: "You have to do your share of the chores around the house."). As the example suggests, parent-child negotiation of quid pro quo exchanges may turn out to be similar in result to reciprocal tasks involving parental management of contingencies, discussed later.

Research on the effectiveness of reciprocal tasks of the symmetrical variety has focused largely on their use with marital pairs within the context of behavioral treatment. Most experiments have compared couples treated by contracting approaches (reciprocal tasks) with those receiving communications/problem solving training or no treatment.

In a controlled study, Jacobson (1978) compared two treatments in which couples received problem-solving training and a form of contracting, either quid pro quo or "good faith" (Weiss, Birchler, and Vincent 1974), against a control group which received a nonspecific form of treatment. The treatment groups surpassed the control group on outcome measures but not each other, leading Jacobson to speculate that problem-solving training, which both treatment groups had in common, was the "primary active ingredient." An alternative explanation would be that both forms of contracting were equally effective.

In two other random allocation studies, O'Leary and Turkewitz (1981) and Russell et al. (1984) compared contracting and communications training approaches against a wait-list control. In both studies treatment groups were found to be superior to the control groups on measures of change in marital problems and communication patterns. Of particular interest in the first study were differential effects relating to the age of the couple. For younger couples, contracting appeared to be more effective; for older couples, the communications approach worked better. Younger couples, according to the authors, might have responded relatively better to the contracting approach because of greater flexibility in their relationships. In neither study were there general differences in effectiveness between the treatments.

In perhaps the most ambitious study to appear to date on the relative effectiveness of these different approaches, Baucom (1982) randomly assigned seventy-two maritally distressed couples to four alternative conditions: problem-solving/communications training plus contracting, problem-solving/communications training only, contracting only, and a wait-list control group. Each approach was found to be generally superior on the outcome measures (which included standardized self-reports and observational measures of couple interaction) to the wait-list controls. Although there were no significant differences between the treatment groups, the groups receiving problem-solving/communications training did do somewhat better in reducing negative communication than the contracting-only group. The latter finding is not surprising in view of the emphasis placed on communication training in those groups. It also should be noted that the group experiencing the most change in communication variables was the one that received both communications training and contracting.

The research reviewed suggests that reciprocal tasks offer promising means of reducing marital conflict, although this approach has not been adequately tested with seriously distressed couples or with other dyads. Also little data have been accumulated on the duration of effects over time. As yet no clear differences in effectiveness between contracting and communications approaches have emerged. There is some evidence from Baucom (1982) to suggest the effects of these two approaches used in combination may be stronger than either used in isolation. This notion has received support from a recent controlled (multiple baseline) study involving two distressed couples (Bornstein et al. 1983). A combination of both approaches brought about significant changes in negative aspects of the interactions of both couples, changes that were maintained during a year follow-up period.

To these studies, one can add the Southampton experiment (Gibbons et al. 1978) discussed earlier (chapter 3). Although reciprocal tasks were not used uniformly in that study, they did constitute a major treatment method (Butler, Bow, and Gibbons 1978). Measures of change significantly favored the experimental group a year following treatment. Moreover, the study involved a test of reciprocal tasks within the framework of the task-centered model.

The second major grouping of reciprocal tasks consists of exchanges based on the premise of a complementary relationship. One family member, normally a parent, occupies an authority position, and the other, normally a child, is in a subordinate position. The child agrees to act in conformity to certain rules; the parent's reciprocal task is to monitor the child's behavior and to provide appropriate rewards and sanctions. Normally, the use of such *complementary tasks* combines principles of parent training, in which the parent essentially manages, under the practitioner's guidance, the contingencies of the child's behavior (chapter 8) with the negotiating-contracting methods that have been considered thus far. Unlike conventional parent training, the parent and child work out agreements together, but unlike the first type of reciprocal task, the exchanges are between a superior and subordinate in a hierarchy.

Exchanges of this kind have been widely used with families where issues of parental control of children have been salient (Tharp and Wetzel 1969; Stuart 1971; Alexander and Parsons 1973; Alexander and Barton 1980; Gant et al. 1981). These tasks can be used for a variety of home problems, including parent-child conflict and difficulties in sibling interaction, as well as for problems the child may be having in certain community settings, such as school. At the same time they are designed to help parents exercise more effective and humane control over the behavior of their children and to provide children with the opportunity to have some say about the rules they are expected to follow. They can serve as a means of putting parents back in charge while avoiding excesses of parental authority. Some examples will illustrate the variety possible in simpler task designs and will serve as points of reference in subsequent discussion of principles of task planning.

Mrs. A agrees to let Jennifer watch TV after her regular bedtime for as long as she spends on her math homework, up to half-an-hour.

Barry agrees to be home from school by 4 p.m. to look after his younger brother until his mother gets home from work at 5:15. Every day he does this he will get five points; every day he fails to, five points will be deducted. For twenty-five points he can have an extra trip to the movies.

Cindy will not push, kick, or hit her sister. At the end of each day she does not she will have a dish of her favorite ice cream for dessert. If she does so more than once in a day, she will not be allowed to watch TV that day.

Dave will be allowed to use the car Saturday night if he makes his payment for the extra cost of the insurance by Thursday.

Whenever possible, rewards for task compliance are emphasized over sanctions, as the examples illustrate. Concrete rewards in the form of privileges, money, food treats, and so on may be earned directly or through accumulation of points (Barry). Following basic principles of operant learning, the interval between task compliance and the corresponding reward should not be too long.

Lengthy or demanding task performance should not be required for some large reward—for example, parents' promising to give a boy who is constantly being sent out of class a minibike if he is not sent out once during the next three months. If one large reward would be a strong motivation, as is often true of adolescents, it can be worked toward through point systems, with some intermediate cash-in provisions for lesser rewards.

When sanctions or penalties are used, it is preferable that they take the form of response costs rather than punishments. With response costs the child loses something of value, points earned (Barry) or a privilege (Cindy). With punishment, something aversive is added to the child's situation—extra chores, for example. As a rule, response costs are easier to enforce and are less likely to provoke counterproductive anger and resentment.

In task planning, the practitioner attempts to help the parent(s) and child arrive at a mutually acceptable exchange. It is important that the participants agree explicitly to the terms. It should be determined that rewards do in fact constitute an adequate incentive for the children and are not viewed as excessive by the parents. Penalties should be seen as fair by the child. How the child's performance is to be monitored, which is generally part of the parents' task, needs to be clarified.

Several potential limitations and obstacles encountered within planning or review stages need to be kept in mind. Although parents usually are willing to become involved in setting up tasks for their children, and have no trouble thinking up penalties for noncompliance, they may balk at the idea of giving rewards on grounds that the child should be doing these things anyway, that rewards are a form of bribery, or that the child's siblings also will expect to get some payoff for good behavior. Such concerns need to be dealt with carefully. It can be pointed out that the rewards are part of a time-limited therapeutic program. Their purpose is to bring about immediate change, not necessarily to set a permanent pattern. Often, siblings can be brought into the reward system if questions of favoritism arise. Task designs that provide small rewards for "good behavior," but stiff penalties for noncompliance, or that tolerate some degree of noncompliance may satisfy some parents yet still may be seen by children as an improvement over the harsh or capricious parental punishment they would otherwise expect. Verbal reinforcement for compliance in the form of praise or expressions of approval (which ideally should be a part of the parents' tasks in any case) may provide enough incentive, even if not accompanied by tangible rewards.

Complementary tasks require that parents have control of resources their children want or that they can successfully impose sanctions as a way of influencing their children's behavior. Often it is hard for parents to meet these requirements. Parents already may have satisfied their children with tangible rewards in unsuccessful efforts to control their behavior. They have little more to offer that children would find strongly motivating. Delinquent youth pose a particular challenge. The observations of Alexander and Barton (1980) apply to many youngsters in this category: "parents have only slightly more control over the adolescents than the adolescents have over the parents. It can be argued, of course, that parents still maintain control over the basic reinforcers (money, food, shelter, etc.), but even these reinforcers become incredibly nonsalient in situations where teenagers simply refuse to be reinforced by them, and develop alternatives through such means as running away or developing their own sources of income" (p. 58). Through a careful elicitation of what such youth want from their parents, some points of remaining parental leverage may be found. Symmetrical exchanges, as discussed above, may work in some cases. Sometimes independent tasks focusing on the youths' own problems, in combination with environmental tasks, may present the best options.

Because complementary exchanges generally lead to a greater exercise of parental authority over the child's behavior, their use may be contradicted with older adolescents who are struggling to secure greater freedom from parents who already may be heavily involved in their lives. The need for autonomy may override whatever rewards or sanctions the parents can give and, perhaps of greater significance, the process of monitoring, rewarding, and sanctioning behavior can result in magnifying the sort of parental oversight the adolescent is trying to be free of. If the adolescent openly rejects and refuses to budge, then there is little choice but to consider other strategies. Often the case is not this clear-cut, however. Adolescents may go through processes of negotiating exchanges with their parents but then fail to perform tasks agreed on. If needs for approval from parents or the practitioner also are strong, noncompliance may be expressed in subtle ways or covered up with deceptive maneuvers. If they are used, complementary exchanges may need to be designed to allow adolescents sufficient autonomy. For example, in one case a teenage girl was able to accept her mother's limits regarding a curfew in exchange for removal of restrictions about friends she would associate with while she was out. The removal of a restriction was preferable to a reward. As with seriously acting-out youngsters, more emphasis may need to be placed on symmetrical and individual tasks.

An examination of research relating to complementary tasks will give a sense of the empirical basis of this intervention strategy. The research also provides additional varieties of the forms and uses of the strategy. Perhaps the most concentrated and rigorous testing of this approach has been carried out by Stuart and associates in their studies of behavioral contracting with delinquents and their families (Stuart 1971; Stuart and Lott 1972; Stuart and Tripodi 1973, Stuart et al. 1976). The behavioral contracts evaluated in these studies fit the concept of complementary tasks; contracts involved exchanges of privileges (rewards) for responsibilities (actions). Provisions were made for sanctions for noncompliance, but also bonuses (extra rewards) for compliance at a high level. As Stuart (1971) describes them, contracts tended to be fairly comprehensive, covering several areas of interaction between youth and their parents. Exchanges involved behavior of the adolescents not only at home but also at school. Performance at school, which covered deportment as well as academic work, was tracked by daily report cards signed by teachers.

In the major controlled test of this strategy, families randomly assigned to either experimental (n = 57) or control conditions (n = 45) were compared. The principal treatment component in the experimental program was the kind of contracting described. Results significantly favored the experimental group on most measures of adult (teacher and parent) evaluations of the youth's behavior, but differences were not large and were not found in respect to grades and attendance. Further analysis revealed that treatment effects were stronger for younger children (ten-to-twelve-year-olds) and low-income families. Lack of teacher cooperation in effecting the school note or report card system was cited as one reason for failure to demonstrate a treatment effect on grades. Follow-up at the end of a year based on a portion of the sample (Stuart 1974) suggested that gains achieved by the treated families were likely to attenuate. In their concluding statement, Stuart et al. (1976) pointed to the need to make "contracting a part of a more comprehensive intervention package that includes techniques aimed at modifying communication patterns within the family, academic skill building at school, and improving peer experiences for the adolescent" (p. 260).

In other controlled studies, complementary tasks involving parents and children have been part of larger intervention strategies. In an experiment reported by Alexander and Parsons (1973), court-referred delinquent adolescents and their families were randomly assigned to a short-term behavioral intervention program (n = 46), a client-centered family group program (n = 19); a psychodynamic family treatment program (n = 11). The behavioral treatment in family sessions emphasized communication training designed to "modify the family communication patterns in the direction of greater clarity and precision, increased reciprocity, and presentation of alternative solutions." The purpose of this approach was "to constitute a pattern of contingency designed to modify maladaptive patterns and institute more adaptive behaviors" (p. 473).

The principal outcome measure was recidivism of the referred adolescents during a six- to eighteen-month interval following treatment. Cases receiving the experimental program had a recidivism rate of 26 percent, half that for the alternative treatment programs, the control group, and the county as a whole. Moreover, the experimentals had better results than other groups on measures of communication processes, and the more successful experimental cases did better on these measures than the less successful experimental cases.

Although the study does not isolate the contribution of complementary tasks, it provides evidence for their efficacy as part of a broader intervention approach in which communication and negotiation in the session were stressed. Because this combination of intervention makes up the core of the task-centered approach, the study provides general support for that model, as well as for others sharing features of the program evaluated. In that respect it is interesting to note that this single study has been cited as evidence of the effectiveness of three other presumably distinct family therapy approaches: Wells (1981) viewed it as evidence for behavioral methods; Stanton (1981b), as supporting strategic family therapy; and Barton and Alexander (1981), as underpinning functional family therapy, a model derived from the study itself. Although it is amusing to see that success begets popularity here as elsewhere, the approach tested does contain elements that appear in each model that has used it to support its case.

Another controlled study demonstrating the effectiveness of programs in which complementary tasks were central features was conducted by Gant et al. (1981). A "multi-component behavioral, skill oriented" treatment program was built around a "home accounting system" (pp. 102–103). "Rewards (reinforcements) were identified and made contingent on the expression of desirable behavior. The loss of privileges—though used reluctantly and judiciously—was also utilized." The practitioners also encouraged parents "to increase their expressions of affection, to give more praise, to give appropriate rationales or reasons for their actions, to engage their children in dialog and negotiation, and to increase the level of feedback to their children" (p. 103). Treated court-referred families (n = 10) outperformed an equal number of equivalent control families on measures of family communication, though data on the effects of treatment on the youths' problems were not yet available.

A study reported by Polster and Pinkston (1979) made use of a complementary task structure: school notes, training in study skills, and self-management techniques in family treatment of pupil underachievement in a school social-work setting. The complementary tasks took the form of a token economy in which students earned points for academic achievement and home study. The points could be cashed in for rewards negotiated by the parents and children. School notes were used to inform parents about the child's progress and homework assignments. Students were taught how to acquire and retain information from reading assignments. In a subset of cases, monitoring procedures were placed under the management of students, with parents making only periodic checks. Random allocation procedures were used to form experimental (n = 12) and comparison (n = 26) groups of children in seventh and eighth grades. Experimental children achieved significantly better grades than children in the comparison group; children in the self-management variation did slightly better on grades than students in the variation, in which parents exercised greater control. Although some of the improvement in grades may have been an artifact of the teacher's involvement in the program, genuine effects appear to have been achieved.

This body of research suggests that complementary tasks are an effective means of helping parents and youth resolve problems relating to their interaction and to the youth's behavior. Given the recommendations by Stuart et al. (1976) and the findings of subsequent studies that in effect incorporated them, it can be argued that effects of complementary tasks are enhanced by attempts to alter communication and negotiation processes between parents and youth. Because studies of use of symmetrical tasks with marital couples seemed to point in a similar direction, one might conclude more generally that the effectiveness of any type of reciprocal task is augmented by in-session work on interaction among family members.

In summary a respectable empirical base can be found for a central strategy of the model—structured problem-solving communication among family members within the session followed by external tasks relating to the problems worked on. Intervention programs that have used some variation of this strategy have been among the more successful in effecting change, often demonstrably durable, in distressed families (Alexander and

Parsons 1973; Jacobson 1977, 1979; Robin 1981; Baucom 1982; Bornstein et al. 1983). Given the variations among programs tested, however, it is hard to make more precise generalizations. It is not yet clear, for example, how much of their effectiveness is due to helping family members learn specific communication and problem solving skills as opposed to enabling them to solve actual problems. Moreover the significance of associated changes in ways family members may perceive or interact with one another is still poorly understood.

Individual Tasks

The essential characteristics of an individual task is that the performance by one family member is not tied in any explicit way to the task performance of another family member. When done in the home setting, individual tasks can provide opportunities for family members to take initiative in working on family problems; a family member may offer to take on added chores to work on a problem. The tasks may be useful, if not critical, regardless of their motivation—a sense of responsibility, altruism, guilt, or whatever. Shared and reciprocal task structures do not allow for such individualistic, volunteer efforts, which are, of course, very much a part of family life. Although family members expect that their contributions to the family's welfare will be reciprocated at some point, they are more likely to expect reciprocation to occur in the long run rather than the short run (chapter 4).

The practitioner may well want to take advantage of voluntary initiatives and to encourage their development. On the other hand, the practitioner must be careful about suggesting individual tasks. They may be interpreted by clients as unfair requests unless other family members also have tasks to do. If other family members have agreed to do shared or reciprocal tasks, then individual tasks can often be conveniently used to give the remaining members a "piece of the action."

At a more dynamic level, individual tasks serve the general function of preserving or promoting autonomy in family relations. When family members are not able to work effectively together because of a need to maintain distance or because of intense conflict, individual tasks can help each work on different aspects of the problem, perhaps as a means of laying the groundwork for more collaborative efforts. For example, in one case, a couple married twenty years was torn by conflicts that affected all aspects of their relationship as well as their relationships with their adolescent children. After attempts at shared and reciprocal tasks had failed, the husband and wife were each asked to come up with at least one thing they might do as individuals that would be of help to the family. Two individual tasks evolved from this exploration: the wife agreed to talk to her brother about his promise to wire the attic, and the husband agreed to have an old car in their yard hauled away for junk. The tasks, which they were able to do, served to get the couple moving in constructive directions and to demonstrate to themselves and to each other a degree of competence in family affairs. Unlike reciprocal tasks, one task was not exchanged for the other; each partner did something that he or she thought should be done, not something the other partner wanted. The fact that one partner's task produced a benefit for the family was noted by the other. The tasks became depositable in the "reciprocity bank account," which at the time appeared to have a negative balance.

Individual tasks of this kind incorporate "good faith" or "parallel" contracts developed by Weiss, Birchler, and Vincent (1974) for use in behavioral marital treatment. In parallel contracts each partner has his or her own task, with rewards and possibly penalties attached. For example, if the husband accompanies his wife on a visit to her mother on Sunday morning, he can watch an extra sports event on TV in the afternoon without negative comment from his wife. If he does not accompany the wife, he will not watch the extra event and agrees to scrub the laundry floor. If the wife calls the husband's mother to reestablish contact, she can buy a new pair of earrings. If she doesn't, she agrees to wash the car. A more straightforward exchange (husband will go with wife to her mother's, if she will call his) might be riskier if conflict around the issue were intense. The refusal of one partner to do the task would likely result in a corresponding refusal of the other partner; or if one partner followed through and the other did not, a good deal of resentment could result, possibly aggravating the conflict. The parallel structure avoids a head-on clash over the issue, and allows for the possibility of progress if only one partner does his or her task. Thus the wife might call her mother-in-law, find the task not so unpleasant, and enjoy her earrings. Consequently, she might not feel too resentful if her husband fails to go with her to visit her mother, particularly if he forgoes some Sunday TV and scrubs the floor. Seeing his wife and mother back on speaking terms, the husband may be more inclined to join his wife on her next visit.

Use of rewards and penalties may lead to some difficulties, however. They increase the complexity of the planning process and the task plan. More time must be invested in the former, and there are more opportunities for the latter to go awry. Moreover, some clients object to the "artificiality" of using rewards and penalties to influence their actions, or feel such schemes treat them like children. Although these objections often can be overcome by explaining that rewards and penalties simply are temporary devices to help them begin to change their behavior toward one another, the necessary discussion still takes time. As Weiss, Birchler, and Vincent (1974) suggest, this form of contract may be useful for couples who are too conflicted to engage in reciprocal exchanges, but one can add that if conflict occurs at too high a level, it may well engulf the implementation of rewards and penalties ("You call *that* scrubbing the floor!"). As a rule it is best to keep contingencies, if used at all, as simple as possible in individual tasks. Because rewards provide incentives, penalties tend to be gratuitous and can often be omitted.

The use of individual tasks in systems too conflicted for shared or reciprocal tasks can be extended to problems involving parents and children. As suggested earlier, youth who are overtly or continually rejecting parental authority may not accept complementary tasks, or may pay them lip service and then not comply with them. They may do individual tasks that will have some visible benefit for themselves. In these situations an effort should be made to help youth identify and articulate personal incentives for constructive actions. For example, an adolescent may be asked, possibly in an individual session, to state what he wants to achieve for himself, and tasks can be designed around his own goals, thus helping to break the pattern of reacting to perceived expectations of the parents. In the foregoing applications, individual tasks are used in situations in which an increase in collaborative effort is not possible. They can also serve to stimulate greater autonomy when involvement between family members is excessive.

A frequently encountered problem in the practice of medical social work is conflict between sick or disabled young people and their parents around autonomy issues. When the young person has a long-term, incapacitating medical problem, it is not unusual for parents to "come to the rescue" by taking over. The parents may assume responsibility for their offspring's financial affairs, social engagements, children, and so on. Help of this kind may be gratefully (or passively) accepted at first, but tensions are likely to develop as the young person tries to recapture some freedom of action, particularly in areas where the parents have always "known what was best" and are now trying to prove their point. Such cases may call for a series of individual tasks to enable the young person to resume functioning, and at the same time to demonstrate an ability to do so to the parents. The parents may be asked to do nothing or to do only what the young person asks them to do in the area being worked on. Thus in one case a young woman suffering from a kidney disease and associated blindness wanted to resume responsibility for caring of her infant son according to her own methods, and not her mother's. A graduated series of tasks was devised to this end, beginning with those the patient could do most readily without her mother's assistance.

Similar considerations apply when parents are in the dependent role, as may happen in family work with aged parents and adult children. As Rathbone-McCuan (1985) suggests, combinations of individual and shared tasks can be used to effect a balance between the older parent's need for autonomy and for family support.

In general, individual tasks provide one solution for excessively dependent relationships. They direct energies away from unwanted reliance on another into autonomous activity. Task requirements are based not on the expectations of the other but on the person's own goals and standards.

Finally, individual tasks provide a means of engaging members of the family who might be otherwise left out, or of balancing task responsibilities. It is not always necessary, of course, that all family members do tasks, but contextual considerations might suggest the wisdom of making sure that certain members of the family do them. For example, a problem may be centered on a mother-and-daughter relationship, and they undertake a reciprocal task to resolve it. At the same time it may be important for the father to demonstrate to the mother, who feels overburdened, his willingness to do something for her. So father agrees to undertake a home improvement project that mother very much wants. Such a move might also lay the basis for strengthening the parental relationship, which may facilitate solutions for the mother-daughter conflict.

Almost all of the research on the effectiveness of individual tasks has been conducted in relation to individual treatment in which such tasks are the norm. A number of controlled studies have suggested that individual tasks done both at home and in the environment are an effective means of bringing about change in a variety of individual and family problems (Reid 1975, 1978; Reid et al. 1980; Wodarski et al. 1982). One survey, limited to marital cases, found that individual tasks had somewhat better outcomes than reciprocal or shared tasks (Fortune 1977) in marital cases. This finding is perhaps not surprising, since reciprocal and shared tasks are more likely to relate to family conflicts where progress is harder to realize. As Rooney (1978) has observed, reciprocal tasks in such situations offset a high risk of failure with opportunity for substantial gain.

"Paradoxical" Tasks

The tasks considered thus far have been "straightforward" (Haley 1977) in the sense of constituting relatively obvious courses of action to solving problems. If two family members disagree about an issue, the usual straightforward task would call for them to negotiate their differences. Under certain circumstances, however, a practitioner might take a different tack.

For example, she might set up a task in which the family members would quarrel about the issue for a specified period of time. The connection between the task and problem solution is by no means clear. If the tasks were successful in resolving the problem, one might naturally say it accomplished its purpose in a "paradoxical" way.

Paradoxical tasks, variously called paradoxical directives or injunctions, have been extensively used and discussed in individual and family therapy (Haley 1963, 1977; Watzlawick and Fisch 1974; Madanes 1980; L'Abate and Weeks 1978, 1982). What is the nature of these tasks, and what place do they have in the present model?

Like many of the terms used in family therapy, paradox lacks precise meaning, to put it mildly. To put it more strongly, we can use the words of Dell (1981): "The label of 'paradox' is currently applied to such a wide range of therapeutic and interactional phenomena that the meaning of the term has been blurred and corrupted beyond usefulness. Today any unconventional therapeutic intervention is likely to be called a paradox" (p. 37). Or consider a recent statement by exponents of the "Palo Alto" school of brief therapy (Fisch, Weakland, and Segal 1982), who make extensive use of techniques that most clinicians would regard as "paradoxical." In introducing their major methods, they comment that "many of the interventions to be described below will appear complex, indirect, or even 'paradoxical,' though in our own view the use of paradoxes as interventions is relatively rare" (p. 127).

These definitional perplexities are not surprising considering the diversity of points of view, theories, and techniques that have been brought to bear on the subject. Behavioral psychology (Dunlop 1932), existential psychotherapy (Frankl 1965), the Adlerian school (Mozdzierz et al. 1976), communication theorists (Watzlawick, Beavin, and Jackson 1968), family therapists (Haley 1963, 1977), and the unconventional therapy of Milton Erickson (Haley 1973) have created an abundance of ideas and techniques but little in the way of a coherent theory.

At a practical level, however, a fairly simple definition of a paradoxical task appears to encompass most intervention considered to be paradoxical. Following Ascher and Efran (1978), a paradoxical task is one that "requires clients to perform responses that appear to be incompatible with the goal for which they are seeking assistance" (p. 547). The paradoxical element arises from the apparent incompatibility between response and goal. Thus, if the goal is to reduce X, responses that appear to require X to be continued, increased, ignored, and so on seem incongruous and, hence, paradoxical. Asking the insomniac to "make every effort to stay awake" is a classic example.

In the context of family treatment, tasks to "practice the problem" can take many forms. For example, the practitioner may suggest that an interactional or individual problem be "performed" at certain times, places, at a certain intensity, or with some specific variation. As Rohrbaugh et al. (1981) suggest, tasks of this kind may be based on quite different rationales. One rationale assumes that clients will *comply* with the task. If compliance occurs, then some positive benefits may follow. By producing the problem, clients presumably can convert spontaneous reactions into deliberate behavior, thereby, increasing their control of it. By deliberately engaging in problem behavior, they may gain new insight into it, perhaps an appreciation of its inappropriateness, or they may become simply tired of it. For some problems, such as inability to achieve orgasm or to fall asleep, attempts to overcome the difficulty through assiduous effort may only make matters worse. Efforts to "intensify" the problem, such as a task to stay awake to complete a boring job, can remove the effect of trying too hard and, "paradoxically," bring about a solution. Similar explanations underlie certain behavioral methods, such as negative practice, massed practice, and implosion.

In all these methods, the client's experience with a problem is deliberately intensified in order to bring about voluntary or self-control, extinction through satiation, or lack of reinforcement, among other possibilities (Raskin and Klein 1976). Putting paradoxical methods in the context of behavioral treatment tends to demystify them because learning theory can be introduced to explain their operations, although it should be noted that consensus has not been reached on which learning principles apply to these phenomena.

A second rationale is based on the assumption that clients will *defy* the task (Rohrbaugh et al. 1981). Defiance may result from oppositional tendencies, resistance toward the practitioner, or conflict with another family member. The rationale resembles that of "reverse psychology"—telling a rebellious youngster not to do what you wish him to do.

In the context of family treatment, Papp (1980) provides an example of a defiance-based task: Billy's failing in school was seen as an outgrowth of his mother's focusing disappointment on him rather than her withdrawn and apathetic husband. To disengage the mother from Billy and to bring the latent marital conflict into the open, the mother was told to "continue to express her disappointment in Billy because otherwise she might begin to express her dissatisfaction with her husband. This would be risky as her husband might become depressed, and since Billy was more resilient than her husband, he could take it better." The task and her husband's support of it so angered the mother that she began to fight with her husband. "The conflict was refocused onto the parents and Billy was released from his middle position."

As the example illustrates, more sophisticated uses of the techniques are related to an assessment of the systemic functioning of the family. The tasks are presented with rationales carefully tuned to the perceptions of family members. It should be noted that the task still takes the form of "continue the problem," but is used with the assumption that it will be disobeyed rather than complied with.

Other kinds of tasks have elements that may be considered paradoxical. For example, some tasks are based largely on assumptions of compliance but contain clauses that serve one therapeutic function if they are followed, another if they are disregarded. In one case, a young woman who wanted to leave her parents' home, but was having a difficult time breaking her dependency ties, took on a task of looking in the newspaper for apartments to rent with the understanding that she was not to make inquiries since she was "not ready" for that step. The "restraining clause" was intended to allay her anxiety about going too fast, but if defied, could be a way of asserting her independence from both parents and practitioner. Other varieties of such "two-sided" tasks have been used in the model (Brown 1977; Reid 1978).

In another kind of task, an attempt is made to locate some positive aspect in problem behavior and to use that aspect as a basis for a task, while accepting the rest of the behavior as given (Haley 1973). An example of such a task in a family context is provided by a case involving a husband who would spend most evenings constructing or repairing electronic gadgets for his own amusement or benefit. His behavior, which was quite patently an effort to withdraw from family contact and responsibilities, infuriated his wife. She wanted him to sharply reduce time on such projects, which he was unwilling to do. He was persuaded, however, to undertake a project—constructing a burglar alarm system—which was something his wife had expressed an interest in having. The project, a slight alteration in the pattern, provided a small but significant shift toward greater involvement with his wife.

In the last example, the paradoxical element arises from using apparent problem behavior as the basis for a constructive step. A variety of tasks may be labeled as paradoxical simply because they call for actions that are aimed at the problem, or its contextual bases, in an oblique manner. A term like "indirect" (Fisch, Weakland, and Segal 1982) perhaps does descibe these tasks more accurately than "paradoxical." For example, in the work just cited, a wife in one case was instructed to "forget" to fix breakfast for her husband, a recent stroke victim who had become excessively dependent on his family. The rationale for the task was to push the husband into doing more for himself. The task achieved this purpose, whereas previous efforts by family members to persuade the husband "to try harder" had failed. The task was not paradoxical in the sense of running counter to the goal of treatment. However, it attempted to achieve this goal through an indirect maneuver (withdrawing support) and deception (not revealing the purpose of the task to the husband). Qualities of indirectness and deception give it a paradoxical coloring because it does not appear to be a straightforward solution effort. In common with true paradoxical tasks, tasks of this kind require clients to act in novel ways. Whether or not defined as paradoxical, tasks that require a person to behave "out of character," as Weiss (1980) has put it, may disrupt habitual responses and stimulate new solutions.

Still other kinds of interventions thought of as paradoxical may not take the form of tasks, such as reframing, exaggerating the seriousness of a problem, or "predicting" a relapse (Fisch, Weakland, and Segal 1982). Restraining or advising clients to "go slow" in making progress, a defiance-based strategy that is intended to stimulate change efforts, may take the form of advice rather than a task, although restraining elements may be a part of tasks as in the example above. For a detailed discussion of these and other paradoxical techniques, see L'Abate and Weeks (1982).

In the task-centered framework, "straightforward" tasks are generally tried first; "paradoxical" tasks may be used if the former fail to accomplish desired results. Under certain circumstances, more paradoxical varieties may be used initially. In some cases, family members have already tried all the obvious task possibilities that may occur to them or to the practitioner. Similar tasks along the same lines might have a low probability of success, if for no other reason than the pessimism or apathy that clients might have toward them. In other instances, there may be empirical evidence that a "paradoxical" approach is effective with a particular problem. Insominia is an example, as discussed below.

When paradoxical tasks are used, they are generally based on assumptions of compliance and, following the collaborative principles of the model, the way the task is supposed to work is shared with the participants. For compliance based tasks this openness usually presents no difficulties—and, in fact, is assumed to increase the likelihood of compliance and of a positive outcome. Here we note that paradoxical tasks have been self-applied with apparent success (Frankl 1975) and will shortly review some research that further supports the usefulness of client awareness of how parodoxes work. The rationale given is based on available knowledge and is "non-deceptive", bringing out in non-technical terms, or by example, some of the considerations discussed above. As noted in chapter 3, when an explanation is withheld for clinical reasons, such as when the task contains a restraining clause, a debriefing is given subsequently so that the client knows what was done and why.

Tasks based primarily on defiance assumptions have a highly limited place in the model. They are considered as one option at the last resort stage of intervention choices. As noted in chapter 3, they run counter to the collaborative stance of the model and, further may seem out of place in a relationship that has stressed collaboration.

Although paradoxical approaches have been in use for over half a century, surprisingly little controlled research has been done on their effectiveness. What little has been done has related largely to use of paradoxical methods to treat individual problems, such as insomnia (Ascher and Turner 1979; Rellinger and Bornstein 1979), agoraphobia (Ascher 1981), and encropresis (Bornstein et al. 1981). These studies, most of which are controlled, single-case experiments, support the efficacy of paradoxical tasks against no treatment and placebo conditions. Their relative effectiveness against alternative methods has not been really tested.

One of these studies (Ascher and Turner 1979) is of particular interest in relation to how paradoxical tasks are used within the present model. Subjects (n = 40) with complaints of insomnia were randomly assigned to two treatment and two control conditions. Treatment consisted of the use of paradoxical tasks that required subjects to remain awake as long as possible. The rationales given for the tasks differed, however, between the treated groups. One group was given a straightforward explanation that revealed the logic of the paradoxical approach as understood by the therapist. The other group was given a rationale based on a "reframe"—they were to remain awake in order to become aware of the discomforting thoughts causing their sleeplessness; these thoughts were to be desensitized in later sessions. The group given the straightforward explanation clearly had better outcomes than the remaining groups, which did not differ in results. The findings of the study, as the authors suggest, were not a definitive test of reframing techniques since the clients were not resistive and the reframe was not individualized. The results do suggest, however, that an "open" explanation of the rationale for paradoxical tasks does not inhibit, and may well enhance, the effectiveness of such tasks.

Almost all of the evidence for the effectiveness of paradoxical tasks in family treatment consists of anecdotal case reports (Papp 1980; Haley 1977) with their well-known limitations. Considering the oft-cited potency of the method as well as its equally oft-cited risks, it is unfortunate that so little is known about its actual effects.

An exception to this observation can be found in a study reported by Kolko and Milan (1983), who conducted a controlled multiple baseline evaluation of paradoxical intervention in a family therapy context: three cases in which an adolescent family member was presenting problems of poor school attendance and failing academic performances constituted the experimental sample. Contingency contracts (complementary tasks) which involved rewards for better school attendance and performance failed to produce much change. When defiance-based paradoxical tasks were introduced (at different points in each case) noticeable improvement occurred. The tasks were presented with careful reframing of the problem. In one case, for example, the adolescent was advised to continue not attending school in order to complete a childish phase of behavior he needed to pass through before becoming a mature adult. It should be noted that the contingency contracts remained in effect and appeared, in the researchers' judgment, to reinforce improvement once it occurred. Also the tasks, while occurring as a part of family therapy, were individually oriented. This small but well designed study provides a measure of empirical support for the effectiveness of paradoxical tasks with adolescents, although it is not clear what contribution was made by the use of the contingency contracts before and during the experimental intervention.

My allocating a restricted role to paradoxical tasks generally is based in part on the lack of much research evidence as to their effectiveness. It also has been influenced by the recommendations of clinicians who have experimented extensively with these approaches. Fisher, Anderson, and Jones (1981), for example, observe "that all of the therapeutic interventions we have tried, paradoxical interventions constitute the highest risk for subsequent no-show appointments and premature terminations." While acknowledging their potency in many situations, they view them as "contraindicated when marked resistance, power struggles, and oppositional behavior are minimally present, when family structure is so disorganized that family solidarity is minimal, or when a potential for sharp escalation of symptoms or other severe forms of acting-out behavior with strongly negative consequences is possible" (pp. 33–34). Papp (1980) and her coworkers "reserve paradoxical interventions for those covert, long-standing repetitive patterns of interaction that do not respond to direct interventions such as logical explanations or rational discussion" (p. 46). In advising a restricted use of paradox in work with families with a schizophrenic member, Haley (1980) makes the general point that "the average therapist, working in a situation where he must deal with social control agents, colleagues with power over his case—and families only tentatively involved and uncommitted, should approach paradoxical interventions with caution" (p. 247).

Relation to Target Problems

Some tasks tackle the target problems directly; others are aimed not directly at the problem but rather at contextual factors that presumably underlie the problem. The distinction between "problem-focused" and "context-focused" tasks can be illustrated with an example of a school avoidance problem. A task strategy that is problem-focused would concentrate on returning the child to school through direct means. The child may have a task of going to school for a reward. A parent may undertake a task of taking the child to school and remaining with him for a certain period of time. A context-focused strategy might generate tasks concerned with modifying family relationships or the school environment presumed to give rise to the problem. For example, tasks might be designed to help the parents resolve differences concerning the child on the assumption that school avoidance was reactive to parental conflict.

This aspect is quite different from the previous distinction between paradoxical and nonparadoxical tasks. For example, a paradoxical task can be focused either on the problem or context. A depressive wife can be instructed to bring on a depression or can be instructed to quarrel with her spouse on the assumption that conflict avoidance is reponsible for the depression.

Issues in choice of task targets are complex and profound. Problem-focused tasks can produce rapid change with a high degree of efficiency, when they work. Often they do not, forcing the practitioner into a sequence of trial and error with other tasks of the same type, or into a search for contextual factors. Using tasks aimed at contextual change from the outset runs the risk, as has been noted (chapter 3), of selling short more direct solutions. Using them at all runs the risk of placing intervention strategy on unverified assumptions.

In the task-centered approach, this issue has been addressed through a two-track intervention strategy (Reid 1981; Mills 1985). On one track, the practitioner begins with straightforward tasks addressed directly to at least one target problem. At the same time, she begins to move along a second track, which is directed at increasing understanding of contextual factors. As this understanding increases, the practitioner may begin to work toward development of tasks focused on contextual concerns, particularly if the more direct tasks do not appear to be working, or if the context-focused tasks seem likely to bring about more significant change. Also, tasks focused on the problem may be retained while context-oriented tasks are introduced.

The Brock-Walters family was referred by the school because of behavior problems presented by Jon, age twelve. Holly Walters, his mother, had assumed most of the responsibility for disciplining Jon at home (where his behavior also presented difficulties) and for handling the school situation. Jon had been a problem while she had been a single mother. When she remarried (the previous year), it was with the understanding that she would continue to assume responsibility for dealing with Jon. Her husband, Dave Brock, had two children from a previous marriage whom he visited on weekends. The relationship between Dave and his stepson was generally distant, which Dave traced to Jon's resentment of him prior to the marriage. Reciprocal tasks centered on the school problem were set up between Jon and his mother but progress was slow. Because there were indications that Jon's current behavior was in part being fueled by his anger at his stepfather, greater involvement between Jon and David was seen as a way of building a relationship that might dissipate Jon's hostility as well as bring David into a more active parental role. Tasks focused on these contextual considerations were devised. David was to invite Jon to go along with him and his own children to a ball game, something Jon would like. Also, David was to take over supervision of Jon's chores at home.

ENVIRONMENTAL TASKS

"Work with the environment" has been a traditional concern of social work and one of the hallmarks of the profession. Perhaps one of the distinctive features of family treatment conducted by social workers is the interpenetration of family and environmental concerns. As has been frequently observed, however, the environmental domain of social work practice has been relatively neglected in social work practice theory (Grinnel 1973; Grinnel, Kyte, and Bostwick 1981). Although many reasons can be cited, a major barrier has been the difficulty in generating theory and research in an area as vast and complex as "the environment," which is, after all, nothing less than everything left over after some client system has been isolated. Progress has been made over the years through efforts to conceptualize environmental work as part of clinical practice (Hollis 1968, 1972; Hollis and Wood 1981; Reid 1978), the evaluation of generalist perspectives (Pincus and Minahan 1973; Middleman and Goldberg 1974; Siporin 1975), the development of ecological and ecosystems approaches (Germain and Gitterman 1980; Maluccio 1981; Meyer 1983a), and the appearance of a specialized literature dealing with environmental interventions (Grinnel, Kyte, and Bostwick 1981). In the present section, an attempt is made to extend this work through development of the notion of an environmental task as it may be applied to work on family problems. Basic concepts and methods usually presented in introductory practice courses will not be dealt with in detail.

Client Tasks

In an environmental task a family member, a family unit, or the practitioner plans to take action in the family environment, however that may be defined in a given case. Regardless of who does them, environmental tasks serve the general function in the model of utilizing the environment as a means of problem resolution. More specific functions include exchanging information with environmental sources, securing and using tangible services and other resources, learning to cope with environments in which family members participate, and inducing beneficial changes in those environments.

As can be seen, the functions allocated to environmental tasks are many indeed. In fact, this area encompasses most of the wide variety of client tasks used in one-to-one work—clients who are having difficulty at school, at work, in institutions, in the community, and so on. Thus, basic strategies and methods used in task-centered practice are germane (Reid and Epstein 1972, 1977; Reid 1978; Epstein 1980). What will be emphasized here is the result of more recent work on the role of the family in helping its members define and carry out environmental tasks, and on the contribution the practitioner can make to this process.

In practice of family therapy, the family tends to be viewed as a cause of problems a member is experiencing in the environment. In some cases the tracking of such problems back to family dysfunctions makes sense and provides a logical basis for intervention. In many others, however, this formulation sells reality short. The problem often can be better seen as an outgrowth of an interactional process between the identified client, his or her family, and the environmental situation—a view which opens up greater possibilities for change.

Many such problems have some elements that are responsive to family influences and other elements that are more reactive to the external environment. Problems of children and youth in school settings provide common examples. Although shared and reciprocal tasks have an important contribution to make toward resolution of those problems, they have their limits. We have seen, for example, that "school notes" contracts requiring daily report cards and home reinforcements failed to affect school grades in one study (Stuart et al. 1976). Both academic and behavior problems may involve complex interplays among child, subject matter, peers, teachers, and other school personnel that may not be amenable to a home-based system of rewards and sanctions. Environmental tasks carried out by the children themselves have proved to be effective in alleviating a wide range of such problems (Reid et al. 1980). Often some combination of shared/reciprocal and individual tasks can be advantageous. For example, school notes can be used in combination with individual tasks undertaken by the child; family conferences can be used to help a member plan a task regarding a job search, school problem, and so on. Within this broader perspective, particular attention should be given to the family's resources in coping with environmental problems that affect it. Even if the cause of the problem can be justifiably attributed to interactional processes within the family, it may not be possible to alter these processes. It may be possible, however, to help the family modify their consequences.

One way of bringing the resources of the family to bear on environmental problems is to make use of family members as models and coaches through role plays (as illustrated in chapters 2, 5, and 6). Here the family helps a member learn more effective ways of coping with the environment. The principle can be extended by having family members, particularly parents and older siblings, recall how they handled similar problems. Although this method may not work when the family members who are to serve as resources are in conflict with the one to be helped, the presence of conflict itself should not automatically rule out its consideration. Through role play or structuring recollections, the practitioner attempts to generate a temporary conflict-free atmosphere. By keeping the family members' contributions limited to acting out or recalling specific situations, the practitioner can avoid lecturing, preaching, and other responses on the part of family members likely to generate conflict. The point can be made that, despite their differences, family members can learn from one another, and in attempting to do so they may discover new ways of relating.

In addition to these specific procedures, the input of the family can be obtained in work with an individual family member concerning the planning and implementation of his or her environmental tasks. For example, family members may be asked to suggest task possibilities, contribute to the development of implementation strategies, and so on, in much the same way that task-centered groups are conducted (Rooney 1977; Reid 1978; Garvin, Reid, and Epstein 1976; Fortune 1985).

Another approach, one that can be used either with or instead of the first, is to help the family deal directly with the environment in which a member is having troubles. Frequently, such interactions involve school problems. Conferences involving the parents, child, teachers, and other school personnel, which the practitioner arranges and attends, are useful devices. A vital part of the practitioner's contribution is to create a cooperative, problem-solving climate in which the purpose is to develop ways of helping the child. The same principle can be extended to work with families who have children or an aged member in institutional settings.

Practitioner Tasks

When feasible, environmental activities of the practitioner on behalf of the family are structured as *practitioner tasks*, which are analogous to client tasks in the sense of being problem-solving actions that are set up and agreed to in the session and carried out and reviewed subsequently. The advantages of using a parallel task structure for the practitioners' environmental work are several: it enhances the symmetrical and collaborative aspects of the relationship, requires the practitioner to be explicit about possible environmental interventions, provides a way of insuring client feedback and consent, increases practitioners' accountability, and provides a systematic record of the environmental intervention for case reviews and research purposes. The value of the concept in research was demonstrated in one investigation. In a developmental study of task-centered practice with families in child welfare settings, Rooney (1978) found that the degree of success of practitioner tasks was significantly predictive of reduction in target problems and more predictive than any other variable. Not all the environmental work undertaken by practitioners needs to be formalized as tasks, however. Falling outside this structure would be minor activities as well as environmental opportunities or problems that require immediate responses.

Two general structures for practitioner tasks have been identified: *facilitating* and *independent* (Reid 1978). In facilitating tasks, practitioners help clients with the implementation of their own environmental tasks. In this structure, practitioners work with persons in the environment such as teachers, employers, or service providers with whom the client will interact in carrying out his or her tasks. The practitioner eventually tries to structure environmental responses that will facilitate the client's task work. For example, a practitioner and teacher may develop a reward system for a child's tasks in the classroom. If a client's task is to ask his physician to explain details of proposed surgery, the practitioner may consult with the physician beforehand concerning the nature of the client's concerns. Other examples include arranging conferences involving family members and organizational personnel or locating and explaining resources that family members will attempt to secure. Facilitating tasks may also involve accompanying family members to conferences, agency or clinic visits, and the like. Such tasks can provide incentive and structure for client action and can give the client on-the-spot emotional support and assistance. Although elements of the task may be shared, the practitioner and client have different purposes and perform different roles.

Independent tasks call for practitioner action in the environment that is not related to complementary client tasks, although it is still done with the client's consent. In independent tasks the practitioner acts as the family's agent in the environment. The occasion for independent tasks arises when action on the client's part may accomplish little or be counterproductive. The family may, in fact, already have tried and failed and is not ready to try again. The practitioner may be able to move with greater efficiency and effectiveness in certain areas of the environment than family members who may be better able to do tasks in other areas.

Finally, independent tasks may be called for when crises or multiple problems prevent the family from acting on its own behalf. As can be surmised, a facilitating task structure is preferred to the practitioner's doing the job herself. If it is assumed the practitioner's involvement is necessary, it is better done in support of client tasks. In this way, family members can retain greater control over their affairs and have the opportunity to learn how to deal with environmental problems, while still being able to draw on the practitioner's support. Situations calling for action in the environment should be assessed to determine if family members can do what is needed on their own or through a facilitating task before independent practitioner tasks are undertaken.

Either task structure can be used to perform the usual range of environmental interventions subsumed under such roles as broker, mediator, and advocate (Grinnel, Kyte, and Bostwick 1981; Germain and Gitterman 1981). Thus in helping connect the family to external resources (brokerage), the family can apply for a service, with the practitioner's task being to contact the agency to facilitate the application, or the practitioner can explore resources and arrange for services herself. In mediation, the practitioner can serve as a go-between to help the family iron out differences with persons or organizations in the environment or take action to support the clients' efforts to do so. Although advocacy usually relies on independent practitioner actions, clients can take on tasks to present their own cases, with practitioner tasks used for groundbreaking, reinforcement, and follow-up.

The knowledge and skills required for environmental work with families and individuals have been well-mapped at a general level (Grinnell, Kyte, and Bostwick 1981; Germain and Gitterman 1981; Maluccio 1980; Reid 1978). Less well described has been the use of environmental intervention in conjoint work with families concerning psychosocial problems of individual members or interactional issues.

When problems of individual members involve the community, the practitioner usually is part of a situational system that includes the family and persons and agencies in the environment. Environmental intervention may easily run afoul of the complex and faulty communication networks that characterize such situations. The focal problem in work with Allen and his parents was Allen's behavior problems at school, which led to frequent suspensions. The school guidance counselor had been notifying the parents of serious disciplinary incidents. Shortly after family treatment had begun, Allen was caught destroying school property and again suspended. The practitioner was told of this development by the counselor, who assumed that the practitioner would somehow convey the information to the family. The practitioner assumed that the family had been advised. After having carefully planned the session around a family discussion of this latest crisis, the practitioner was stunned when informed by the parents that things had been going fine with Allen both at home and at school. Instead of confronting everyone with what she knew, or asking to see Allen alone briefly, the practitioner, rattled by this unexpected development, started to question Allen closely about the week at school with the hope that he would reveal the difficulty. Allen blithely denied all. To avoid such predicaments, the practitioner needs to set up a workable communications network and to maintain its operation. She should clarify who informs whom about what kind of events and make sure messages arrive at the right place at the right time. A contingency plan for handling breakdowns in communication should be in place.

An environmental intervention, like any intervention, has implications for family interaction—a generalization that needs to be taken into account in planning practitioner and family tasks in the environment. In some situations, the structural component may be a secondary, but important, theme of the task. For example, tasks that involve the family and practitioner in transactions with the external system concerning resources, planning for family members, and the like can be set up in particular ways to achieve a desired impact on family interaction. They may affect the opportunity to involve an isolated parent, to engage parents in a cooperative and boundary-strengthening venture, or to enable them to exercise constructive authority on behalf of their children. The practitioner can vary the nature and level of her activity in facilitating tasks in line with desired effects on family interaction patterns. These structural components, of course, need to be balanced against criteria of effectiveness and efficiency in getting the task done.

In other cases, environmental intervention can be applied directly to interactive difficulties. When overinvolvement among family members is an obstacle, consideration should be given to environmental resources, such as self-help or recreational groups, that might direct energies outside the family and reduce the amount of family interaction. For a child who lacks adequate involvement with a parent or who is being scapegoated, one might consider a "big brother" or "big sister" who could work under the supervision of the practitioner. For children and parents involved in mutually coercive and potentially explosive struggles, the family's social network (Swenson 1981) may be of immediate help. It may be possible for the child to stay with a friend for a few days as a means of interrupting escalation of the conflict, avoiding a runaway, or forestalling a parental move toward placement.

In complex situational systems, the practitioner may need to assume responsibility for orchestrating the activities of a network of actual and potential helpers. As Tavantzis, Tavantzis, and Brown (in press) have suggested, it may be necessary to "organize helpers before families," especially when the helping network is operating in an uncoordinated or dysfunctional fashion. Usually the practitioner will have no special mandate for assuming this role, and there may be others in the network in a more advantageous position to take it on. Generally the practitioner who is working with the family as a whole is in the best position, inasmuch as she has a conception of the needs and involvements of different family members.

TASK PLANNING

Planning considerations unique to different types have been dealt with in the preceding portion of this chapter. In this section I shall take up generic aspects of planning home and environmental tasks.

General and Operational Tasks

A basic distinction in the model is made between *general tasks* and *operational tasks* (Reid 1978). The former set an overall direction but provide no procedural details for action (Dick and Beth will come to a mutually satisfactory decision about having a baby; Sally will leave her parents' home and begin to live independently). Tasks at this level usually serve to put basic treatment goals into action form and to fix responsibility for achieving them. Once formulated, they may continue through the life of the case unlesss revised.

Operational tasks are specific, structured activities that are to be carried out between sessions. They may be derived from general tasks (Sally and her mother will discuss when Sally will leave) or can be generated from problem or goal statements, bypassing the need for general tasks. In recent years, developmental work on the model has stressed operational tasks, and this emphasis is reflected in the present volume (in which the term "task" is in fact generally used in the sense of "operational task"). Some practitioners and families prefer to limit the amount of structure in treatment to the level of general tasks, and may not reach the operational level of task development. Other components of the model still can be used. We note that a similar distinction, between "macro" and "micro" tasks, has appeared in a recently developed family treatment approach (Pinsof 1983).

Task Planning and Implementation Sequence

A basic planning format used in the task-centered model is the *task planning and implementation sequence,* a series of steps for helping clients plan tasks (Reid 1975; Reid 1978; Brown 1980; Rzepnicki 1985). Some aspects of this sequence already have been considered, and others will be examined subsequently in this section. The outline below, which summarizes the steps as adapted to family work, will help pull the parts together. The steps may not necessarily occur in the order presented, and seldom are all used in a given session.

Generating Alternatives. Family members and the practitioner identify and discuss alternative task possibilities. The best alternatives are identified (see Family-Practitioner Collaboration, below).

Task Agreement. An *explicit* agreement on the tasks is reached. This step often occurs after the one below.

Planning Details of Implementation. The specifics of how the task(s) will be done are planned in detail (see Structure and Detail, below).

Establishing Incentives and Rationale. The purpose and value of the task(s) from the participants' point of view are clarified. The procedure may be omitted if these aspects seem clear to clients, but it is important in use of paradoxical and other tasks whose function is not apparent.

Anticipating Obstacles. Potential obstacles to task completion are considered, particularly in situations where there is a high risk of failure (see below).

Simulation and Guided Practice. Brief try-outs of the task(s) or components in the session through role play or practice and feedback.

Summarization. A final step in which the task plan is summarized. The procedure is particularly useful if multiple tasks are involved or if the plan has undergone revision. It may be augmented by putting the task(s) in written form.

Family-Practitioner Collaboration

Collaboration between the practitioner and family members is the key to successful task planning. The source of ideas for tasks—whether they originate with the practitioner or family members—is of secondary importance. What matters is the process by which the idea is shaped into a final plan.

The practitioner generally takes the initiative in getting the process underway. One option, as noted, is to structure the family's work on a plan by means of a session task (Discuss what each of you can do about this problem and try to come up with a plan). A second option is to invite suggestions from family members. A third is to propose one or two possibilities and have the family react to them. Finally, the practitioner can present a task plan in an authoritative fashion, in the form of a directive (Haley 1977) (I would like to have you do this between now and next time).

As can be seen, these options became progressively more restrictive in respect to the amount of choice the family is given in developing a plan. The first enables the family to move ahead with its own solutions, the option of choice when the development of problem-solving and communication skills is being emphasized. Or either the first or second may be used when the practitioner really has no clear ideas herself about task possibilities. The family's problem-solving efforts may produce a workable plan or provide the practitioner with ideas. Note that the second option offers the practitioner both more stimulus and control than the first, since she can be selective in her response to the ideas offered or add her own, but gives the family less opportunity to do its own problem solving. The third option (practitioner suggestion) can vary in directiveness: one possibility can be presented with some or considerable tentativeness, alternative possibilities can be offered, and so on. In this option the practitioner is less sanguine about the family's ability to generate workable tasks—for example, the level of conflict may be high, or it may seem likely that one member may take over. Theory or experience may suggest to her a task that seems particularly well-suited to the situation.

The final option, in which the practitioner is clearly the expert very much in control, is typically used in strategic and structural approaches, but only under certain circumstances in the task-centered model—when, for example, the family seems clearly unable to proceed constructively with its own problem-solving efforts. Collaborative planning is a part of all these options, however. When the family develops a task, the practitioner may make suggestions about implementation or ask for clarifying details. When the practitioner proposes a task, she may ask the family to react to it, or if it is presented more assertively, she will ask the family members participating how they think they might do it. In any event, the participants' explicit agreement that they will attempt the task is obtained. Throughout, the practitioner is sensitive to ways of incorporating and building upon the contributions of family members, not only to stimulate their own problem solving but also to attain the most effective task plan possible.

Structure and Detail

Tasks at the operational level can be planned with a varying amount of structure and detail or left at a relatively global level. A fair degree of structure (who does what, when) and detail (how is it to be done) is usually indicated for most tasks. In particular, vague areas that are likely to create uncertainty, confusion, or conflict should be clarified. For example, key terms in the task statement should be spelled out. If a child's part of a reciprocal task is to get "good grades" on tests and homework, what is meant by "good grades" needs to be made clear. If his reward is to be able to "watch TV", then how much and when should be discussed.

Generally, reciprocal tasks require the greatest amount of structure and detail since they involve considerations of equity and coordination between the partners. Shared tasks tend to play themselves out according to how participants interact or how the project goes, and may not call for more structure than a statement of what participants are to do generally, when, and where. Individual tasks (and also reciprocal tasks) vary in structure and detail according to their complexity, the extent to which participants are familiar with the actions being called for, and the preferences and styles of the participants. Some clients prefer or need to have things spelled out in detail; others are more comfortable with tasks at a less specific level.

These factors generally become clearer after initial tasks have been tried. In fact, de Shazer (1982) has argued that task designs can be fitted to the family's response style, and has suggested a system of matching designs and styles. For example, if a family tends to modify tasks, then tasks that are easily "modifiable" can be designed, such as tasks that take the form of accounts of what other families have tried (p. 52).

In the interest of developing the family's own problem-solving abilities or preparing for the practitioner's withdrawal, task plans ideally should give greater discretion to participants as the case progresses. It is usually a good prognostic sign when family members reshape or replace tasks to achieve better resolutions. The desired goal is, after all, to help family members learn more effective ways of coping with problems on their own rather than develop their capacity to comply with therapeutic regimens.

Some care should be exercised in allowing task designs to become too loose when interpersonal conflict still is at a high level. Participants may then refashion the tasks into weapons.

Mrs. Arthur and her fifteen-year-old daughter, Linda, had made some progress through reciprocal tasks in which Linda had agreed to meet a curfew during the week in exchange for being able to stay out later on weekends. There was still a good deal of bickering about Linda's tendency to come home a little later than the agreed-upon time, as well as conflict over other issues. Mrs. Arthur thought that Linda should have some penalty for being late and Linda, after protesting mildly, accepted the idea. The practitioner, who was impressed with Mrs. Arthur's competence, suggested that Mrs. Arthur and Linda "work out an appropriate penalty for Linda's lateness." In the next session Mrs. Arthur reported that "things had fallen apart." Linda had been twenty minutes late, and Mrs. Arthur had grounded her for the rest of the week but Linda had gone off without permission. Exploration revealed that Mrs. Arthur had interpreted the last-minute addendum to the task to mean that she herself should set a penalty for Linda's lateness, and she did so with a vengeance. In hindsight, it became clear that Mrs. Arthur's need to punish Linda had been underestimated; negotiation in the session about what the penalties should be as well as some exploration of Mrs. Arthur's anger toward Linda would have been preferable.

Anticipating Obstacles

An important practitioner function in task planning is to help the family identify potential obstacles to the task and to shape plans so as to avoid or minimize these obstacles. This function is implicitly addressed when the practitioner presses for specificity in the task plan. As details of how the task is to be done are brought out, possible obstacles can be identified and dealt with. A more explicit approach is to ask family members to think of ways that a task might fail. This "anti-sabotage" procedure, as Birchler and Spinks (1981) call it, can be done through discussion or take the form of a session task. If substantial obstacles appear, techniques of contextual analysis (chapter 5) can be used. Alternatively, the task can be modified or another developed.

As previous studies have suggested (Reid and Epstein 1972; Reid 1978), the degree of apparent commitment to the task may be the best single indication that the task will be accomplished. Commitment is inferred through such evidence as the client's enthusiasm and involvement in discussing the task, in planning its details, in their expressed confidence that it will work, or other comments made about it. Lack of apparent commitment may suggest the presence of unexpressed obstacles and may prompt a search for them, particularly in the motivational area.

8. *The Single Mother Family*

William J. Reid and Kathleen DuFresne

It has long been a goal in the development of practice theories and models to construct intervention strategies specific to particular types of cases. For the practitioner the question becomes, "What are the best methods available for the type of situation I am facing?" In the family therapy field there are numerous examples of case-type approaches. Among the better known are methods of structural intervention for families with psychosomatic children (Minuchin, Rosman, and Baker 1978) and Haley's (1980) paradigm of strategic intervention for families with eccentric young adults. Examples from the social work literature include approaches to work with "poverty level" families (Janzen and Harris 1980; Orcutt 1977), with Hispanic families (Hardy-Fanta and MacMahon-Herrera 1981), and with the aging family (Kirschner 1979). A combination of categories can be used for a given case type—for instance, a family that is poor, Hispanic, and aging.

As the examples suggest, a case type in the present context is any way of classifying (or cross-classifying) a family or its problems that may be useful for diagnostic or treatment purposes. It is assumed that a categorization conveys general information that may be helpful in the case at hand. Thus, if the family is second generation Italian-American, one can expect certain values to be present (Speigel 1981). The usefulness of a type, therefore, expands on generalizations presumably accumulated through clinical observation or research. Although many types have been identified and are used to inform practice, there still is not an adequate empirical basis for establishing treatment of choice for any given type.

In the evaluation of the task-centered model, a typology for classifying problems has been used as one basis for relating targets to treatments (Reid and Epstein 1972; Reid 1978). Thus, a problem categorization of interpersonal conflict would suggest one intervention approach; a problem defined as "inadequate resources" would suggest another. Although the problem typology can be applied to work with families, a more discriminating method of classifying target situations is needed. In view of limitations of knowledge and assessment techniques, the most promising approach seems to lie in constructing selected "case types" without regard for what they might look like in the aggregate. Because the model is problem-focused, it seemed to make sense to develop a case type consisting of a problem configuration that might be found in a given class of family. To be useful, the resulting type would need to be readily identified, appear with some frequency in the case loads of practitioners, and be related to specialized knowledge and research. On the other hand, it could not be so heterogeneous that meaningful and valid generalizations would be difficult to develop. This thinking led us to select, as a starting point, the single mother with problems of interaction with one or more of her children.

In this chapter, we shall examine theory and research relative to a variant of this type of case situation (which will be delineated later on) and show how the task-centered approach can be applied to it. By so doing, we hope to make a beginning at developing more specific variations of the model and to demonstrate how one might go about building such variations. At the same time, the chapter should provide an extended illustration of how different components of the model come together in relation to a particular kind of case. Our intent is not to formulate prescriptions on the order of "if faced with X, do Y." What is done in a case should always be a function of its specific characteristics. Rather, we hope to present considerations that may be taken into account in developing particularized assessments and treatment plans. (For a task-centered group treatment approach with single parents, see Macy-Lewis 1985.)

PERSPECTIVE

The single mother family historically has been defined within a deficit-model framework. This perspective has described the single mother family as a "broken home" that awaited the expected adverse reactions to "father absence." Single mother families were presumed progenitors of juvenile delinquency, inappropriate sex-role identification, and poor academic achievement. There does not appear, however, to be an adequate empirical basis for this view. (Blechman 1982; Herzog and Sidia 1973).

In many situations the terms "single mother," "female-headed," or "single parent" may be misleading descriptors of actual family structure. Often such families are better thought of as "post-divorce family systems," in view of the considerable amount of significant interaction that may occur between the divorced parents and between the noncustodial parent and children (Goldsmith 1982:297). Single parents closely involved with their families of origin or with friends of the same or opposite sex suggest additional types of systems.

Whatever its structure the single-mother family need not be a deleterious arrangement, and in fact, many such families are successful in meeting family members' needs. There can be positive elements within these family systems. These include relief from marital conflict, increased self-esteem derived from one's competency in managing work and family matters, greater autonomy and independence, opportunities for increased self-growth, and closer relationships with children (Cherlin 1981; Kaslow and Hyatt 1982; Weiss 1979). It would even appear a misnomer to describe the single mother family as a "nontraditional" family form. Thompson and Gongla (1983) point out that the number of single-parent families from the mid-nineteenth century through 1970 remained fairly constant, approximately one in ten families.

What has been "nontraditional" about this family form in recent years has been its growth within the general population. Whereas the number of households consisting of married couples and their own children under 18 declined between 1970 and

1982, female-headed households with children under 18 increased by 105 percent. In 1982 there was nearly six million such female-headed households (U.S. Bureau of Census 1983:2). If current trends continue, it is estimated that one-half of all children born in the 1970s will live for some time in a single-parent family (Pett 1982).

All family forms have areas of strength and weakness. The traditional two-parent family can draw on the combined efforts of two parents in child-rearing and wage earning, and can offer children male and female role models, but it is vulnerable to marital conflict, scapegoating alliances of parents against a child, or the alliance of one parent and child against the other parent. The female-headed family is spared these problems in their usual forms and may enjoy special advantages, as noted above. But other difficulties must be faced: the mother is more apt to have total responsibility for child care with its attendant hazards, is more likely to face financial hardship and role overload, and must contend with often trying and unstable relationships with ex-spouses and male friends. Although the philosophical question of which family form is inherently superior need not be answered, it probably is true that the mother-headed family is especially vulnerable to the kinds of problems that are likely to bring people to human service agencies.

For example, Guttentag et al. (1980) have reported that single mothers have higher rates of anxiety and depression than other marital status groups, that single mothers are the major consumers of mental health services, and that children of single-parent mothers are recipients of mental health services at four times the rate of children living in two-parent households. In their national survey of family service agencies, Beck and Jones (1973) found that 23 percent of applicant families were single-parent (overwhelmingly single-mother), whereas such families made up only 11 percent of the general population.

Theme and Variation

A case type is identified by elements that cases have in common, such as single mothers with a problem child, families with delinquent members, or separated couples considering reconciliation. Presumably, special knowledge exists about such groupings. This knowledge provides answers to such questions as, "What can I expect from a case of this kind?" "What kinds of interventions might be indicated?" In order to have utility, a type must lead the practitioners to actions that differ from and surpass what she would ordinarily do.

Knowledge relating to case types takes the form, however, of "tendencies" that have far less than universal application. The theme expressed by the case type is replete with variations that need to be recognized.

With a single mother, there are no universals beyond what follows directly from being a single mother—for example, not having the father present to share in the day to day child-rearing responsibilities. Efforts have been made to develop more discriminating subtypes.

In the light of her research, Pett formulated a composite of the "high risk single parent" (1982:14). This individual, usually a mother, feels depressed and emotionally out of control. Her relationships with her children are tense and difficult. She has a poor relationship with her family of origin. She perceives herself as socially isolated and is concerned that there are few people that she can turn to in an emergency. She is likely to be an AFDC recipient. When such mothers live in the inner city, data provided by Dill et al. (1981) suggest that additional environmental stressors, associated with urban poverty and crime, can be added to the profile.

The profile is of interest in its own right, and also introduces important sources of variation in the single mother family: degree of emotional distress, amount of difficulty with children, extent and kind of relationships with her social network, socioeconomic status, and whereabouts. Single mothers may have relationship problems with their children, but not be exclusively distressed, isolated, or poor, or may have some of these characteristics but not others. Still other important sources of variation concern the origins and developmental stage of the single-mother family. Most such families have been formed as the result of marital separation or divorce. This origin-in-crisis generally is accompanied by emotional upheaval and an abrupt restructuring of parent-child relationships. As the crisis attenuates, a new stability is found, though the process may take years and for some families is never attained (Cherlin 1981). Single mother families formed as a result of "out-of-wedlock" births have a different course. Although the mother's relationship with the father may be a source of considerable stress in her life, an ongoing family unit is not disrupted.

In subsequent discussion, our focus will be on single-mother families created through separation or divorce. Even though it may not have occurred recently, the marital break-up, we assume, is still an active ingredient in terms of its emotional fall-out for the family and its relationships with the absent father. We also assume that the mother is under stress (or could be) from her employment, her financial situation, her relationships within her social network, and the accumulated challenges of solitary coping with family and external systems. In addition, the mother has at least one child of school age with whom she is having a problem. We shall first take up problems and contextual factors that one might expect to find in such single-mother families. With this profile in mind, we will then discuss how these factors might influence problem formulation and intervention. Most of our observations can be extended to other variations of the single-mother family.

Problems and Contexts

With the single mother, as with any kind of client, target problems are whatever become the agreed-on foci for work. All other issues become part of the context of these problems. For the present, we assume, as noted, that the problem involves the mother's relationship with a child. Obviously, factors bearing on this difficulty could themselves become problems.

The break-up of the marriage—the cataclysm creating the single-mother family—is a logical place to begin contextual considerations. The time period following separation or divorce normally is a stressful one. The family must proceed through a process of reorganization that may appear to be "disorganization" (Hetherington et al. 1982, p. 224). Some studies have suggested that this adjustment process usually occurs over a two-year period (Hetherington et al. 1982; Pett 1981). During the first year after the break-up, findings from this research indicate that mothers are likely to experience anger, anxiety, and depression and to perceive themselves as incompetent. One source of the mother's negative emotions and perceptions are realistic stresses encountered in day-to-day living, such as economic difficulties (Epenshade 1979), limited employment opportunities (Halem 1982), and work-family role strain (Keith and Shafer 1982). In attempting to fulfill child care, household maintenance, and employment obligations, mothers frequently feel overwhelmed (Halem 1982; Berman and Turk 1981). Depression and anxiety are likely correlates of this state of affairs.

Another potential source of distress are cognitive and attitudinal factors. It has been suggested that successful adaptation may be hampered by an unrealistic evaluation of goals and resources available (Buehler and Hogan 1980). This frequently takes the form of the mother despondently referring to "how things were then" (while married) versus "how things are now." Additionally, a cognitive adherence to traditional male-female roles has been cited as a correlate of depression among single mothers (Keith and Shafer 1982) perhaps because women with a traditional orientation are likely to equate being a wife and homemaker with selfworth. As Morawetz and Walker (1984) suggest, women from Hispanic and other cultures in which traditional values are stressed may be especially vulnerable to such feelings of guilt. Other women may perceive the child as a burden that they have been unfairly saddled with and may as a result resent the usual responsibilities of mothering. Resentment can be compounded if the child is also identified with the hated father (Morawetz and Walker 1984).

Children likewise experience negative emotional consequences following the marital break-up (Wallerstein and Kelly 1980). In fact, it appears that it is frequently the resulting acting-out behavior of a child that prompts the single mother to seek agency assistance (Guttentag et al. 1980). The practitioner must be wary of rationalizing the child's behavior as a reaction to parental loss, however. Research suggests that post-divorce relationships will have as great an impact on the child's well-being as the divorce itself (Hess and Camara 1979; Wallerstein and Kelly 1980).

The mother-child interaction represents one facet of the total family environment wherein adjustment may be impaired or facilitated. Pett (1982), for instance, found children's adjustment to be predictive of satisfactory maternal social adjustment. Hetherington et al. (1982) observed that mother-child interactions during the year following divorce were often mutually coercive. In this study, investigators noted that the single mother

. . . . was harrassed by her children, particularly sons. In comparison with fathers and mothers of intact families, her children in the first year didn't obey, affiliate, or attend to her. They nagged and whined, made more dependency demands and were likely to ignore her. (p. 258)

One mother in the study described her relationship with her children as akin to "being bitten to death by ducks." Mothers for their part provided positive reinforcement for compliance by children less than one-half of the time. Boys received less positive reinforcement than girls and were given more positive and negative commands and sanctions. This coercive pattern likely contributes further to mother's feelings of depression and incompetence, which in turn serve to exacerbate the pattern. As Griest and Wells (1983) suggest, parental depression may lower the parent's tolerance level for child behavior and incline the parent to employ more punishment. Also, these investigators point out that the child may accelerate his or her output of negative behavior in an effort to elicit some response from the indifferent parent.

Such cycles are perhaps more likely to occur, and may prove more difficult to check in a single-parent family, because the single parent lacks the power of the "united front" that is possible in the two-parent family. Without the support of a partner, the single mother is likely to cede some measure of power to her children. Symmetrical interactions between the mother and children are therefore more likely to occur.

Another dimension pertinent to post-divorce adjustment is the level of involvement among family members (see chapter 4).

During the period following the end of the marriage, the changes in family structure and accompanying emotional turmoil may cause family levels of involvement to be altered. The mother, feeling despondent or anxious, may turn to her child for emotional support. The child, having experienced the loss of a father, is more than willing to become closer to the mother. Although this phenomenon appears to be time-limited for most families, it may stabilize into a pattern that is dysfunctional for both mother and child. For example, the mother may rely on her relationship with the child as a means of fulfilling emotional or social needs that would normally be met by adults. If the child responds, his or her own development may be thwarted. The child may be the pursuer. Thus, Isaacs (1981) reports an instance of an eight-year-old daughter who slept nightly in her mother's bed and gave up her friends in order to be "a sister to her mother" (p. 256).

The high mutual involvement may shift to a conflict over involvement as either the mother or child begins to make moves toward greater independence. In one of our cases, the mother treated her nine-year-old daughter "as a pal" during the initial period following her separation. Later, when the mother became involved with a male friend, she began to resent the daughter's "pal-like" behavior—for example, her wanting to be a part of mother's conversations with the boyfriend. She now saw the daughter not as a "little pal" but as a "nine-year-old going on thirty-nine," that is, as inappropriately assuming adult prerogatives. With children moving toward adolescence, a common pattern is that the child desires more freedom and the mother is reluctant to let go.

Increased involvement between mothers and children, as well as changes in patterns of control, are normative and probably inevitable characteristics of single-parent families. As Weiss (1979) discovered in his in-depth study of over 200 single parents from a nonclinical population, the consequences can be positive. A common theme in these families (mostly female-headed) was greater participation of the children in the kind of family decision making that normally would be the province of the parents in a two-parent household. Children were given greater responsibility, and as a result gained greater authority and more rights than children in two-parent families. One favorable result was an acceleration in the child's maturation ("growing up a little faster") (p. 97). This phenomenon was more likely to have clearly positive consequences in adolescents than younger children, perhaps because adolescents were more ready for the responsibility. Younger children, Weiss concluded, may have had to suppress needs for parental nurturance in carrying out roles as "junior partners," with mixed results developmentally—an enhanced ability to function autonomously paid for with "a persisting need for the care and investment of a nurturing figure" (p. 109).

When there is more than one child, the presence of alliances involving mother and children needs to be considered. (We take up alliances subsequently involving the mother and other adults, such as ex-spouses, male friends, or members of the extended family.) The more common patterns consist of cross-generational alliances. An alliance between the mother and an older sibling is often used as a means of family management. The older sibling, or "parental child" as structural therapists might say, is given certain responsibilities for younger children. Although this arrangement is often seen as problematic by family therapists, it may be quite functional in many situations. As has been noted (Weiss 1979), older children can be given responsibility that may be beneficial for their own development while relieving the mother from some of the burdens of child care. Here, as elsewhere, one needs to consider how the problem is affected by the contextual feature. The alliance may become an obstacle if it keeps the mother from giving necessary attention to the needs of a younger problem child, but it may be a resource particularly if the "parental child" can be used in a helping role. Often it may be a question of modifying the role of the parental child without disrupting it.

A pattern that is generally more deleterious involves a scapegoating (two against one) coalition between the mother and one child against another child, who usually is presented as the problem. The child allied with the mother, who actually may be younger, is not given responsibility for the other but is used by the mother as a source of support for her feelings and actions toward the problem child. The relationship between the siblings is typically hostile or distant. The mother and the allied child (who is usually conforming) join together to blame the scapegoated child for causing distress in the family. In more complex variations, the allied child may support the scapegoated sibling in certain situations, sometimes to gain tactical advantages in family power struggles. (As discussed in chapter 4, an extension of our triadic form of analysis can yield patterns even more complex.)

The last pattern of alliance to be mentioned is a variation of the "two-after-one" coalition. In this pattern, siblings compete to form alliances with the parent and may succeed temporarily. What is characteristic is not a stable pattern of alliance but constant jockeying between one sibling to gain an advantage over another through a parental alliance. Although rivalrous siblings can seek parental alliances in two-parent families, a single mother is more vulnerable because of her greater dependence on her children for support. And being the only parent, her children's efforts are concentrated on her. Understandably, she may find herself joining with one or another from time to time which, of course, serves to fuel the fire.

In addition to the immediate family of the mother and her children, the practitioner often needs to consider alliances within a larger family or quasi family context involving the extended families of the mother and the former spouse, as well as the former spouse himself. To these possibilities can be added male or female friends who may be deeply involved with the family, perhaps sharing the same household.

The practitioner needs to be alert to both potential obstacles and resources in considering alliances within these broader contexts. The position of the mother and children in relation to the separated father should always be explored. The mother and children may be allied against the father, or one or more of the children may be allied with father against mother. Alliances of the latter kind may not be readily apparent since the father may seem to be out of the picture.

To complete our examination of contextual factors, we shall broaden our attention to the family's relationships with "outside" persons and agencies. In general, the relationship with the ex-spouse, the establishment of a satisfying intimate relationship, and the presence of a peer or familial support network have been shown to mediate maternal and child adjustment (Wahler 1980; Pett 1982; Hetherington et al. 1982; McLanahan et al. 1981). Each of these aspects may be viewed as potential resources or obstacles which will indirectly influence internal family functioning.

Wahler's (1980) study provides an intriguing illustration of such influences on the mother-child relationship. His investigation involved eighteen low-income mother-child dyads. The mothers had sought help for child management problems. The results of the parent training procedure showed a significant decrease in oppositional child behaviors. Unfortunately, at follow-up the problematic behaviors had returned to baseline levels. Self-report findings indicated that on days when the mothers had several contacts with friends, aversive mother-child interactions were lower in frequency. Additionally, child improvement seen in treatment continued into the follow-up phase during mother's high friendship days.

Wahler (1980) describes two groups of parents: "insular" parents and "noninsular" parents. Insular parents have few social contacts outside the home, and those that do occur are largely aversive. Noninsular parents are those parents who experience frequent and largely positive interactions outside of the home. Baseline observations in the homes of these families indicated that children of insular households evidenced more oppositional behavior than did children from noninsular households. Also, there is evidence to suggest that continuing conflictual interaction between the parents after divorce is linked to problem behavior in children. Hetherington (1980) reports that sons of divorced parents who continue a conflictual relationship show more behavior problems than sons from divorced low-conflict households. (For a thorough review of this literature, see Emery 1982.) Other research on maritally intact but conflictual households supports the notion that aversive dyadic interaction has some relationship to observed child difficulties (Oltmans, Broderick, and O'Leary 1977; Porter and O'Leary 1980; Christensen et al. 1983).

Although active involvement in a social network may be a valuable resource for the single mother, the quality of her relationships and the support she receives from them are the critical factors. A social network or some parts of it may constitute obstacles. Thus, Spanier and Hanson (1982) found that interaction with extended families did not help the mother's post-separation adjustment on the average. Some mothers found the interactions to be helpful; others did not. The prior relationship of the extended family members, particularly her parents, and their attitudes toward the break-up of the marriage were influencing variables.

Similar considerations apply to relationships with former spouses. An interaction with a former spouse who is responsible about financial obligations and visitation, and who provides support in other ways, can be an asset. A difficult relationship—which is, of course, more common—can be an additional source of stress.

In the world of work, the single mother may face a special set of stresses. In addition to the well-known overload problem of having responsibility for children as well as a job (Smith and Reid 1973), she must deal with conflicts between job and child care needs. Child care arrangements break down, children may need medical attention, schools and social agencies must be visited, and so on. These conflicts are more difficult to resolve if the mother, as is often the case, has a low-level job or lacks seniority or other job protection: "taking off a little time" to attend to personal affairs is much more easily accomplished if you are a boss, or an old hand, or if your skills are badly needed.

Relationships to social agencies often are a vital part of the single mother's life, particularly if her income is low. Public and child welfare departments, medical clinics, housing authorities, courts, and schools may be sources of support or frustration, depending on the agency or circumstances. Accommodating to agency office hours, appointment schedules, and waiting rooms may be especially difficult for the single mother because of constraints at work (as noted above) and her child care responsibilities. Discrimination and negative labeling by agency personnel may pose additional obstacles. Her distress may be augmented by fears, sometimes justified, that questions will be raised about her adequacy to care for her children (Dill et al. 1980). Failures to cope with her organizational environment are more likely to be internalized without a partner to reinforce her own position.

This review of contextual factors has attempted to abstract those that may be of special concern in work with single mother families in general. It has hopefully provided a base for consideration of assessment and intervention strategies.

Practice Implications

The special characteristics of a case type should provide the practitioner with guidance in her work with the family and her problems. As suggested, the guidance is at best partial, given the amount of general knowledge available about any type of situation, uncertainties about what the knowledge should lead to in the way of intervention, and idiosyncratic features of the case at hand.

A general principle, one that is basic to all others, is that the practitioner should be sensitive to the kind of contextual features discussed, and if they appear to be present and pertinent, to learn more about them. As with any theory, one needs to pin abstractions down to the situation at hand. What the single mother may be feeling and facing may be a helpful guide to exploration, but it is essential to determine what is actually going on.

Problem formulation with the single mother, as with any client, is controlled by the issues the client wants to work on, although the practitioner may take an active role in identifying areas of possible concern to the client. When the problem concerns her relationships with one of her children, the practitioner tries to help her identify interactional elements but does so with awareness of possible feelings of inadequacy and guilt the mother may have. Lacking a partner with whom to share responsibility and blame, the mother may take a defensive position that the problems lie in her child. This position may need to be accepted initially. Session tasks involving communication between parent and child early in treatment may provide a means of focusing on interactive elements without directly confronting the mother's defenses. An actual demonstration of communication difficulties (which are likely to emerge) can be referred to, rather than undertaking a threatening exploration of the mother's role in the problem.

In exploring the context of the problem, the practitioner should routinely inquire about the circumstances of the divorce or separation (including the mother's and children's emotional reactions), the mother's and children's current relationship with the father, and the mother's social network, including male and female friends and interactions with her own and her ex-husband's families. These contextual factors almost always have bearing on the mother's difficulties with the child.

Beginning with the divorce or separation itself enables material to be elicited sequentially. Even if this event occurred some time ago, attitudes and feelings generated at the time may still be active. Whatever current distress about her life situation the client may be having is explored, with an effort made to relate these to her problems with her child or to other target problems.

Following the initial phase, the practitioner and family will begin to concentrate on tasks in the session, at home, and in the environment and will make use of contextual analysis to facilitate work on these tasks. As suggested, single mothers may find it difficult to deal with relationship problems on an interactional basis and may need to see the problem as one of the child's misbehavior. If this position is accepted, and particularly if the child is preadolescent, then a parent-training approach can be used within a task-centered framework (Berkowitz and Graziano 1972; Henry 1981; Griest and Forehand 1982). The practitioner puts her role in terms of helping the mother find more effective ways of bringing her child's behavior under control. Although the child's views of the problems are elicited, the mother's definition of the problem (as child misbehavior) is legitimated. The practitioner takes greater responsibility than is customary for setting up the mother's and child's tasks. Tasks for the child are generally pointed toward more compliant behavior.

The mother's tasks usually include the following sequence of activities: (1) informing the child which specific behaviors are expected, and which are not acceptable; (2) making clear to the child rewards for proper behavior and penalties for non-compliant behavior; (3) giving the child reasons for the desired behavior; (4) asking for the child's understanding of these explanations and correcting misperceptions through feedback; (5) following through with consequences, including verbal praise for acceptable behavior. The program is presented to the mother in general terms, and an effort is made to involve the mother in working out the particulars. In task planning and review the practitioner helps the mother develop realistic expectations and consequences for the child, and emphasizes the importance of follow-through. Session tasks involving both mother and child may be used to practice elements of the plan. If interaction between mother and child in the session proves to be problematic, the mother may be seen alone or the mother and child may be seen separately. This training format may be accompanied by shared tasks aimed at increasing mutually satisfying contact between mother and child.

This approach can be extended to the mother's relationship with additional children. When the mother feels that the children are "out of control," as in Pett's (1982) profile, emphasis may be placed on helping the mother set up and enforce prescriptive rules for the household. Rules concerning chores, bedtime, curfews, television, sibling relations, and so on are developed with the mother alone or with children present. Emphasis initially is on shaping up and making clear a few key rules that would appear to have the greatest immediate impact on the central problem. Usually, rules in some form do exist but are no longer in force, or the mother has been unable to articulate rules she would like to see in place. Thus, one begins with the kinds of rules the mother is trying to implement or would like to have. Children are involved if possible, but the mother's wishes are given preference and her authority position is strongly supported. The practitioner may make suggestions about the kinds of rules to set up rewards and penalties, and so on.

The parent-training and rule-making approaches are not greatly dissimilar from the use of complementary tasks discussed in the preceding chapter. The difference is one of emphasis. The approaches just described provide more immediate and direct support to the mother. They are intended for single mothers who may be too vulnerable to criticism to engage in examination of their own roles, or too overwhelmed to become involved in negotiation with children or to implement complicated task agreements. For other single mothers, methods described earlier may work better and achieve greater contextual change because they may deal more effectively with the interactional basis of the difficulty. With older or recalcitrant children, a more interactional focus may be needed in any case.

If the mother has problems in other areas and is receptive to discussing them, the practitioner may be tempted to move away from focus on the parent-child relationship on grounds that these other issues are more important or that they need to be resolved before any real headway can be made with the child-related problem. In keeping with the basic strategy of the model, we suggest that such areas be dealt with selectively as they constitute obstacles to work on the target problem, which in the present discussion presumably concerns the child.

In some cases these other issues, while causing the mother distress, will not intrude as major obstacles to resolving the problem with the child. The mother either can handle them on her own or, if she wants professional help with any of them, the practitioner can suggest an extension of the service contract or referral elsewhere *after* the problem with the child has been dealt with.

In other cases, however, movement on the child-related problem is blocked by other difficulties. Contextual analysis then is used to sort out potential obstacles, identify those that appear to be impeding problem resolution, and work on them in the session. The mother may find herself unable to do tasks that would improve her relationship with the child for any number of underlying reasons: her resentment of the child as a burden, her depreciated self-image, overwhelming difficulties at work, and so on. Focused exploration, explanation, encouragement, direction, and other techniques of contextual analysis may help her work through such obstacles to the degree necessary to enable her to make progress with the target problem. Extended use of contextual analysis for this purpose may be best done through individual sessions with the mother. A continual effort should be made, however, to connect the results of this analysis to the problem concerning the child. It is also possible, of course, that difficulties the mother has apart from her relationship with the child will have been identified as target problems in their own right, and can be worked on accordingly.

As suggested earlier, the practitioner needs to expect, as normative, higher levels of mutual involvement between the mother and children than might obtain in a two-parent family. In designing tasks directed at greater independence, the practitioner may want to protect functional areas of involvement—for example, mother's reliance on an older child may meet her dependency needs without overwhelming the child. Such relationships may need to be modified but not fundamentally altered.

A general strategy for reducing high levels of mutual involvement between mother and child is to help both develop relationships or interests outside the family. Exploration of the social networks of both is used to locate possible resources for this purpose. Reduction of involvement can be accomplished in ways that preserve areas of involvement that the mother or child may be unwilling to relinquish. In the case cited earlier of the daughter who slept with her mother (Isaacs 1981), the practitioner devised a task that met this requirement. The mother was to make arrangements for the daughter to have friends overnight and to have the daughter spend the night with friends. In this way the mother was not made to feel left out, and her investment in the child was used constructively.

In some cases, the mother appears to have locked herself into the child's world out of guilt or need to compensate for the absent father by becoming a "double parent." The mother may be the pursuer, the child or children may be seeking greater distance. At the same time, the mother may resent the self-imposed burden of child care and forgoing of other interests, which she may see as a sacrifice she is making for the children. Displays of independence on the children's part may be interpreted by her as lack of appreciation.

Tasks that simply direct the mother toward outside involvement may run aground of her guilt and other feelings that keep her entangled. These feelings perhaps can be relieved by presenting the valid rationale that she can be a better parent if she can achieve a better balance in her life. By developing other interests—forcing herself, if necessary—she can acquire vitality that will benefit her relationships with her children. Thus, the mother's defenses are redirected rather than challenged. In another variation the practitioner can elicit from the mother activities apart from the children she would like to engage in "if she had the time." These activities then can be used as self-rewards for successful completion of child management tasks. Again, the mother's striving to be a conscientious parent can serve as a means of gaining entitlement to more of a life for herself. Individual sessions with the mother or seeing the mother alone for part of the session can be used to accentuate the mother's self-boundaries as well to enable exploration of the mother's concern about the nonchild part of her life.

Alliances involving the parent and one child against another of her children can be addressed through session tasks if the child left out is present. (We continue a triadic form of analysis to simplify discussion; the mother may be allied with two children against a third, and so on.) The tasks may call for interaction between mother and the triangulated child in which they deal with a problem directly. Tasks involving the child allied with mother and the triangulated child can be used for the same purpose. The usual goal for such tasks is to restructure communication patterns that may constitute problems or obstacles. Thus, in one family the mother avoided speaking directly with her fourteen-year-old problem daughter but would instead use her younger siblings as messengers. This arrangement, which the mother used to avoid conflict, made the daughter feel resentful and served as an impetus for further acting out. A session task in which mother and daughter discussed several issues, including the mother's using the younger siblings as messengers, helped to break up this pattern. The task accomplished its purpose even though the other siblings were not present. It is usually preferable, however, if the allied child or children participate in the session. Their presence provides the practitioner with more options, such as enactments of the coalitional pattern or tasks involving the siblings. Moreover, tasks between the mother and the isolated child and the post-task discussion can give the sibling(s) an understanding of the changes that are being attempted.

There is sometimes need to build alliances rather than to break them up. In some situations, for instance, an older child can accept greater responsibility for care of younger children as a way of easing the burden on the mother. An alliance between the mother and the child (the deliberate creation of a parental child, if you will) can be fostered through a session task in which the mother and older child plan out collaborative actions. Similarly, session tasks can be used to develop alliances between siblings for such purposes as providing mutual aid or working together on household tasks. By thinking of positive contributions that family members can make, the practitioner can increase her awareness of possibilities for functional alliances to achieve particular objectives. Work on alliances begun in session tasks can be pursued through home tasks. If session tasks do not prove feasible or productive for this purpose, home tasks alone can be used (see chapter 7).

The same principles are followed in work on alliances that go beyond the immediate family. If alliances constitute obstacles, or if alliance building would be useful, the practitioner may take steps to involve "outsiders" such as members of the extended family or former spouses. Sessions involving the divorced parents sometimes can be productive. The usual goal is to promote a functional coalition concerning their joint responsibilities for the children or at least to reduce negative consequences of dysfunctional coalitions, which are typically cross-generational in form. For this step to be productive, there normally needs to be some form of a working relationship between the divorced parents—something to build on. Otherwise, a joint session may lead only to a renewal of old marital warfare. Seeing the former spouse in an exploratory session alone may help determine if a joint meeting would be worthwhile.

Given the kind of external situations faced by many single-mother families, a good deal of use is made of environmental tasks designed to help the mother develop interests and activities outside the family and to cope with health and welfare organizations. The social isolation or overabsorption with children that one may find does not lend itself, however, to simple environmental prescriptions. Most single mothers whose social lives appear to be undernourished know of such resources as Parents Without Partners and usually have been enjoined by friends and relatives to "get out and meet people." If lack of external involvement appears to be a problem or obstacle, the practitioner needs to learn first about her feelings and wishes. Is there any interest in expanding her social horizons? Or if not, does she think there should be? Here, as elsewhere, the practitioner challenges but does not pursue. The last thing a single mother needs is another person prodding her into social activities.

If the client verbalizes some readiness to move in this direction, the practitioner then asks what she might like to try or has tried. This discussion generally leads to consideration of obstacles—lack of time and energy, concerns over child care, feelings of not belonging in a world of couples, and so on. Resources in line with the mother's interests are explored. Tasks evolve from such considerations, following an inward-outward progression. Beginnings may be small; the client's calling to inquire about a program or introducing herself to someone at work may suffice at the start. The practitioner should actively contribute suggestions, but they should reflect the client's preferences and readiness as they become clear and not presumptions about what the client really needs.

In helping clients deal with organizations, the practitioner should enable them, as Dill et al. (1980) put it, "to distinguish situations where control may be effectively exercised from those over which they have little control, so that responsibility would not be assumed without control" (p. 508). This principle, which grew out of a study of the coping efforts of low-income mothers, provides a basis for allocating tasks between clients and practitioners. Where the client can exercise some measure of control over an organization's response, a client task should be considered. The client's autonomy and sense of competence in dealing with her environment can be reinforced. If the client lacks control, a practitioner task is indicated. Although the practitioner may also lack control, and hence her task runs the risk of failure, the client is protected from wasted effort and an experience that may further deflate her self-esteem. Preliminary exploration by the practitioner of the organizational realities may be necessary to make this decision or to determine if some action on the practitioner's part can facilitate a client task. How responsive does an organization appear to be to a client's initiative? Can anything be done to make the organization more responsive? Additional criteria concern the kind of organizational response in question and the nature of the client's relationship with an organization or its personnel. In some situations, on-the-spot decisions must be made about what may be involved in a resource or service. There may then be good reason in the client's doing the task. Arranging for child care is an example. In others, such detail may not be so important, as in getting a utility company to restore service.

Organizations may expect clients to act on their own behalf for certain purposes, or it may be to the client's advantage to do the task herself as a way of developing a relationship with an organization. It may be important, for example, for a client to become involved with her child's school system. Of these criteria, the client's capacity to influence the organization's response is fundamental. Only if there is some evidence of that capacity do the other criteria apply.

The application of the model to the case type of the single mother and a problem child has illustrated how the various components of the model work together in a given kind of practice situation. A strategy for constructing case types, has been demonstrated, which can be used in the development of this and other models of practice.

As work on this particular case-type evolved, it became clear that certain approaches developed for this single mother family had broader application. For example, the parent-training methods, as well as methods of environmental intervention, could be adapted to other situations. Thus, efforts to build applications to case types can serve to add depth and range to the model as a whole.

9. *Model Development*

The task-centered model was designed to undergo continual modification as a result of experience in using it, systematic study of its use, and the incorporation of selected theories and methods from other approaches. In this chapter I shall focus on a strategy for model development within the context of family treatment. These strategies, which rely largely on single-case designs, can be implemented by practitioners and students who apply the present model or can be adapted to trials with other practice models. In a larger sense, the chapter offers methods of improving one's own practice from systematic study of his or her own cases.

DEVELOPMENTAL RESEARCH

Model development as a goal of research is a somewhat new idea in social work (Thomas 1978; Rothman 1980; Briar 1980; Reid and Smith 1981). The essence of this research strategy is the use of ongoing study to provide feedback for model-building efforts. Preliminary versions of the model are tried out. Data on its operations and apparent effects are obtained and used as a basis for progressive modifications in the approach. While many standard research methods may be used, the end product is practice technology and not research reports. This process usually is conceived of as progressing through stages, starting with an initial formulation of the model followed by preliminary or pilot testing. After a series of such trials and subsequent revisions, the model then may be evaluated through more rigorous, controlled designs.

My own experience over the past decade in developmental research with the task-centered model has led me to a different view. It makes sense to start with pilot trials of a model before conducting experiments. It does not follow, however, that one then necessarily shifts to more rigorous, formal studies. A variety of research methodologies are needed in the continuing development of a model. More flexible methods are needed, for example, to adapt the results of particular experiments, or of research conducted on similar approaches, into the mainstream of the model. Moreover, as a model continues to evolve it becomes applied in new forms or to new problems or populations. To evaluate such beginning applications through rigorous research designs may not be feasible or wise, even though designs of this kind may have been used earlier to study the operations of the model in other contexts.

This conception of model development has been illustrated by the evolution of the task-centered approach. Pilot studies (Reid and Epstein 1972) preceded controlled experiments (Reid 1975, 1978; Reid et al. 1980; Tolson 1977; Gibbons et al 1978). New branches of the model, in child welfare settings for example, began with pilot work (Rooney 1978) followed by a controlled study (Rzepnicki 1981). Work on conjoint family treatment, another branch, began with a reasonably well developed model that had been extensively tested in both uncontrolled and controlled studies. Additional theoretical and practice elements were incorporated in adapting the approach for work with family members seen together. This version has been tested in a series of uncontrolled case studies. These studies have been guided, however, by the earlier controlled studies previously cited.

The progression of research from "soft" to "hard" seemed to be followed in the early stages. Then more complicated patterns began to appear, in which "softer studies" were used to extend the results of "harder" research.

A PARADIGM FOR DEVELOPMENTAL RESEARCH

This experience has led me to conceive of a paradigm of developmental research in which more flexible experimental designs would be the major modality, and more rigorous (controlled) studies would have an adjunctive role. This paradigm might fit well to the development of complex forms of intervention, such as family therapy, where well-tested knowledge is a relative rarity. Also such a paradigm might make sense in settings in which more elaborate studies might be difficult to implement because of cost or feasibiity considerations. The principal users of this paradigm are intended to be instructors, students, and practitioners in agency settings operating without significant amounts of research funding.

The approach to be described has evolved from the methods of the Task-Centered Family Treatment Project (chapter 1) which is still in progress. In this project, the task-centered model has been applied to over thirty cases, a number which have been used as examples in this book. Some of the methods of the project as well as some of its findings will be introduced for illustrative purposes, but a full-scale report will not be presented here. However, in keeping with the purposes of developmental research, most of the important findings to date already have been incorporated in the model presented in the previous chapters.

The developmental research program essentially is accumulating single-case trials of the model over time within the context of ordinary agency service. Each case is a study in its own right and can be used as a basis for developing hypotheses about the model or for revisions. As cases accumulate, data from each can be combined and analyzed as one might from a group study.

The basic design is a single case study similar to Bergin's "elaborate, objectified case study approach" (1971:255). It may also be seen as a variation of the AB design as it is used in behavior modification research (Herson and Barlow 1976). Data are collected at the beginning of service on the family's problems and functioning. The opening picture includes retrospective information on the occurrence of the problems prior to the initial contact. As the case progresses, data on changes in the problem and on service events are obtained. At termination, changes in these problems are reviewed, another measure of family functioning is taken, and the family's reactions to treatment are secured. The result is a considerable amount of data on the operations and apparent effects of the model. The qualifier "apparent" is used in recognition that the design is not sufficiently controlled to permit definitive statements about treatment effects.

The design differs from an ordinary case primarily in the following respects: (1) an attempt is made to apply a designated model of practice and stick with it, unless there is good reason to suppose that its continuation would not be in the family's best interest; (2) systematic data are collected from clients through paper-and-pencil instruments, reviews of progress on problems, consumer questionnaires, and tape recordings of interviews; and (3) practitioners complete structured recording forms. All of these features, have clinical as well as research benefits. Commentary on each of these features will make their role clearer and will provide a means of introducing additional aspects of the design.

Model Application. Minimal criteria for case selection are developed, and an effort is made to have the participating practitioner pick the first case meeting these criteria. In this way one can avoid handpicking good cases for the model or cases that would make any model look good.

In the application, the practitioner makes a conscientious effort to follow the guidelines of the model but tries not to "force" the situation to fit the model. If what the model offers does not seem appropriate to the practitiioner, she uses her own judgment in deciding what to do. In this way, one avoids use of procedures that have an obviously poor fit to a situation not anticipated by the model. Moreover, it usually is better for the practitioner to follow her own clinical sense than to try to do something she has little confidence in. Finally, a flexible position on how religiously the practitioners are to follow the procedures is helpful in practitioner recruitment and retention.

As long as the model provides a reasonable fit to the family's situation, can be applied with discretion, and its use does not deny the family an opportunity to receive treatment that is demonstrably more effective, no ethical issue arises. It is hard at this point to foresee a situation in which the practitioner would have a grasp of a family treatment model clearly superior in effectiveness to the one under development. At best, other models contain components whose effectiveness has been demonstrated, as is the case with the task-centered approach. It can also be argued that the data collection procedures and attention given to the application can be expected to *enhance* the service provided to the family.

The training and supervision given practitioners in use of the model can vary considerably in intensity and amount. In the present program I meet in weekly group sessions with student practitioners, each of whom applies the task-centered model to a single case. Students receive help with their individual cases as well as training in the model. Individual supervision is used to supplement this format. Other modes have included individual supervision only and, with experienced practitioners, an initial all-day workshop with follow-up sessions after the practitioners have started to apply the model to cases.

A test of a model involves a test of how well its strategies and methods are communicated to practitioners. The written word is crucial to the widespread dissemination of a practice approach; lack of clarity and specificity in written guidelines and their failure to address frequently occurring contingencies are common shortcomings. While guidelines need to be supplemented by case discussions, taped illustrations, role plays and so forth, it is important to try to modify and expand the written material, which pretty much becomes the model in the world of practice at large.

Client Instruments and Tape Recording. Data obtained from clients or tapes provide a picture of the case that is free from the subjective impressions of the practitioner. Available paper-and-pencil instruments may be used to obtain profiles of family functioning at the beginning and the end of service. Comparisons of these profiles can yield measures of change, usually along several dimensions. In addition, responses of family members on particular items in the initial administration may provide clinically helpful clues about problem areas and attitudes of family members not dealt with in the session. The practitioner may in fact use family members' responses as a basis for additional exploration.

To minimize research intrusiveness, we generally restrict ourselves to one instrument that can be completed by family members in less than fifteen minutes. For most cases we use the Family Assessment Device (Epstein, Baldwin, and Bishop 1983), a sixty-item self-report instrument that yields scores on several aspects of family functioning: problem solving, communication, roles, affective responsiveness, behavior control, and general functioning. For cases limited to marital difficulties, a more specialized instrument, the Dyadic Adjustment Scale, is used (Spanier 1965). Other standard instruments can be added depending on the case and the interests of the practitioner. (See, for example, Moos 1974; Hudson 1982.)

Measures of change on these instruments are used to evaluate the apparent effectiveness of the model, particularly in respect to contextual change. In single-case analysis, an attempt is made to relate emphasis in treatment with change in related dimensions in family functioning. For example, if training in problem-solving communication was the major modality in a case, we would expect to see greater amounts of change in this dimension than in others on the Family Assessment Device. This kind of relationship can be tested with a group of cases once sufficient numbers have accumulated.

If there is interest in aggregating cases, there is an obvious advantage in using the same instrument for a given type of case. Other instruments, as noted, can be added to provide supplementary data.

Family members can supply data based on their own observations of behaviors and interactions at home. Use can be made of client logs designed by the practitioner (Bloom and Fischer 1982). Client recording devices can be integrated with task plans. For example, a parent can record instances of a child's performance or nonperformance of a task. Client-supplied data may be used as measures of problem change as well as of the apparent effectiveness of particular intervention strategies.

Audio or (more rarely) video recordings of family sessions serve several research purposes in our program. They provide a check of the practitioners' ratings of problem change, task progress, and recording of other data based on client self-report. They also present detail on the process and content of family members' communication for use in qualitative analysis of events in the case, as will be shown. Finally, recorded segments of client communication can be used as a basis for analysis of communication skills, problems, and so forth. Also, clients can tape-record communication sessions at home, and these tapes can be analyzed.

Practitioner Recordings. The practitioner obtains and records data on client characteristics, problems, service processes, and outcomes. For this purpose she makes use of structured recording guides (Reid 1978; Videka-Sherman and Reid, in press). The guides used in the present project are found in the appendix. The recording format serves both clinical and research purposes. As a clinical tool, they provide a structure for practice by requesting information on different steps of the model. The guides are keyed to the outline provided in chapter 2. In order to complete the guides, the practitioner must follow the model. Thus, the recording of target problems, and how family members ranked them, the information requested on session and home tasks, and data for the terminal interview could only be honestly provided if the practitioner were in fact making use of central elements of the model. The organization of content provided by the recording format is also helpful in clinical supervision. The supervisor knows where to look to locate key information. She can quickly determine what has been done and with what results. The record does not, of course, provide all the details that may be needed in supervising students or beginning practitioners, but this deficit can be compensated for by supplementary devices such as sample tape recordings of the practitioner's interviews, or logs containing interview process or other information not recorded in the guides.

As a research instrument, the record yields quantified practitioner ratings of task progress, problem change, and the like. It also organizes data in a form that can be readily coded.

Data useful for qualitative analysis can be obtained by requesting the practitioner to complete open-ended items. For example, if clients disagree on problem priorities, the practitioner is asked to record how priorities were arrived at (Initial Phase Schedule, see appendix). Such items can be revised or replaced depending on the focus of attention in model development. Thus, the recording guides presented in the appendix were designed for developmental work on the initial phase and session tasks. Hence, more detail is elicited for those components than for others. Although items can be used to achieve developmental purposes, certain features, such as task and problem ratings, remain constant in order to accumulate data over cases.

Quantitative Analysis. Data for each case contains already quantified elements, such as scores from client self-report instruments and ratings of task progress and problem change. These data may be used in the monitoring and analysis of single cases and aggregated across sets of cases. Outcome data can provide a picture of how the model as a whole as well as how different components appear to be working. More discriminating analysis in which characteristics of clients, problems, interventions, and the like can be correlated to outcome begin to make sense as the case pool achieves a respectable size—twenty or so cases.

An interesting example of an early yield from cases completed thus far in the present project had to do with reactions of family members to the length of service. Adult members indicated that service lasted about the right length of time or was a little brief, responses consistent with earlier studies in which clients responsed to this item (Reid 1978). The great majority of problem children in these families, however, indicated that service went on "too long," even though the median number of sessions per case was about six. Overall, the children indicated they had found service helpful (as did the parents), supporting previous findings that evaluations of the length of service were not necessarily related to perceptions of its helpfulness (Reid 1978; Reid and Shyne 1969). Also, in previous studies the response that service went on too long rarely was selected, not even by children (when seen in individual treatment). These data supported qualitative analyses (discussed later) that suggested that children often were reluctant participants in the family sessions. While they may have seen some benefits resulting from the sessions, they were glad to be through and perhaps thought that service had gone beyond the point of diminishing returns.

In addition to already available ratings, scores, and the like, quantitative data can be generated through additional coding, either of tape recordings or of the practitioner's written statements. The tape recordings offer a particularly rich resource for various kinds of analysis of communication processes relevant to model development. A number of schemes for coding problem skills in family communication have been developed (Hops et al. 1972; Thomas 1976; Gottman 1979).

Qualitative Analysis. Much of the analysis in this form of developmental research is qualitative. The search is for ideas that would improve the model. Case data are examined in terms of what they might suggest rather than in terms of what they might prove.

The main approach we have used is *analysis of informative events*. The methodology, which is an attempt to systematize the use of case material in model development, evolved from our efforts to make use of data to improve the task-centered approach. Although the findings of formal research undertakings provided ideas about how the model could be improved, these results were most useful in providing evidence, as they frequently did, that the methods we were using indeed were effective agents of change. The process of revising, elaborating on, and adding to the methods of the model seemed to receive more direction from intensive qualitative analysis of individual cases or small sets of cases. The case studies seemed to provide the detail essential to this process, because from them we could gain some ideas about the workings and apparent effectiveness of specific methods, observe inadequacies of the model in given situations, or note promising innovations. Moreover, new elements could be rapidly incorporated in the model and tried out, sometimes almost at once, on a new case.

We attempted to make this case review more systematic by developing a method of recording and classifying incidents or events that seemed to provide particularly useful information. For example, if a component (that is, a method or procedure) of the model was tried and failed to work as planned, the failure was examined to glean from it clues that might be useful in model development. Even though only a single instance of applying the component might be involved, the failure in itself would produce a negative signal. An accumulation of enough of them without offsetting positive results, would argue for a modification.

Procedure

An informative event is any occurrence in a case that provides information useful for the development of the model. Informative events have both factual and generative aspects. They provde specific facts that are themselves of interest—for example, a particular method fails to work in a particular situation. Their generative value lies in what they may suggest. An instance of failure may raise questions about the method or the assumptions on which it is based. The use of an innovation may suggest either ways in which the innovation may be varied or other applications of it. An event may also suggest connections to available theories and methods or stimulate a search of the literature for something similar. The generative aspect is an essential ingredient. It is what makes an event informative. Thus, failures or successes must in some way be "instructive," that is, offer ideas for model development.

What an event generates provides input for the model in the form of suggestions for revisions, additions, and so forth. Although all events, by definition, should be generative and provide input, the input may not necessarily lead to a change in the model. A single event may do so, if it points up an obvious deficit or reveals a clear improvement over existing procedures. Generally, one waits for input to accumulate to see what patterns are formed. Also, it is important to remember that in an active model-building program, changes in the model may be introduced provisionally, tried, and later withdrawn.

In the present effort, data from which events are generated consist largely of structured records completed by the practitioner and tape recordings of interviews. The records, which can be reviewed more quickly, are examined in their entirety; tapes are listened to selectively, often to probe particular events in greater detail. Additional data may be obtained from discussions with practitioners whose cases provided the events.

Each event is recorded on a card along with information to identify the case and locate the event within the case. The event itself is simply a factual description of what occurred. For example: The practitioner, parents, and Rich (age fourteen) met with school personnel at the school's suggestion. Discussion of Rich's behavior problems and possibility of placement in a special school.

The input provided by the event is then recorded. For example: The model contains no provisions for conferences involving practitioner, family members, and school or other community personnel.

The event is classified according to type of event. In this instance the event suggests a limitation of the model because it has no guidelines to cover the contingency. As can be seen, the event generates the observation that the model is lacking in respect to conferences involving the family and community personnel in general, not just school personnel. The event and input could have been elaborated on in greater detail. For example, the event might have stimulated the idea that such conferences might be suggested by the practitioner in some cases.

What is considered to be an informative event and what is recorded are subjective decisions made by the case analyst, a person who must be knowledgeable about the model and the field. A case may yield no events or it may produce a dozen or more. Conventional notions of reliability do not apply to this kind of analysis. If two analysts are used, one does not expect them to agree on what events in a case are informative. The contributions of each may differ but both may be useful. Special weight may be given, however, to events on which there is agreement.

After a set of cases has been examined, events that have been recorded are reviewed. This review guides a focused reexamination of the cases. The reexamination, which goes fairly quickly because the analyst is already familiar with the cases, accomplishes two purposes. First, it ensures that components that have been singled out are systematically examined, thus controlling to some extent for bias resulting from selectivity. Second, by making comparisons between cases, the analyst can continue to develop and test hypotheses relating to the model. The process draws on qualitative methods of analysis described by Glaser and Straus (1967) and by Butler, Davis, and Kukkonnen (1979) for study of patterns through case comparisons. In addition, use can be made of input from experts and from practitioners participating in the model-development undertaking.

What is done can be most readily grasped from an example. The initial review of a set of cases revealed instances of difficulty in how the client (usually a preadolescent or adolescent) responded in the initial problem survey. In two cases, the child either refused to respond or denied any problems.

The reexamination of cases located sixteen in which a child was present with one or both parents in the initial interview. When all cases were considered, three types of initial responses could be discerned: most children replied to initial query about their views of the problem with defensive explanations, justifications, or downplays of their misbehavior, usually in response to parents' description of the problem which put the blame on them. A much smaller group of children (four) "stonewalled" by denying that they saw any problems, voicing protests about being there or simply saying nothing. A couple of children readily acknowledged themselves as the problem. The initial survey was almost always structured by the parents' complaints and the childrens' responses. Rarely, at the beginning, did a child define a problem that was not reactive to problems brought up by parents. A typical response was Betty's reply to her mother's statement that she seldom obeyed curfew: "There is no reason to come home. You're out yourself to 2 or 3 o'clock in the morning." Only later in the session did some children reveal other kinds of difficulties, such as parents' favoring a sibling. Some gender differences were also noted: the stonewallers were all boys.

The child very much occupied the position of the accused and in fact used the options of an accused person—defense, remaining silent, or confession. This observation raised some questions. Should the structure of the initial interview be changed? For example, the parents could be seen alone initially, a structure advocated by some therapists (Weakland, Fisch, and Segal 1982). If not, could anything be done to involve the child in a more productive way at the beginning?

To generate ideas on this point, use was made of a panel of four to six experienced therapists familiar with the task-centered model but reflecting different points of view about family therapy. This group met regularly over a two-month period as part of the model development program. Selected areas of difficulty with the model were presented and illustrated by written and tape recordings. The panel reacted to these situations and suggested possible solutions. For instance, responding to a situation involving a noncommunicative adolescent boy and his mother, different members of the panel offered the following suggestions.

"Comment humorously on his fighting spirit".

"Ask him why he came in joking away, for example 'Did your mom tie you up and bring you here?'"

"Feign mild shock at mom's recital of her punitive efforts as a means of joining with son."

"Try to engage son around some topic of interest to him."

The panel also considered ways in which the initial interview might have been structured:—seeing the boy alone first, then the mother, then both together; seeing the mother only for the first interview; and so on. Additional situations that revealed other facets of the difficulty were also given to the panel for its reactions and suggestions. Additional input was obtained from the group of student practitioners carrying the cases. Although the focus of the meetings was on learning the task-centered model and case supervision, a good deal of time was devoted to critiquing model components and considering ways of improving them. Also, the students were able to provide supplementary information about events in the cases.

To continue the example, the analysis of the cases and contributions from practitioner and student groups resulted in a rethinking of how best to engage children in family treatment. It was decided as a rule to stick with the format of an initial session involving parents and children. Despite the initial difficulties experienced, the initial session seemed to work reasonably well in most cases. Moreover, the advantages in working with the parents and child from the beginning as an interactive system seemed compelling. One modification was to discuss the initial session at somewhat greater length with parents on the phone when setting up the appointment for it. The child's reluctance about attending might be explored, and if this appeared to be a problem the practitioner might consider several options, including a brief session with the child and parents separately before seeing them together or calling the child herself to invite him to the session. Other elaborations were developed. When parents and child are seen together, in the first interview, the practitioner should anticipate that parents will blame and that the child will defend himself or remain silent. While not challenging the parent's definition of the problem, at that point the practitioner should make an attempt to engage the child through some overt recognition of his situation—his being on the spot, his not wanting to be there, and the like. Any attempt to draw the child into participating should be done lightly and not forced. The interview should continue with an eye to an opening that would permit the practitioner to involve the child.

Also opening the initial interview by engaging the family in some preliminary informal conversation concerning, for example, the parents' work and the children's interests, may establish a pattern for total family participation that will hold when problems are discussed. Support for use of such a "warm-up period," especially when recalcitrant children or adolescents are present, can be found in recent literature on interviewing (Hepworth and Larsen, in press).

A major goal of practice research is to establish different interventions for different situations. What is the best way to proceed with *this* kind of client or problem as opposed to *that* kind? Although this goal is seldom attained in any definitive sense, it provides a helpful point of reference to guide inquiry. In qualitative analysis of small numbers of diverse cases, only beginning approximations of the goal can be achieved; one hopes that progress will advance as cases accumulate. The development of procedures (just illustrated) for involving children in the initial interview is one example of movement towards this goal, although clearly contrasting situations and intervention approaches have not yet emerged in the present program.

Another example is provided by analysis of events involving fathers in disciplining children. A contrast emerged between stepfathers and natural fathers. The former tended to take a standoffish position on discipline on grounds that the child was "the mother's problem." Unless this obstacle was recognized, it seemed difficult to get these fathers involved in tasks. Even though they might not be actively involved in discipline, natural fathers assumed they had a responsibility to be so, hence a different approach on the practitioner's part was called for.

Once a component is identified as one of continuing interest, it may be routinely reviewed in each new case in which it may be relevant. As information is added, previous conclusions may be modified.

How much of a data base should be established before changes are introduced in the model varies according to type of event. In the case of obvious defects or promising innovations, one event may be sufficient. In fact, an innovation needs to be introduced at least provisionally in order to obtain experience with it. When events relate to established components as in the example of seeing family members together in the first interview, more of a data base is obtained before changes are introduced. As data accumulate, ideas about what changes may be desirable become strengthened and refined. On the other hand, one wants to modify questionable components as soon as possible. Moreover, the longer the delay in introducing a change, the less testing the modification can receive. No rules have yet been devised to provide guidance on this point.

Informative Event Categories. The major categories thus far developed for analysis of informative events are described below. The categories, which are meant to be more illustrative than exhaustive, can be modified or added to, depending on the kind of model to which applied or the model's stage of development.

Instructive Failure. A component of the model does not work as expected. In some instances there is nothing in the model or underlying theory that would anticipate the failure or suggest what can be done about it. The previous example of children refusing to participate in the initial problem survey applies here. In other instances, it is expected that a component will fail to work some of the time, but the failure in the case at hand is informative for one reason or another, often because clues are provided to suggest how subsequent failures might be avoided. For example, in one case a reciprocal task involved a mother's rewarding a child if the child did a particular chore. As the task review revealed, implementation soon broke down. The child claimed he started out by doing the chore but did not receive his reward. The mother responded that he did the task only after being reminded repeatedly, to the point that she no longer felt he deserved anything. The reasons for failure were instructive because they pointed out the need to take the "reminding" factor into account in planning tasks of this type. Because chores are frequently used as tasks and parents frequently nag children about them, the failure became particularly instructive. Had the task or reasons for its failure been less common, the event might have been legitimately passed over.

Lessons learned from the failure are made clear. Possibilities for corrective action are suggested.

Limitations in Model Development. Certain events may reveal omissions or deficiencies in the model or simply the lack of guidelines for certain contingencies. The circumstances of a case may call for a certain practitioner response but no provision is made for it in the model, or the approach suggested may appear to be inappropriate. For example, in some problem explanations, family members would mention things happening at about the time the problem began, such as a marital separation. These occurrences were explored, but practitioners did not specifically ask family members themselves what connections they saw between the occurrences and the problem. The model did not preclude such inquiry but still did not specify that the clients' own perceptions of these connections be explored. Other events in this category may arise when the model is applied to unfamiliar populations, settings, and the like.

These informative events differ from *instructive failures* in that they represent errors of omission rather than commission. Unlike innovations (see below), the practitioner does not introduce novel approaches worth incorporating.

The input statement on the card spells out the limitation revealed by the event. Drawing on his or her clinical knowledge and judgment, the analyst may suggest what might be done under the circumstances identified.

Practitioner Noncompliance. Practitioners may depart from the guidelines of the model to handle unanticipated contingencies. If so, the reason for the departure usually is evident, and may result in events of the types already considered. But they may also go off track for no apparent reason. Such deviations can be caused by several factors. The practitioner may lack proper understanding of the model, may believe that the model is off the mark, or may try a component but change course when difficulties are encountered. Whatever the reason, the event is recorded under this category if guidelines of the model are ignored without apparent reason. Evidence in the case or the accumulation of events across cases may give clues as to where the problem lies, although some discussion with the practitioner usually is necessary. If the problem appears to be the practitioner's misunderstanding, the resulting input may relate to modifications of how relevant components are presented or to the need for more careful training. If the problem is the lack of sufficient guidance for implementing a method, explication of specific procedures may be suggested.

Instructive Success. Because components of a model generally are supposed to work, routine successes are not particularly instructive. Successes exert influence on model development when there is uncertainty about how well a component works, particularly if data are present that might help account for the success. The uncertainty may arise from the newness of the component, failures in previous trials, or doubts generated from studies or from clinical experience reported in the literature. For example, in a case discussed earlier (chapter 6), a session task between father and son succeeded in effecting an apparent reconciliation, despite evidence of long-standing conflict and the presence of a coalition between mother and son. The resulting home task in which the son was to come home "dry" and spend the weekend with the family also was completed as planned.

Given the history of the problem and characteristics of the family structure, the task strategy had a high risk of failure. Its success provides some support for the model's position that straightforward problem-solving tasks are capable of achieving positive results in the face of what might appear to be formidable resistance. Analysis of possible reasons for the success brought two factors to light. First, both father and son had reached a point of readiness to work out their differences. Second, the mother-son coalition seem to be limited to protecting the son against the father's anger and rejection. When the father-son interaction took a turn for the better, this coalition seemed to dissolve, revealing elements of a stronger alliance between the parents.

In addition to providing support for the component, the event and its analysis would point to the need to examine the strength of client motivations and coalitions in such circumstances. In general, input for the model from instructive successes consists of a signal of encouragement for the component. Factors that may have facilitated its success, and ways of utilizing these factors, are suggested.

Innovation in Method. Practitioners and students who use the model are continually adding innovations, as alternatives or embellishments to standard procedures, or in response to contingencies not covered in the model. Innovations that become informative events are generally those that add significant and promising new elements to the model. They may be in use in other approaches but are new to the model. If so, there should be evidence that they can be implemented within the framework of the model and are in accord with its principles. An innovation may consist of a new way of carrying out a method that already is part of the model—an ingenious type of task, for example. A successful outcome in the case at hand makes the innovation more attractive but is not necessary for its selection.

One of the best examples of an innovation in developmental studies of the present model was the utilization of parents as models in role play with their children. This intervention, introduced by Kenneth Jacobs, one of our practitioners, was subsequently incorporated into the model (chapter 6). Different varieties of the intervention yielded a series of informative events. It was thus possible to put together pictures of both its actual and potential range.

Input for the model consisted not only of descriptions of the innovation but also implications for other components of the model. Thus more attention was given to identification of resources in contextual analysis, particularly in respect to how parents might help their children.

Other. An event that appears to be informative to the analyst, but does not seem to fit any of the preceding categories, should be recorded here. Examples might include events that (1) have implications for the value assumptions or theory underlying the model, (2) illustrate unusually skillfull (or outstandingly inept) applications of the model, and (3) demonstrate successful or unsuccessful uses of approaches that are not a part of the model.

Assessing Effects: Designs and Strategies. The single-case design that has been presented was not intended to provide definitive data on the effects of intervention. Although, as has been seen, quantitative measures can be used within the design, no provisions are made for the control of various factors that might offer alternative explanations for changes associated with intervention. A family receiving task-centered treatment might experience changes for the good that may be the result of positive developments in the family system or in its environment that might have occurred whether or not treatment was provided. Design controls are used to rule out such possibilities.

In single-case research design, controls are achieved through various procedures. Data on the level and variability of target problems prior to an intervention may be collected to provide a baseline for assessing change after intervention is begun. If only this control is used (the simple time series design), it may be difficult to rule out placebo effects, contemporaneous events and other factors that may occur when treatment is begun.

More powerful controls involve greater manipulation of treatment. Intervention may be applied and then withheld to determine if its presence makes any difference in the problem—the withdrawal/reversal design. Or several families, or several problems within a family, may be selected. Intervention may be introduced at different times across clients or problems to see if expected changes occur when it is introduced—the multiple baseline design. These designs and their application to social work intervention have been well described in the literature (Bloom and Fischer 1982; Reid and Smith 1981; Wodarski 1981; Jayaratne and Levy 1979). Discussion of their use in family treatment can be found in Nelson (1982). For illustrative applications to this form of treatment, see Tolson (1977), Jacobson (1978).

Because controlled designs can provide more definitive evidence on the effectiveness of interventions than uncontrolled designs, they have an important role to play in model development. They are particularly helpful after an intervention has been developed and used with apparent success. The question of whether the intervention is actually the effective ingredient of change may arise. A controlled design provides a powerful means of answering that question.

In the present paradigm, however, the use of such designs has an ancillary, specialized role. They help settle questions about the effectiveness of certain procedures. They are not seen as the mainstay of the developmental research effort.

The use of controlled single-case design in the development of family treatment approaches is constrained by several factors. As Thomas (1978) has suggested, single-case designs that involve the manipulation of intervention may interfere with service requirements. This factor becomes particularly limiting in a developmental effort that must depend upon regular service programs for its cases. It is difficult to sell such designs to agency personnel who staff or administer programs. Even if permission is secured, it is hard to hold practitioners, whether agency or student, to the requirements of the design, when it appears to conflict with what they regard as best for the family. Designs that require intervention to be withheld or applied sequentially within a case are often confounded by the systemic properties of the families being treated.

Once introduced, an intervention may set in motion systemic phenomena that may make it difficult to assess the effects of withdrawing the intervention or withholding it from certain problems. For example, in one such design, the across-problems multiple baseline, two or three problems may be targeted and baseline data obtained on each. The problems then are treated in sequence, under the hypothesis that each problem will show positive change over baseline levels only after it receives its "turn" to be treated. The difficulty that frequently arises is that when the first problem is treated, various changes in the other problems occur. These changes may be the result of the intervention or of several system changes due to other causes. But the fact that the family system has undergone a holistic change involving all its problems vitiates the logic of the design. One solution is to target problems that are relatively narrow and discrete to minimize overlap—for example, deficits in different kinds of communication skills. But this solution runs the risk of restricting intervention to limited problems that may not be central to the family's concern.

Another solution is to use across-case multiple baseline designs in which treatment is applied sequentially to several families. Intervention can deal simultaneously with multiple problems of a given family, since the logic of the design calls for change in family measures when the family as a whole is treated. This design requires, however, that some families must agree to postpone their needs for genuine service but still participate in measurement procedures during their baseline periods. If not the family, then the practitioner is likely to have serious reservations about this demand. Although these difficulties can be overcome at least to some extent, they constitute real impediments to routine use of controlled single-case designs in developmental research on models of family treatment.

The feasibility problems associated with across-case multiple baseline designs occur with greater force in group experiments that compare treated and control groups. To these problems one must add, of course, the cost and time of these experiments. Like their single-case counterparts, controlled group experiments provide definitive data on the effectiveness of intervention and do so with a better basis for generalization. Their advantage in generalization may make them, in fact, more attractive than a series of single-case studies. Despite the importance of this function, feasibility and time and cost considerations limit their utility. They are best reserved for "final tests" of a model with a given problem or population after their model has been shaped up by previous developmental work.

The restricted role of controlled designs in developmental research does not mean, however, that efforts to determine the effectiveness of interventions should be forsaken. It means, rather, that more reliance must be placed on reasoning from whatever evidence can be brought to bear on the effectiveness question.

A control group may be lacking, but data from other studies might shed light on average rates of recovery for particular problems. For example, in a well-known study by Minuchin, Rosman, and Baker (1978), a pediatric family-therapy program was associated with impressive rates of recovery for anorectic children. Although a control group was not used, these rates appeared to be sufficiently better than the usual rates for recovery, to provide strong evidence that the program contributed to the alleviation of the anorexia.

In some cases the presumed effects may be so well matched with the intervention that design controls are not necessary to make reasonable inferences that intervention was the cause. This kind of situation arises when effects are very specific, detailed, and highly unlikely to have been produced by anything but the intervention. For example, a program may be devised to help couples acquire specific communication skills that they would not likely acquire on their own. If such skills are acquired on completion of the program, it may be reasonable to assume that the program was responsible for the change. Cook and Campbell (1979) refer to such explanations as "signed causes," because the effect bears the stamp or the signature of the cause.

Another situation involves a test of interventions whose effectiveness has already been demonstrated in controlled studies. Such tests may be conducted to determine if an intervention evaluated in one setting works in another or with a different population. If the method tested conforms to expectations based on prior controlled research—that is, if it is implemented in the same way and produces results similar to those achieved in the controlled test—then one has a basis for inferring that the methods were effective, even though controls were not used. The argument here is that the controlled test provided a prior probability that the methods work.

In a formulation relating specifically to single case studies of clinical intervention, Kazdin (1981) has cited several conditions that can be used to argue for treatment effectiveness even if design controls are lacking: reliance on objective measurement, a problem that has followed a stable course prior to treatment, the use of continuous assessment to monitor problem change before and after treatment, the occurrence of immediate and marked effects after the intervention is introduced, and the replication of effects with multiple cases. Not all of these conditions need be present. For example, a large, dramatic effort following an intervention—a slam-bang effect, as Gilbert, Light, and Mosteller (1975) have called it— may obviate the need for objective measurement.

These ideas, as well as those examined previously, are ways of ruling out alternative explanations in group or single-case experiments. Design controls generally are the most efficient and effective means of achieving this end, but in their absence, other considerations can be brought to bear.

If controlled designs are not used, one must be more guarded about the effectiveness of the model. But in family treatment models, like the present one, the effectiveness question seldom can be answered in a "yes" or "no" fashion. If a model is integrative, follows hierarchial principles (try A first, then use B), suggests different options for different situations, and is continually evolving, the question is more one of, "how effective are given elements of the approach in given situations." The effectiveness of the "model as a whole" requires an accumulation of evidence of varied levels of rigor.

For the time being we must be content with family treatment models whose components, whether original or borrowed, have received some testing in some applications and that can produce some evidence for their effectiveness. We have little choice but to use them while we push on with our research and development efforts.

Appendix

The appendix contains structured recording guides used in developmental research on the task-centered family practice model. The face sheet, which is relatively standard, has been omitted. To conserve pages, space provided in the originals for practitioner recording has been reduced. The guides illustrate how data can be obtained on selected components of the model; they are not designed to provide a full-scale case record.

INITIAL PHASE SCHEDULE

Name of Practitioner ⸺⸺⸺⸺⸺⸺⸺⸺⸺⸺⸺⸺⸺⸺

Name(s) (disguised) of Client(s) Participating ⸺⸺⸺⸺⸺⸺

Date of Interview(s) ⸺⸺⸺⸺⸺⸺⸺⸺⸺⸺⸺⸺⸺⸺

I. Initial Problem Survey

    A. Record each family member's initial expressions of problem in order of who had floor first, second, etc. Use family members' names as headings. Summarize using client's own words as much as possible. Use reverse of page and additional pages if necessary in this and subsequent sections of recording guides.

    B. Why did clients seek help at present. Use client's own words, note who said what.

    C. Describe difficulties, if any, in enabling each client to express his or her view of the problem—e.g., were there frequent interruptions, did one client take over?

II. Initial Problem Exploration

    Indicate below your activities during this step. For each activity checked, give critical examples.

_____A. Helped clients pin down global descriptions of difficulty.

_____B. Helped clients focus on central aspects of concern.

_____C. Helped clients expand excessively limited concerns.

_____D. Pointed out possible aspects of problem clients did not verbalize.

_____E. Reformulated individual problems as interactional problems.

_____F. Other activities important in problem formulation.

III. Target Problems and Goals

    A. List in final order of priority the problems (up to three) that you and the family agreed to work on. Identify problems in a single sentence or phrase.

        1.

        2.

        3.

    B. How were these problems rank ordered?

	PROBLEMS		
	1	2	3
Clients	_____	____	____
	_____	____	____
	_____	____	____
	_____	____	____
Practitioner	_____	____	____

    C. List and number additional problems of concern to family or to collaterals.

    D. Problem Formulation and Prioritization Processes

        1. Clients' response to practitioners' initial formulation.

        _____a. Clients pretty much accepted formulation

        _____b. Problems were altered as a result of client response

2. Prioritization

___a. Clients agreed on priorities

___b. Clients disagreed on priorities

If "b" above was checked, explain how priorities were determined.

E. Problem and Goal Specification

Record data requested for each problem listed under A above.
Use separate forms for each problem.

1. Problem #_____

2. Specification of details of the problem, including specific indicators or conditions to be changed and frequency and severity of each indicator for preceding 7 days.

3. Goals agreed on (if different from simple problem reduction)

4. When did problem begin and what has family done about it? Include relevant historical data.

5. Obstacles preventing solution of the problem and other relevant contextual factors.

F. Contract

The contract includes problems and goals previously specified. Indicate here other aspects of agreements with clients, including time limits, number of sessions, family members participating in treatment.

NOTE: Record initial session task on Session Task Recording Guide.

G. Practitioner's Assessment

Assess family's problem situation, including interrelation among problems, factors contributing to problems, and strengths that may be utilized in problem solving. Material previously covered in schedule may be summarized or referenced.

PROBLEM REVIEW SCHEDULE

Name of Practitioner _____

Review status of each problem beginning with second session. Record frequency and severity of problem occurrence in respect to each condition specified. Describe any major developments as well as any reformulation of problem conditions. If problem was replaced, describe new problem using item III E, IPS, and attach. Record review of each problem until termination. Use a separate form for each problem.

Problem #_____ (as numbered in Initial Phase Schedule)

Session 2   Date_____

Session 3   Date_____

Session 4   Date_____

Session 5   Date_____

SESSION–TASK SCHEDULE

Session #_____   Date_____

Session Task #_____   Related problem #_____   _

A. Nature of task
   (Briefly describe task as initially set up and indicate who participated.)
   (Note special instructions given participants.)

B. Task description
   (How did participant carry out task? Summarize process of implementation.)

C. Task length _____minutes

D. Task outcome rating _____

   Use following scale: (4) Successful—produced most results intended; (3) Partially successful—produced some intended results; (2) Uncertain—task carried out but results uncertain; (1) Participants unable to carry out task.

E. Post-Task intervention

   Describe main post-task interventions and clients' responses (what you said and how clients responded.)

	Intervention	Clients' Responses
1.		
2.		
3.		
4.		

HOME AND ENVIRONMENTAL TASK SCHEDULE

Practitioner name_____ Case name_____

Supply data requested and rate each task using the following scales.

Client's initial commitment to task:

1	2	3	4	5
Low				High

Task progress rating:

    0—No opportunity to carry out task
    1—Minimally or not achieved
    2—Partially achieved
    3—Substantially achieved
    4—Completely achieved

Task #_____

Task statement (begin with client name(s) or "I" if practitioner task)

_____

_____

_____

_____

Problem # to which related _____ When task formulated, Sess. #_____ Date_____

Who suggested idea for task? Client (specify)_____
                                    Practitioner_____
                                    Other (specify)_____

Client's initial commitment to task:

_____ _____ _____

(If different family members involved in task, specify commitment for each)

Comments on task planning:

When task reviewed, sess. # ＿＿ ＿＿ ＿＿ ＿＿ ＿＿ ＿＿ ＿＿ ＿＿ ＿＿
Progress rating (use ＿＿ ＿＿ ＿＿ ＿＿ ＿＿ ＿＿ ＿＿ ＿＿
additional lines if ＿＿ ＿＿ ＿＿ ＿＿ ＿＿ ＿＿ ＿＿ ＿＿
different ratings for
different clients)

Details of task review (indicate obstacles identified or significant variations between task statement and how task carried out):

TERMINAL INTERVIEW SCHEDULE

Name of Practitioner ＿＿＿＿＿＿＿＿＿＿＿＿＿＿＿＿＿＿＿＿＿

Name(s) of Client(s) Participating ＿＿＿＿＿＿＿＿＿＿＿＿＿＿

Session # ＿＿＿＿＿ Date ＿＿＿＿＿＿

I. Current Problem Assessment

A. How does family view its problems now? In eliciting family's view of problems, repeat procedure used for Initial Problem Survey.

B. What areas of difficulty, if any, have occurred since initial interview?

C. How does each family member assess change in each target problem since initial interview? (Note revisions in problem definitions and priorities.)

Problem 1:

Problem 2:

Problem 3:

D. How do collaterals, if any, assess change in target problems since initial interview?

E. Ratings of Problem Change

Use the following scale to rate degrees of problem change:

1. Problem greatly aggravated
2. Considerable aggravation
3. Some aggravation
4. Slight aggravation
5. No change
6. Minimal alleviations
7. Some alleviation
8. Considerable alleviation
9. Substantial alleviation (problem almost resolved)
10. Problem no longer present (completely alleviated)

(completely alleviated)

	Each Client's Assessment	Collateral's Assessment (if relevant)	Your Assessment
Problem 1	___ ___ ___	_____	_____
Problem 2	___ ___ ___	_____	_____
Problem 3	___ ___ ___	_____	_____
Overall problem situation (taking into account change in all target problems and changes in other problems present)	___ ___ ___	_____	_____

II. Review of family's accomplishments. (What was reviewed in the last session? How did clients react?)

III. Planning clients' and collaterals' work in remaining areas of difficulty. (What remaining difficulties and strategies, tasks, etc. for working on them were discussed and how did clients react?)

IV. Review of family learning of problem-solving skills. (Discussion of use family can make of treatment experience in regard to future problems.)

V. Plans for additional or future help, if any; rationale. (Summary of discussion, including clients' reactions.)

References

Alexander, James F. and Cole Barton. 1980. "Systems-Behavioral Intervention with Delinquent Families: Clinical Methodological and Conceptual Considerations." In John P. Vincent, ed., *Advances in Family Intervention Assessment and Theory* vol. 1. Greenwich, Conn.: AJAI Press.

Alexander, James F. and Bruce V. Parsons. 1973. "Short-Term Behavioral Intervention with Delinquent Families: Impact on Family Process and Recidivism." *Journal of Abnormal Psychology* 81:219–225.

Anderson, Carol and Susan Stewart. 1983. *Mastering Resistance*. New York: Guilford Press.

Aponte, Harry J. and John M. Van Deusen. 1981. "Structural Family Therapy." In Alan S. Gurman and David P. Kniskern, eds. *Handbook of Family Therapy*. New York: Brunner/Mazel.

Ascher, Michael L. 1981. "Employing Paradoxical Intention in the Treatment of Agoraphobia." *Behavioral Research and Therapy* 19:533–542.

Ascher, Michael L. and Jay S. Efran. 1978. "Use of Paradoxical Intention in a Behavioral Program for Sleep Onset Insomnia." *Journal of Consulting and Clinical Psychology* 46:547–550.

Ascher, Michael L. and R. M. Turner. 1979. "Paradoxical Intention and Insomnia: An Experimental Investigation." *Behavioral Research and Therapy* 17:408–411.

Azrin, Nathan H., Barry J. Naster, and Robert Jones. 1973. "Reciprocity Counseling: A Rapid Learning-Based Procedure for Marital Counseling." *Behavioral Research and Therapy* 11:365-382.

Bach, George R. and Peter Wyden. 1981. *Intimate Enemy: How to Fight Fair in Love and Marriage*. New York: Avon.

Barton, Cole and James Alexander. 1981. "Functional Family Therapy." In Allen S. Gurman and David P. Kniskern, eds., *Handbook of Family Therapy*. New York: Brunner/Mazel.

Baruth, Leroy G. and Charles H. Huber. 1984. *An Introduction to Marital Theory and Therapy*. Monterey, Calif.: Brooks/Cole.

Bass, Michael. 1977. "Toward a Model of Treatment for Runaway Girls in Detention." In William J. Reid and Laura Epstein, eds., *Task-Centered Practice*. New York: Columbia University Press.

Baucom, Donald H. 1982. "A Comparison of Behavioral Contracting and Problem-Solving/Communications Training in Behavioral Marital Therapy." *Behavior Therapy* 13:162–174.

Baumrind, D. 1973. "The Development of Instrumental Competence Through Socialization." In A. D. Pick, ed., *Minnesota Symposia on Child Psychology*, vol. 7. Minneapolis: University of Minnesota Press.

Beavers, W. Robert. 1977. *Psychotherapy and Growth: A Family Systems Perspective*. New York: Brunner/Mazel.

Beck, Aaron T. 1976. *Cognitive Therapy and the Emotional Disorders*. New York: International Universities Press.

Beck, Dorothy Fahs and Mary Ann Jones. 1973. *Progress on Family Problems: A Nationwide Study of Clients' and Counselors' Views on Family Agency Services*. New York: Family Service Agency of America.

Bell, John E. 1975. *Family Therapy*. New York: Jason Aronson.

—— 1981. "The Small Group Perspective: Family Group Therapy." In Eleanor Reardon Tolson and William J. Reid, eds., *Models of Family Therapy*. New York: Columbia University Press.

Bell, Linda G. and David C. Bell. 1982. "Family Climate and the Role of the Female Adolescent: Determinants of Adolescent Functioning." *Family Relations* 31:519–527.

Bergin, Allen E. 1971. "The Evaluation of Therapeutic Outcomes." In Allen E. Bergin and Sol L. Garfield, eds., *Handbook of Psychotherapy and Behavior Change*. New York: Wiley.

Berkowitz, Barbara P. and Anthony M. Graziano. 1972. "Training Parents as Behavior Therapists: A Review." *Behavior Research and Therapy* 10:297–317.

Berman, William H. and Dennis C. Turk. 1981. "Adaptation to Divorce: Problems and Coping Strategies." *Journal of Marriage and the Family* 43:179–189.

Berne, Eric, M.D. 1961. *Transactional Analysis in Psychotherapy*. New York: Grove Press.

Birchler, Gary R. 1979. "Communication Skills in Married Couples." In A. S. Bellack and M. Hersen, eds., *Research and Practice in Social Skills Training*. New York: Plenum Press.

—— 1981. "Paradox and Behavioral Marital Therapy." *American Journal of Family Therapy* 9:92–94.

Birchler, Gary R. and Suzanne H. Spinks. 1981. "Behavioral-Systems Marital and Family Therapy: Integration and Clinical Application." *The American Journal of Family Therapy* 8:6-28.

Blechman, Elaine. 1982. "Are Children with One Parent at Psychological Risk? A Methodological Review." *Journal of Marriage and the Family* 44:179–195.

Bloom, Martin and Joel Fischer. 1982. *Evaluating Practice: Guidelines for the Accountable Professional*. Englewood Cliffs, N.J.: Prentice-Hall.

Bornstein, Phillip H., Cynthia A. Sturm, P. D. Retzlaff, K. L. Kirby, and H. Chong. 1981. "Paradoxical Instruction in the Treatment of Encopresis and Chronic Constipation: An Experimental Analysis." *Behavioral Research and Therapy* 12:167–170.

Bornstein, Phillip H., J. Scott Hickey, Michael J. Schulein, Steven G. Fox, and Michael J. Scolatti. 1983. "Behavioral-Communciations Treatment of Marital Interaction: Negative Behaviors." *British Journal of Clinical Psychology* 22:41–48.

Boszormenyi-Nagy, Ivan and David N. Ulrich. 1981. "Contextual Family Therapy." In Alan S. Gurman and David P. Kniskern, eds., *Handbook of Family Therapy*. New York: Brunner/Mazel.

Bowen, Murray. 1960. "A Family Concept of Schizophrenia." In Don Jackson, ed., *The Etiology of Schizophrenia*. New York: Basic Books.

—— 1978. *Family Therapy in Clinical Practice*. New York: Aronson.

Briar, Scott. 1980. "Incorporating Research into Education for Clinical Practice in Social Work: Toward a Clinical Science in Social Work." In Allen Rubin and Aaron Rosenblatt, eds., *Sourcebook on Research Utilization*. New York: Council on Social Work Education.

Broderick, Carlfred B. 1983. *the Therapeutic Triangle*. Beverly Hills, Calif.: Sage.

Bross, Allon. 1982. *Family Therapy Principles of Strategic Practice*. New York: Guilford Press.

Bross, Allon and Michael Benjamin. 1982. "Family Therapy: A Recursive Model of Strategic Practice." In Allon Bross, ed., *Family Therapy: Principles of Strategic Practice*. New York: Guilford Press.

Brown, Lester B. 1977. "Treating Problems of Psychiatric Outpatients." In William J. Reid and Laura Epstein, eds., *Task-Centered Practice*. New York: Columbia University Press.

—— 1980. "Client Problem-Solving Learning in Task-Centered Social Treatment." Ph.D. dissertation, University of Chicago.

Buehler, Cheryl A. and M. Janice Hogan. 1980. "Managerial Behavior and Stress in Families Headed by Divorced Women: A Proposed Framework." *Family Relations* 29:525–532.

Burr, Wesley R., Reuben Hill, Ivan F. Nye, and Ira L. Reiss. 1979. *Contemporary Theories About the Family: Research-Based Theories*, vols. 1 and 2. New York: Free Press.

Butcher, James N. and Mary P. Koss. 1978. "Research on Brief and Crisis-Oriented Psychotherapies." In Sol L. Garfield and Allen E. Bergin, eds., *Handbook of Psychotherapy and Behavior Change: An Empirical Analysis*, 2d ed. New York: Wiley.

Butler, Harry, Inger Davis, and Ruth Kukkonen. 1979. "The Logic of Case Comparison." *Social Work Research and Abstracts* 15:3-11.

Butler, Janet, Irene Bow, and Jane Gibbons. 1978. "Task-Centered Casework with Marital Problems." *British Journal of Social Work* 8:393–409.

Caplow, Theodore. 1968. *Two Against One—Coalitions in Triads*. Englewood Cliffs, N.J.: Prentice-Hall.

Cattaneo, Dominique, Laurie Haslam, and Janet Young. 1984. *Task-Centered Family Practice: A Study of Session, Home, and Environmental Tasks in Two San Diego Cases*. Master's thesis, San Diego State University.

Cherlin, Andrew. 1981. *Marriage, Divorce, Remarriage*. Cambridge, Mass.: Harvard University Press.

Christensen, Andrew, Susan Phillips, Russell E. Glasgow, and Steven N. Johnson. 1983. "Parental Characteristics and Interactional Dysfunction in Families with Child Behavior Problems: A Preliminary Investigation." *Journal of Abnormal Child Psychology* 11:153–166.

Constantine, Larry L. 1978. "Family Sculpture and Relationship Mapping Technique." *Journal of Marriage and Family Counseling* 40:13–23.

Coopersmith. S. 1967. *The Antecedents of Self-Esteem*. San Francisco: Freeman.

Cormican, Elin J. 1977. "Task-Centered Model for Work with the Aged." *Social Casework* 58:490–494.

Dell, Paul F. 1980. "The Hopi Family Therapist and the Aristotelian Parents." *Journal of Marriage and Family Therapy* 6:123–130.

—— 1981. "Some Irreverent Thoughts of Paradox." *Family Process*, 20:37-51.

—— 1982. "Beyond Homeostasis: Toward a Concept of Coherence." *Family Process* 21:21–41.

de Shazer, Steve. 1982. *Patterns of Brief Family Therapy*. New York: Guilford Press.

—— 1984. "The Death of Resistance." *Family Process* 22:11–16.

Diaz, Carmen. 1980. *Demonstration of Using Single-Subject Research Modality in Social Work Practice*. Ph.D. dissertation, Ohio State University.

Diekring, Barbara, Margot Brown, and Anne E. Fortune. 1980. "Task-Centered Treatment in a Residential Facility for the Elderly: A Clinical Trial." *Journal of Gerontological Social Work* 2:225–240.

Dill, Diana, Ellen Feld, Jacqueline Martin, Stephanie Beukema, and Deborah Belle. 1980. "The Impact of the Environment on the Coping Efforts of Low Income Mothers." *Family Relations* 29:503–509.

Doane, Jeri A. 1978. "Family Interaction and Communication Deviance in Disturbed and Normal Families: A Review of Research." *Family Process* 17:357–376.

Druckman, J. M. 1979. "The Family-Oriented Policy and Treatment Program for Female Juvenile Status Offenders." *Journal of Marriage and the Family* 41:627-636.

Duhl, Frederick J., D. Kantor, and Bunny S. Duhl. 1973. "Learning, Space, and Action in Family Therapy: A Primer of Sculpture." In Donald A. Bloch, ed., *Techniques of Family Psychotherapy*. New York: Grune and Stratton.

Dunlop, K. 1932. *Habits: Their Making and Unmaking*. New York: Liveright.

Emery, Robert. 1982. "Interpersonal Conflict and the Children of Discord and Divorce." *Psychological Bulletin* 92:310–330.

Emery, Robert E. and Daniel K. O'Leary. 1982. "Children's Perceptions of Marital Discord and Behavior Problems of Boys and Girls." *Journal of Abnormal Child Psychology* 10(1):11–24.

Epenshade, Thomas J. 1979. "The Economic Consequences of Divorce." *Journal of Marriage and the Family* 41:615–625.

Epstein, Laura. 1977. "A Project in School Social Work." In William J. Reid and Laura Epstein, eds., *Task-Centered Practice*. New York: Columbia University Press.

—— 1980. *Helping People: The Task-Centered Approach*. St. Louis: C. V. Mosby.

Epstein, Nathan B. and Duane S. Bishop. 1981. "Problem-Centered Systems Therapy of the Family." In Alan S. Gurman and David P. Kniskern, eds., *Handbook of Family Therapy*. New York: Brunner/Mazel.

Epstein, Nathan B., Lawrence M. Baldwin, and Duane S. Bishop. 1983. "The McMaster Family Assessment Device." *Journal of Marital and Family Therapy* 9:171–180.

Ericson, Phillip M., and Edna L. Rogers. 1973. "New Procedures for Analyzing Relational Communication." *Family Process* 12:245–267.

Ewalt, Patricia L. 1977. "A Psychoanalytically Oriented Child Guidance Setting." In William J. Reid and Laura Epstein, eds., *Task-Centered Practice*. New York: Columbia University Press.

Feldman, Larry B. and William H. Pinsof. 1982. "Problem Maintenance in Family Systems: An Intergrative Model." *Journal of Marital and Family Therapy* 7:295–308.

Fisch, Richard, John H. Weakland, and Lynn Segal. 1982. *The Tactics of Change—Doing Therapy Briefly*. San Francisco: Jossey-Bass.

Fisher, Lawrence, Ann Anderson, and James E. Jones. 1981. "Types of Paradoxical Intervention and Indications/Contraindictions for Use in Clinical Practice." *Family Process* 20:25–36.

Fisher, Stuart G. 1980. *"The Use of Time-Limits in Brief Psychotherapy: A Comparison of Six-Session, Twelve-Session, and Unlimited Treatment with Families."* Family Process 19:377–392.

—— 1984. "Time-Limited Brief Therapy with Families: A One-Year Follow-Up Study." *Family Process* 23:101–106.

Fogarty, Thomas. 1976. "Marital Crisis." In Philip Guerin, ed., *Family Therapy: Theory and Practice*. New York: Garden Press.

Fortune, Anne E. 1977. "Practitioner Communication in Task-Centered Treatment." Ph.D. dissertation, University of Chicago.

—— 1981. "Communication Processes in Social Work Practice." *Social Service Review* 55:93–128.

—— 1985. *Task-Centered Practice with Families and Groups*. New York: Springer.

Frankl, Victor. 1965. "Paradoxical Intention: A Logotherapeutic Technique." *American Journal of Psychotherapy* 14:520–535.

—— 1975. "Paradoxical Intention and Dereflection." *Psychotherapy: Theory, Research, and Practice* 12:226–237.

Gambrill, Eileen D. 1981. "A Behavioral Perspective of Families." In Eleanor Reardon Tolson and William J. Reid, eds., *Models of Family Treatment*. New York: Columbia University Press.

Gant, B. L., J. D. Barnard, F. E. Kuehn, H. H. Jones, and E. R. Christophersen. 1981. "A Behaviorally Based Approach for Improving Intrafamilial Communication Patterns." *Journal of Clinical Child Psychology* 10:102–106.

Garvin, Charles D., William J. Reid, and Laura Epstein. 1976. "Task Centered Group Work." In Helen Northern and Robert W. Roberts, eds., *Theoretical Approaches to Social Work with Small Groups*. New York: Columbia University Press.

Garvin, Charles D. and Brett A. Seabury. 1984. *Interpersonal Practice in Social Work—Processes and Procedures*. Englewood Cliffs, N.J.: Prentice-Hall.

Gergen, Kenneth J., Martin S. Greenberg, and Richard H. Willis, eds. 1980. *Social Exchange: Advances in Theory and Research*. New York: Plenum Press.

Germain, Carel B., ed., 1979. *Social Work Practice: People and Environments, An Ecological Perspective*. New York: Columbia University Press.

—— 1983. "Technological Advances." In Aaron Rosenblatt and Diana Waldfogel, eds., *Handbook of Clinical Social Work*. San Francisco: Jossey-Bass.

Germain, Carel B. and Alex Gitterman. 1979. "The Life Model of Social Work Practice." In Francis J. Turner, ed., *Social Work Treatment—Interlocking Theoretical Approaches*, 2d ed. New York: Free Press.

—— 1980. *The Life Model of Social Work Practice*. New York: Columbia University Press.

Gibbons, James S., Janet Butler, Paul Urwin, and Jane L. Gibbons. 1978. "Evaluation of a Social Work Service for Self-Poisoning Parents." *British Journal of Psychiatry* 133:111–118.

Gibbons, Jane, Janet Butler, and Irene Bow. 1979. "Task-Centered Casework with Marital Problems." *British Journal of Social Work* 8:393–409.

Gilbert, J. P., R. J. Light, and F. Mosteller. 1975. "Assessing Social Innovations: An Empirical Base for Policy." In C. A. Bennett and A. A. Lumdsaine, eds., *Evaluation and Experiment*. New York: Academic Press.

Glaser, Barney G. and Ansel Strauss. 1967. *The Discovery of Grounded Theory: Strategies for Qualitative Research*. Chicago: Aldine.

Glueck, Sheldon and Eleanor Glueck. 1950. *Unraveling Juvenile Delinquency*. Cambridge, Mass.: Harvard University Press.

Goldberg, E. Matilda and J. S. Stanley. 1978. "A Task-Centered Approach to Probation." In Joan King, ed., *Pressures and Changes in the Probation Service*. Cambridge, England: Institute of Criminology.

Goldberg, E. Matilda, Jane Gibbons, and Ian Sinclair. 1984. *Problems, Tasks and Outcomes*. Winchester, Mass.: Allen and Unwin.

Goldsmith, Jean. 1982. "Postdivorce Family Systems." In Froma Walsh, ed., *Normal Family Processes*. New York: Guilford Press.

Gordon, Thomas. 1970. *Parent Effectiveness Training*. New York: Peter H. Wyden.

Gottman, John et al. 1976. *A Couple's Guide to Communication*. Champaign, Ill.: Research Press.

Griest, Douglas and Rex Forehand. 1982. "How Can I Get Any Parent Training Done with All These Other Problems Going On? The Role of Family Variables in Child Behavior Therapy." *Child and Family Behavior Therapy* 4:73–81.

Griest, Douglas and K. Wells. 1983. "Behavioral Family Therapy with Conduct Disorders in Children." *Behavior Therapy* 14:37–53.

Grinnell, Richard M., Jr. 1973. "Environmental Modification: Casework's Concern or Casework's Neglect?" *Social Service Review* 47:208–220.

Grinnell, Richard M., Jr., Nancy S. Kyte, and Gerald J. Bostwick, Jr. 1981. "Environmental Modification." In Anthony N. Maluccio, ed., *Promoting Competence in Clients: A New/Old Approach to Social Work Practice*. New York: Free Press.

Guerney, Bernard. 1982. "Relationship Environment." In Eldon K. Marshall and P. David Kurtz, eds., *Interpersonal Helping Skills*. San Francisco: Jossey-Bass.

Gurman, Alan S. 1981. *Questions and Answers in the Practice of Family Therapy*. New York: Brunner/Mazel.

Gurman, Alan S. and David P. Kniskern. 1978. "Behavioral Marriage Therapy: II. Empirical Perspective." *Family Process* 17:139–164.

—— 1981. "Family Therapy Outcome Research: Knowns and Unknowns." In Alan S. Gurman and David P. Kniskern, eds., *Handbook of Family Therapy*. New York: Brunner/Mazel.

—— 1981. *Handbook of Family Therapy*. New York: Brunner/Mazel.

Guttentag, Marcia, S. Salasis, and D. Belle. 1980. *The Mental Health of Women*. New York: Academic Press.

Halem, Lynne Carol. 1982. *Separated and Divorced Women*. Westport, Conn.: Greenwood Press.

Haley, Jay. 1963. *Strategies of Psychotherapy*. New York: Grune and Stratton.

—— 1973. *Uncommon Therapy: The Psychiatrc Techniques of Milton H. Erickson*. New York: W. W. Norton.

—— 1977. *Problem Solving Therapy: New Strategies for Effective Family Therapy*. San Francisco: Jossy-Bass.

—— 1980. *Leaving Home: The Therapy of Disturbed Young People*. New York: McGraw-Hill.

Hardy-Fanta, Carol and Elizabeth MacMahon-Herrera. 1981. "Adapting Family Therapy to the Hispanic Family." *Social Casework* 62:138–148.

Hari, Veronica. 1977. "Instituting Short-Term Casework in a 'Long-Term' Agency." In William J. Reid and Laura Epstein, eds., *Task-Centered Practice*. New York: Columbia University Press.

Hartman, Ann. 1981. "Bowen Family Systems: Theory and Practice:" In Eleanor R. Tolson and William J. Reid, eds., *Models of Family Treatment*. New York: Columbia University Press.

Hartman, Ann and Joan Laird. 1983. *Family-Centered Social Work Practice*. New York: Free Press.

Henry, Stephen A. 1981. "Current Dimensions of Parent Training." *School Psychology Review* 10:4–41.

Hepworth, Dean H. and Jo Ann Larsen. 1982. *Direct Social Work Practice: Theory and Skills*. Homewood, Ill.: Dorsey Press.

—— In press. Ann Minahan ed., *Encyclopedia of Social Work*. 18th ed. New York: National Association of Social Workers.

Herson, Michael and David H. Barlow, eds. 1976. *Single Case Experimental Designs: Strategies For Studying Behavior Change*. New York: Pergamon Press.

Herzog, E. and C. Sudia. 1973. "Children in Fatherless Families." In B. M. Caldwell and N. H. Riccuiti. eds., *Review of Child Developmet Research*, vol. 3. Chicago: University of Chicago Press.

Hess, Robert D. Kathleen A. Camara. 1979. "Post-Divorce Family Relationships as Mediating Factors in the Consequences of Divorce for Children." *Journal of Social Issues* 35:79–96.

Hetherington, E. Mavis, Martha Cox, and Roger Cox. 1982. "Effects of Divorce on Parents and Children." In Michael Lamb, ed., *Nontraditional Families: Parenting and Child Development*. Hillsdale, N.J.: Lawrence Erlbaum.

Hoffman, Lynn. 1980. *Foundations of Family Therapy*. New York: Basic Books.

—— 1981. *Foundations of Family Therapy: A Conceptual Framework for Systems Change*. New York: Basic Books.

Hofstad, Milton O. 1977. "Treatment in a Juvenile Court Setting." In William J. Reid and Laura Epstein, eds., *Task-Centered Practice*. New York: Columbia University Press.

Hollis, Florence. 1972. *Casework: A Psychosocial Therapy*, 2d ed. New York: Random House.

Hollis, Florence, and Mary Woods. 1981. *Casework: A Psychosocial Therapy*, 3d ed. New York: Random House.

Hudson, Walter W. 1982. *The Clinical Measurement Package: A Field Manual*. Homewood, Ill.: Dorsey Press.

Isaccs, M. 1981. "Treatment for Families of Divorce: A Systems Model of Prevention." In I. R. Stuart and L. E. Abt, eds., *Children of Separation and Divorce: Management and Treatment*. New York: Van Nostrand Reinhold.

Jackson, Alice A. 1983. *Task-Centered Marital Therapy: A Single Case Investigation*. Ph.D. dissertation, University of Alabama.

Jacobson, Neil S. 1977. "Problem-Solving Contingency Contracting in the Treatment of Marital Discord." *Journal of Consulting and Clinical Psychology*, 48:92–100.

—— 1978. "A Stimulus Control Model of Change in Behavioral Couples' Therapy: Implications for Contingency Contracting." *Journal of Marriage and Family Counseling* 4:29–35.

——— 1979. "Increasing Positive Behavior in Severely Distressed Marital Relationships: The Effects of Problem-Solving Training." *Behavior Therapy* 10:311–326.

Jacobson, Neil S. and Gayla Margolin. 1979. *Marital Therapy: Strategies Based on Social Learning and Behavior Exchange Principles.* New York: Brunner/Mazel.

Jantzen, Curtis and Oliver Harris. 1980. "Family Treatment for Problem Poverty Families." In Curtis Jantzen and Oliver Harris, eds., *Family Treatment in Social Work Practice.* Itasca, Ill.: Peacock Press.

Jayaratne, Srinika and Rona Levy. 1979. *Empirical Clinical Practice.* New York: Columbia University Press.

Jefferson, Carter. 1978. "Some Notes on the Use of Family Sculpture in Therapy." *Family Process* 17:69–76.

Johnson, Adelaide. 1959. "Juvenile Delinquency." In Silvano Arieti, ed., *Handbook of American Psychiatry*, vol. 2. New York: Basic Books.

Kagan, Richard M. and William J. Reid. 1984. "Critical Factors in the Adoption of Emotionally Disturbed Youth." Paper presented at the Annual Meeting of the American Orthopsychiatric Association.

Karpel, Mark A. and Eric S. Strauss. 1983. *Family Evaluation.* New York: Gardner Press.

Kaslow, Florence and R. Hyatt. 1982. "Divorce: A Potential Growth Experience for the Extended Family." In Esther O. Fisher, ed., *Impact of Divorce on the Extended Family.* New York: Haworth Press.

Kazdin, Alan E. 1981 "Drawing Valid Inferences from Case Studies." *Journal of Consulting and Clinical Psychology* 49:183–192.

Keith, Pat M. and Robert B. Shafer. 1982. "Correlates of Depression Among Single Parent Employed Women." *Journal of Divorce* 5:49–59.

Kerr, Michael E. 1981. "Family Systems Theory and Therapy." In Alan S. Gurman and David P. Kniskern, eds., *Handbook of Family Therapy.* New York: Brunner/Mazel.

Kiesler, Donald J., Michael J. Sheridan, Joan E. Winter, and Michael S. Kolevzon. 1981. "Family Therapist Intervention Coding System (FTICS)." The Family Research Project, Family Institute of Virginia.

Kifer, Robert E., Martha A. Lewis, Donald R. Green, and Elery L. Phillips. 1974. "Training Pre-Delinquent Youths and Their Parents to Negotiate Conflict Situations." *Journal of Applied Behavioral Analysis* 7:357–364.

Kirschner, Charlotte. 1979. "The Aging Family in Crisis: A Problem in Living." *Social Casework* 60:209–216.

Kluckhohn, Florence, R. and Fred L. Strodtbeck. 1961. *Variations in Value Orientations.* Evanston, Ill.: Row, Peterson.

Knopf, Jennifer and William J. Reid. (forthcoming). "Marital Decision Making." In Jon Conte and Scott Briar, eds., *The Casebook.* New York: Columbia University Press.

Kolevzon, Michael S. and Robert G. Green. 1983. "Practice and Training in Family Therapy: A Known Group Study." *Family Process* 22:179–200.

Kolko, David J. and Michael A. Milan. 1983. "Reframing and Paradoxical Instruction to Overcome 'Resistance' in Treatment of Delinquent Youths: A Multiple Baseline Analysis." *Journal of Consulting and Clinical Psychology* 51:655–661.

L'Abate, Luciano. 1981. "Skill Training Programs for Couples and Families." In Alan S. Gurman and David P. Kniskern, eds., *Handbook of Family Therapy.* New York: Brunner/Mazel.

L'Abate, Luciano and Gerald Weeks. 1978. "A Bibliography of Paradoxical Methods in Psychotherapy of Family Systems." *Family Process* 17:95–98.

L'Abate, Luciano and Gerald Weeks. 1982. *Paradoxical Psychotherapy: Theory and Practice with Individuals, Couples and Families.* New York: Brunner/Mazel.

Larsen, JoAnn and Craig Mitchell. 1980. "Task-Centered Strength-Oriented Group Work with Delinquents." *Social Casework* 61:154–163.

Lester, Gregory W., Ernest Beckham, and David H. Baucom. 1980. "Implementation of Behavioral Marital Therapy." *Journal of Marital and Family Therapy* 6:189–199.

Levant, Ronald F. 1984. *Family Therapy: A Comprehensive Overview.* Englewood Cliffs, N.J.: Prentice-Hall.

Lewis, Catherine C. 1981. "The Effects of Parental Firm Control: A Reinterpretation of Findings." *Psychological Bulletin* 90:547–563.

Lewis, Jerry M., W. Robert Beavers, John T. Gossett, and Virginia Austin Phillips. 1976. *No Single Thread: Psychological Health in Family Systems.* New York: Brunner/Mazel.

Lieberman, Robert P., Eugenie G. Wheeler, Louis A. J. M. DeVisser, Julie Kuehnel, and Timothy Kuehnel. 1980. *Handbook of Marital Therapy: A Positive Approach to Helping Troubled Relationships.* New York: Plenum Press.

Lidz, Theodore et al. 1965. *Schizophrenia and the Family.* New York: International Universities Press.

Lorber, R. and Gerald R. Patterson. 1981. "The Aggressive Child: A Concomitant of a Coercive System." In John P. Vincent ed., *Advances in Family Intervention, Assessment and Theory.* Greenwich, Connecticut: JAI Press.

McLanahan, Sara S., Nancy V. Wedemyer, and Tina Adelberg. 1981. "Network Structure Social Support, and Psychological Well-Being in the Single Parent Family." *Journal of Marriage and the Family* 43:601–612.

Macy-Lewis, Jane A. 1985. "Single Parent Groups." In Anne E. Fortune, ed., *Task-Centered Practice with Families and Groups.* New York: Springer.

Madanes, Cloe. 1981. "Protection, Paradox, and Pretending." *Family Process* 19:73–85.

—— 1981. *Strategic Family Therapy.* San Francisco: Jossey-Bass.

Mallon-Wenzel, Charlotte, Marcia M. McCabe, William J. Reid, and Elise M. Pinkston. 1982. "Negotiation: Modification of Communication Processes." In Elise Pinkston, John L. Levitt, Glenn R. Green, Nick L. Linsk, and Tina L. Rzepnicki, eds., *Effective Social Work Practice.* San Francisco: Jossey Bass.

Maluccio, Anthony N., ed. 1981. *Promoting Competence in Clients: A New/Old Approach to Social Work Practice.* New York: Free Press.

Mayer, John E. and Noel Timms. 1970. *The Client Speaks: Working Class Impressions of Casework.* New York: Atherton Press.

Meyer, Carol H. ed. 1983a. *Clinical Social Work in the Eco-Systems Perspective.* New York: Columbia University Press.

—— 1983b. "Selecting Appropriate Practice Models." In Aaron Rosenblatt and Diana Waldfogel, eds., *Handbook of Clinical Social Work.* San Francisco: Jossey-Bass.

Middleman, Ruth and Gale Goldberg. 1974. *Social Service Delivery: A Structural Approach to Social Work Practice.* New York: Columbia University Press.

Miller, Sherod, Elam Nunnally, and Daniel B. Wackman. 1975. *Alive and Aware.* Minneapolis: Interpersonal Communication Program, Inc.

Mills, Paul R., Jr. 1985. "Conjoint Treatment Within the Task Centered Model." In Anne E. Fortune, ed., *Task Centered Practice with Families and Groups.* New York: Springer.

Minuchin, Salvadore. 1974. *Families and Family Therapy.* Cambridge: Harvard University Press.

Minuchin, Salvadore. et al. 1967. *Families of the Slums.* New York: Basic Books.

Minuchin, Salvadore and Charles H. Fishman. 1981. *Family Therapy Techniques.* Cambridge: Harvard University Press.

Minuchin, Salvadore, Bernice L. Rosman, and Lester Baker. 1978. *Psychosomatic Families: Anorexia Nervosa in Context.* Cambridge: Harvard University Press.

Moos, Rudolf H. 1974. *Family Environment Scale Prelminray Manual.* Palo Alto, Calif.: Consulting Psychologists Press.

Morawetz, Anita and Gillian Walker. 1984. *Brief Therapy with Single-Parent Families.* New York: Brunner/Mazel.

Moreland, John R., Andrew I. Schwebel, Steven Beck, and Robert Wells. 1982. "Parents as Therapists: A Review of the Behavior Therapy Parent Training Literature." *Behavior Modification* 6:250–276.

Mozdzierz, Gerald J., Frank J. Macchitelli, and Joseph Lisiecki. 1976. "The Paradox in Psychotherapy: An Adlerian Perspective." *Journal of Individual Psychology* 32:169–184.

Nelsen, Judith C. 1983. *Family Treatment: An Integrative Approach.* Englewood Cliffs, N.J.: Prentice-Hall.

Newcome, Kent. 1985. "Task-Centered Group Work with the Chronic Mentally Ill in Day Treatment." In Anne E. Fortune, ed., *Task Centered Practice wtih Families and Groups.* New York: Springer.

Nichols, Michael P. 1984. *Family Therapy: Concepts and Methods.* New York: Gardner Press.

Northen, Helen, 1982. *Clinical Social Work.* New York: Columbia University Press.

O'Connor, Richard. 1983. "A Study of Client Reactions to Brief Treatment." Ph.D. dissertation, University of Chicago.

O'Leary, Daniel K. and Hillary Turkewitz. 1981. "A Comparative Outcome Study of Behavioral Marital Therapy and Communication Therapy." *Journal of Marital and Family Therapy* 7:159–169.

Olson, David H., Hamilton I. McCubbin, and Associates. 1983. *Families: What Makes Them Work.* Beverly Hills, Calif.: Sage Publications.

Olson, David H., Candyce S. Russell, and Dennis H. Sprenkle. 1980. "Circumplex Model of Marital and Family Systems II: Empirical Studies and Clinical Intervention." In John P. Vincent, ed., *Advances in Family Intervention, Assessment, and Theory,* vol. 1. Greenwich: JAI Press.

Olson, David H., Dennis H. Sprenkel, and Candyce S. Russell. 1979. "Circumplex Model of Marital and Family Systems I: Cohesion and Adaptability Applications." *Family Process* 18:3–28.

Oltmans, Thomas F., Joan E. Broderick, and K. Daniel O'Leary. 1977. "Marital Adjustment and the Efficiency of Behavior Therapy with Children." *Journal of Consulting and Clinical Psychology* 45:724–729.

Orcutt, Ben A. 1977. "Family Treatment of Poverty Level Families." *Social Casework* 58:92–100.

Osborn, A. F. 1963. *Applied Imagination.* New York: Scribners.

Papp, Peggy. 1976. "Family Choreography." In Philip Guerin, Jr., ed., *Family Therapy: Theory and Practice.* New York: Gardner Press.

—— 1980. "The Greek Chorus and Other Techniques of Paradoxical Therapy." *Family Process* 19:45–57.

Papp, Peggy, Olga Silverstein, and Elizabeth Carter. 1973. "Family Sculpting in Preventive Work with Well Families." *Family Process* 12:197–212.

Parihar, Bageshwari. 1983. *Task-Centered Management in Human Services.* Springfield, Ill.: Charles C. Thomas.

Patterson, Gerald R. and Hyman Hops. 1972. "Coercion, A Game for Two: Intervention Techniques for Marital Conflict." In R. E. Ulrich and P. Mountjoy, eds., *The Experimental Analysis of Social Behavior.* New York: Appleton-Century-Crofts.

Patterson, Gerald R. 1976. "The Aggressive Child: Victim and Architect of A Coercive System." In E. J. Marsh, L. A. Hammerlynck, L. C. Handy, eds., *Behavior Modification and Families.* New York Brunner/Mazel.

Perosa, L. M. and Sandra L. Perosa. 1982. "Structural Interaction Patterns in Families with a Learning Disabled Child." *Family Therapy* 9:175–187.

Pett, Majorie G. 1982. "Predictors of Satisfactory Social Adjustments of Divorced Single Parents." *Journal of Divorce* 5:1–17.

Pincus, Allen and Ann Minahan. 1973. *Social Work Practice: Model and Method.* Itasca, Ill.: Peacock.

Pinkston, Elsie M., John L. Levitt, Glenn R. Green, Nick L. Linsk, and Tina L. Rzepnicki. 1982. *Effective Social Work Practice.* San Francisco: Jossey-Bass.

Pinsof, William. 1981. "Family Therapy Process Approach." In Alan S. Gurman and David P. Kniskern, eds., *Handbook of Family Therapy.* New York: Brunner/Mazel.

—— 1983. "Integrative Problem-Centered Therapy: Toward the Synthesis of Family and Individual Psychotherapies." *Journal of Marital and Family Therapy* 9:19–35.

Polster, Richard P. and Elsie M. Pinkston. 1979. "A Delivery System for the Treatment of Underachievement." *Social Service Review* 53:35–55.

Porter, Beatrice and K. Daniel O'Leary. 1980. "Marital Discord and Childhood Behavior Problems." *Journal of Abnormal Child Psychology* 8:287–295.

Rabin, Claire. 1981. "A Behavioral Perspective on the Scapegoat Theory." *International Journal of Behavioral Social Work and Abstracts* 1:109–124.

Raskin, David E. and Zanuel E. Klein. 1976. "Losing a Symptom Through Keeping It." *Archives of General Psychiatry* 33:548–555.

Rathbone-McCuan, Eloise. 1985. "Intergenerational Family Practice with Older Families." In Anne E. Fortune, ed., *Task Centered Practice with Families and Groups.* New York: Springer.

Regensburg, Jeanette. 1954. "Application of Psychoanalytic Concepts to Casework Treatment of Marital Problems." *Social Casework* 35:424–432.

Reid, William J. 1975. "A Test of the Task-Centered Approach." *Social Work* 20:3–9.

—— 1977. "Social Work for Social Problems." *Social Work* 22:374–381.

—— 1978. *The Task-Centered System.* New York: Columbia University Press.

—— 1981. "Family Treatment Within a Task-Centered Framework." In Eleanor Reardon Tolson and William J. Reid, eds., *Models of Family Treatment.* New York: Columbia University Press.

—— 1985. "Work with Families." In Anne E. Fortune, ed., *Task Centered Practice with Families and Groups.* New York: Springer.

Reid, William J. and Laura Epstein. 1972. *Task-Centered Casework.* New York: Columbia University Press.

Reid, William J. and Laura Epstein, eds. 1977. *Task-Centered Practice.* New York: Columbia University Press.

Reid, William J. and Patricia Hanrahan. 1982. "Recent Evaluations of Social Work: Grounds for Optimism." *Social Work* 27:328–340.

Reid, William J. and Ann Shyne. 1969. *Brief and Extended Casework.* New York: Columbia University Press.

Reid, William and Audrey Smith. 1981. *Research in Social Work.* New York: Columbia University Press.

Reid, William J. et al. 1980. "Task-Centered School Social Work." *Social Work in Education* 2:7–24.

Reiss, D. 1971. "Varieties of Consensual Experience: A Theory for Relating Family Interaction to Individual Thinking." *Family Process* 10:1–27.

Relinger, Helmut and Philip Bornstein. 1979. "Treatment of Sleep Onset Insomnia by Paradoxical Instruction." *Behavior Modification* 3:203–222.

Robin, Arthur. 1979. "Problem-Solving Communication Training: A Behavioral Approach to the Treatment of Parent-Adolescent Conflict." *American Journal of Family Therapy* 7:69–82.

——— 1980. "Parent-Adolescent Conflict: A Skill Training Approach." In D. P. Rathjem and J. P. Foreyt, eds., *Social Commpetence: Interventions for Children and Adults.* New York: Pergamon.

——— 1981. "A Controlled Evaluation of Problem-Solving Communication Training with Parent-Adolescent Conflict." *Behavior Therapy* 12:593–609.

Rohrbaugh, Michael, Howard Tennen, Samuel Press, and Larry White. 1981. "Compliance, Defiance, and Therapeutic Paradox: Guidelines for Strategic Use of Paradoxical Interventions." *American Journal of Orthopsychiatry* 51:454–467.

Rollins, Boyd C. and Darwin L. Thomas. 1975. "A Theory of Parental Power and Child Compliance." In R. C. Cromwell and David H. Olson, eds., *Power in Families.* New York: Halsted and John Wiley.

——— 1979. "Parental Support, Power, and Control Techniques in the Socialization of Children." In Wesley R. Burr, Reuben Hill, F. Ivan Nye, and Ira L. Reiss, eds., *Contemporary Theories About the Family,* vol. 1. New York: Free Press.

Rooney, Ronald H. 1978. "Separation Through Foster Care: Toward a Problem-Oriented Practice Model Based on Task-Centered Casework." Ph.D. dissertation, University of Chicago.

——— 1981. "A Task-Centered Reunification Model for Foster Care." In Anthony A. Maluccio and Paula Sinanoglu, eds., *Working with Biological Parents of Children in Foster Care.* New York: Child Welfare League of America.

Rooney, Ronald H. and Marsha Wanless. 1985. "A Model for Caseload Management Based on Task-Centered Casework." In Anne E. Fortune, ed., *Task-Centered Practice with Families and Groups.* New York: Springer.

Rothman, Jack. 1980. *Research and Development in the Human Services.* Englewood Cliffs, N.J.: Prentice-Hall.

Russell, Candyce S., 1976. "Circumplex Model of Marital and Family Systems: Ill. Empirical Evaluation with Families." *Family Process* 18:29–45.

Russell, Candyce S., David H. Olson, Douglas H. Sprenkle, and Raymond B. Atilano. 1983. "From Family Symptom to Family System: Review of Family Therapy Research." *The American Journal of Family Therapy* 11:3–14.

Russell, Candyce S., Dennis A. Bagarozzi, Raymond B. Atilano, Janet E. Morris. 1984. "A Comparison of Two Approaches to Marital Enrichment and Conjugal Skills Training: Minnesota Couples Communication Program and Structured

Behavioral Exchange Contracting." *The American Journal of Family Therapy* 12:13–25.

Rzepnicki, Tina L. 1981. "Task-Centered Intervention in Foster Care Services." Ph.D. dissertation, University of Chicago.

—— 1985. "Task-Centered Intervention in Foster Care Services: Working With Families Who Have Children in Placement." In Anne E. Fortune, ed., *Task-Centered Practice with Families and Groups*. New York: Springer.

Salmon, Wilma. 1977. "Service Program in a State Public Welfare Agency." In William J. Reid and Laura Epstein, eds., *Task-Centered Practice*. New York: Columbia University Press.

Santa-Barbara, Jack, Christel A. Woodward, Solomon Levin, John T. Goodman, David L. Streiner, and Nathan B. Epstein. 1979. "The McMaster Family Therapy Outcome Study: I. An Overview of Methods and Results." *International Journal of Family Therapy* 1:304–343.

Schinke, Steven P., ed. 1981. *Behavioral Methods in Social Welfare*. New York: Aldine.

Segal, Carol Ann. 1983. *Parent Enrichment Project: A Community Based Preventative Service to Families*. Montreal: Allied Jewish Community Services and Ville Marie Social Service Centre.

Segal, Lynn. 1981. "Focused Problem Resolution." In Eleanor R. Tolson and William J. Reid, eds., *Models of Family Treatment*. New York: Columbia University Press.

Segraves, R. Taylor. 1982. *Marital Therapy : A Combined Psychodynamic-Behavioral Approach*. New York: Plenum.

Shaw, M. E. et al. 1980. *Role Playing*. San Diego: University Associates.

Sherman, Sanford N. 1981. "A Social Work Frame for Family Therapy." In Eleanor R. Tolson and William J. Reid, eds., *Models of Family Treatment*. New York: Columbia University Press.

Silverman, Phyllis R. 1970. "A Reexamination of the Intake Procedure." *Social Casework* 51:625–34.

Simon, Robert M. 1972. "Sculpting the Family." *Family Process* 11:49–57.

Siporin, Max. 1975. *Introduction to Social Work Practice*. New York: Macmillan.

—— 1980a. "Marriage and Family Therapy in Social Work." *Social Casework* 61:11–21.

—— 1980b. "Ecological Systems Theory in Social Work." *Journal of Sociology and Social Welfare* 7:507–532.

Smith, Audrey D. and William J. Reid. 1973a. "Child Care Arrangements of AFDC Mothers in the Work Incentive Program." *Child Welfare* 52:651–661.

—— 1985. *The Role-Sharing Marriage* New York: Columbia University Press.

Spanier, Graham B. 1976. "Measuring Dyadic Adjustment: New Scales for Assessing the Quality of Marriage and Similar Dyads." *Journal of Marriage and the Family* 38:15–28.

Spanier, Graham B. and Sandra Hanson. 1982. "The Role of Extended Kin in the Adjustment to Marital Separation." *Journal of Divorce* 5:33–48.

Spiegel, John P. 1981. "An Ecological Model with an Emphasis of Ethnic Families." In Eleanor R. Tolson and William J. Reid, eds., *Models of Family Treatment*. New York: Columbia University Press.

Stanton, Duncan M. 1981a. "Marital Therapy From a Structural/Strategic Viewpoint." *The Handbook of Marriage and Marital Therapy*. G. Pirooz Sholevar ed. Jamaica, N.Y.: Spectrum Publications.

—— 1981b. "Strategic Approaches to Family Therapy." In Alan S. Gurman and David P. Kniskern, eds., *Handbook of Family Therapy*. New York: Brunner/Mazel.

Stanton, Duncan M., T. C. Todd, and Associates. 1982. *The Family Therapy of Drug Addiction*. New York: Guilford Press.

Stedman, James and Thomas Gaines. 1981. "Relationships Between Affiliation and Involvement Among Family Members and Family Pathology." *Family Therapy* 8:159–164.

Stierlin, Helm. 1972. *Separating Parents and Adolescents*. New York: Quadrangle.

Stuart, Richard B. 1971. "Behavioral Contracting Within the Families of Delinquents." *Journal of Behavior Therapy and Experimental Psychiatry*, 2:1–11.

—— 1974. *Final Report: Contingency Contracting in Treatment of Delinquents*. Ann Arbor, Mich.: Behavior Change Labs.

—— 1980. *Helping Couples Change: A Social Learning Approach to Marital Therapy*. New York: Guilford Press.

Stuart, Richard B. and Leroy A. Lott, Jr. 1972. "Behavioral Contracting With Delinquents: A Cautionary Note." *Journal of Behavior Therapy and Experimental Psychiatry* 3:161–169.

Stuart, Richard B. and Tony Tripodi. 1973. "Experimental Evaluation of Three Time-Constrained Behavioral Treatments for Pre-Delinquents and Delinquents." In Richard D. Rubin, J. Paul Brady, and John D. Henderson, eds., *Advances in Behavior Therapy*. New York: Academic Press.

Stuart, Richard B. et al. 1976. "An Experiment in Social Engineering in Serving the Families of Predelinquents." *Journal of Abnormal Child Psychology* 4:243–261.

Summers, F. and F. Walsh. 1977. "The Nature of the Symbiotic Bond Between Mother and Schizophrenic." *American Journal of Orthopsychiatry* 47:484–494.

Swenson, Carol R. 1981. "Using Natural Helping Networks to Promote Competence." In Anthony N. Maluccio, ed., *Promoting Competence in Clients: A New/Old Approach to Social Work Practice*. London: Free Press.

Tavantzis, Thomas N., Martha Tavantzis, Larry G. Brown, and Michael Rohrbaugh. In press. "Home-Based Structural Family Therapy for Adolescents at Risk of Placement." in M. D. Prauader and S. L. Roman, eds., *Adolescents and Family Therapy: A Handbook for Theory and Practice*. New York: Gardner Press.

Taylor, Carvel. 1977. "Counseling in a Service Industry." In William J. Reid and Laura Epstein, eds., *Task-Centered Practice*. New York: Columbia University Press.

Teyber, Edward. 1983. "Effects of the Parental Coalition on Adolescent Emancipation From the Family" *Journal of Marital and Family Therapy*. 9:305–310.

Tharp, Roland G. and R. J. Wetzel. 1969. *Behavior Modification in the Natural Environment*. New York: Academic Press.

Thibault, Jane M. 1984. "The Analysis and Treatment of Indirect Self-Destructive Behaviors of Elderly Patients," Ph.D. dissertation, University of Chicago.

Thomas, Edwin J. 1976. *Marital Communication and Decision Making: Analysis, Assessment, and Change*. New York: Free Press.

—— 1978. "Generating Innovation in Social Work: The Paradigm of Developmental Research." *Journal of Social Service Research* 2:95–115.

Thompson, E. and P. Gongla. 1983. "Single Parent Families: In the Mainstream of American Society." In E. Macklin and R. Rubin, eds., *Contemporary Families and Alternative Lifestyles*. Beverly Hills, Calif.: Sage.

Tolson, Eleanor. 1977. "Alleviating Marital Communication Problems." In William J. Reid and Laura Epstein, eds., *Task-Centered Practice*. New York: Columbia University Press.

—— 1984. "Some Observations about Problem Evolution" *tc Newsletter*. 4:1–2.

Tomm, Karl. 1982. "Towards a Cybernetic Systems Approach to Family Therapy." In Florence W. Kaslow, ed., *The International Book of Family Therapy*. New York: Brunner/Mazel.

Tripodi, Tony and Irwin Epstein. 1980. *Research Techniques for Clinical Social Workers*. New York: Columbia University Press

Tsoi-Hammond, Lisa. 1976. "Marital Therapy: An Integrative Behavioral-Learning Model." *Journal of Marriage and Family Counseling* 2:179–191.

Turner, Francis J., ed. 1979. *Social Work Treatment: Interlocking Theoretical Approaches*. New York: Free Press.

U.S. Bureau of the Census. 1983. Current Population Reports, Series P–20. No. 381. *Household and Family Characteristics: March 1982*. Washington, D.C.: GPO.

Videka-Sherman, Lynn and William J. Reid. In press. "The Structured Clinical Record: A Clinical Education Tool." To be published in the *Clinical Supervisor*

Wahler, Robert. 1980. "The Insular Mother: Her Problems in Parent-Child Treatment." *Journal of Applied Behavior Analysis* 13:207–219.

Wallerstein, Judith S. and Joan B. Kelly. 1979. "Children and Divorce." *Social Work* 24:468–475.

—— 1980. *Surviving the Breakup: How Children and Parents Cope with Divorce*. New York: Basic Books.

Walsh, Froma. 1983. "Family Therapy: A Systemic Orientation to Treatment." In Aaron Rosenblatt and Diana Waldfogel, eds., *Handbook of Clinical Social Work*. San Francisco: Jossey-Bass.

Wattie, Brenda. 1973. "Evaluating Short-Term Casework in a Family Agency." *Social Casework* 54:609–616.

Watzlawick, Paul, J. Weakland, and R. Fisch. 1974. *Change: Principles of Problem Formation and Problem Resolution*. New York: W. W. Norton.

Watzlawick, Paul, Janet Helmick Beavin, and Don D. Jackson. 1967. *Pragmatics of Human Communication*. New York: W. W. Norton.

Weiss, Robert L. 1975. "Contracts, Cognition, and Change: A Behavioral Approach to Marriage Therapy." *The Counseling Psychologist* 5:15–25.

—— 1980. "Strategic Behavioral Marital Therapy: Toward a Model for Assessment and Intervention." In John P. Vincent, ed., *Advances in Family Intervention, Assessment and Theory*, vol. 1. Connecticut: JAI Press.

Weiss, Robert L. et al. 1973. "A Framework for Conceptualizing Marital Conflict, A Technology for Altering It, Some Data for Evaluating It." In Leo A. Hamerlynck, Lee C. Handy, and Eric J. Mash, eds., *Behavior Change: Methodology, Concepts, and Practice*. Champaign-Urbana, Ill.: Research Press.

Weiss, Robert L., Gary R. Birchler, and John Vincent. 1974. "Contractual Models for Negotiation Training in Marital Dyads." *Journal of Marriage and the Family* 36:321–330.

Weiss, Robert S. 1979. "Growing Up a Little Faster: The Experience of Growing Up in a Single Parent Household." *Journal of Social Issues* 35:97–111.

Weissman, Andrew. 1977. "In the Steel Industry." In *Task-Centered Practice*. William J. Reid and Laura Epstein, eds. New York: Columbia University Press.

Wells, Richard A., T. C. Dilkes, and N. Trivelli. 1972. "The Results of Family Therapy: A Critical Review of the Literature." *Family Process* 7:189–207.

Wells, Richard A. and Joan A. Figurel. 1979. "Techniques of Structured Communication Training." *The Family Coordinator* 28:273–281.

Wells, Richard. 1981. "The Empirical Base of Family Therapy: Practice Implications." In Eleanor Reardon Tolson and William J. Reid, eds., *Models of Family Treatment*. New York: Columbia University Press.

Wertheim, Eleanor S. 1975. "The Science and Typology of Family Systems. II. Further Theortical and Practical Considerations." *Family Process* 14285–309.

Wexler, Phyllis. 1977. "A Case From a Medical Setting." In William J. Reid and Laura Epstein, eds., *Task-Centered Practice*. New York: Columbia University Press.

Whitaker, Carl A. and David V. Keith. 1981. "Symbolic-Experiential Family Therapy." In Alan S. Gurman and David P. Kniskern, eds., *Handbook of Family Therapy*. New York: Brunner-Mazel.

Whittaker, James K. 1974. *Social Treatment: An Approach to Interpersonal Helping*. Chicago: Aldine.

Wile, Daniel B. 1981. *Couples Therapy: A Nontraditional Approach*. New York: Wiley.

Wise, Frances. 1977. "Conjoint Marital Treatment." In William J. Reid and Laura Epstein, eds., *Task-Centered Practice*. New York: Columbia University Press.

Wodarski, John S., Marcy Saffir, and Malcolm Frazer. 1982. "Using Research to Evaluate the Effectiveness of Task-Centered Casework." *Journal of Applied Social Sciences* 7:70–82.

Wolman, Benjamin B. and George Stricker, eds. 1983. *Handbook of Family and Marital Therapy*. New York: Plenum Press.

Woodward, Christel A., Jack Santa-Barbara, Davis L. Streiner, John T. Goodman, Solomon Levin, and Nathan B. Epstein. 1981. "Client, Treatment and Therapist Variables Related to Outcome in Brief, Systems Oriented Family Therapy." *Family Process* 209:189–197.

Wynne, Lyman, I. Ryckoff, J. Day, and S. Hirsch. 1958. "Pseudomutuality in the Family Relations of Schizophrenics." *Psychiatry* 21:205–220.

Zuk, Gerald H. 1978. "Values and Family Therapy." *Psychotherapy: Theory, Research and Practice* 15:48–55.

Author Index

Subject Index